The Behaviour Guru

Also available from Continuum

Getting the Buggers to Behave 4th edition, Sue Cowley

Managing Very Challenging Behaviour, Louise Leaman

100+ Ideas for Managing Behaviour, Johnnie Young

The Behaviour Guru

*Behaviour Management
Solutions for Teachers*

TOM BENNETT

continuum

Continuum International Publishing Group
The Tower Building,   80 Maiden Lane,
11 York Road,   Suite 704,
London, SE1 7NX   New York, NY 10038

www.continuumbooks.com

British Library Cataloguing-in-Publication Data
A catalogue record for this book is available from the British Library.

ISBN: 978-1-4411-2860-7 (paperback)

Library of Congress Cataloging-in-Publication Data
Bennett, Tom, 1971-
    The behaviour guru : behaviour management solutions for teachers / Tom Bennett.
        p. cm.
    ISBN 978-1-4411-2860-7 (pbk.)
    1. Classroom management.   2. Problem children--Behavior modification.
    I. Title.

    LB3013.B396 2010
    371.102′4--dc22

                                                    2010007256

Typeset by Fakenham Photosetting Limited, Fakenham, Norfolk
Printed and bound in Great Britain by Ruskin Press Limited

To my parents, Tam and Betty, and Anthony Bennett,
who have often put up with all my very own bad behaviour.
And to Anna.

Contents

Preface

In 2009 the inimitable Gail Robinson at *tslonline* invited me to follow up on my work with *The Times Educational Supplement* by becoming an online 'agony uncle' for teachers who wanted advice and suggestions about behavioural problems they were experiencing in the classroom and beyond. Since that time I have discussed many hundreds of different topics related to achieving civilized behaviour, with many, many more teachers. It's been enlightening for me to be able to discuss these issues with so many people from all over the UK and sometimes the world. What it has taught me is that these problems are ubiquitous; there are no new challenges under the sun that someone somewhere hasn't faced and defeated. It makes perfect sense that teachers should prop each other up, share their experiences, and pass their own learning on to other teachers – after all, that's what we're supposed to be experts in.

I was, and am, amazed by the enormous number of teachers who volunteer their time and thoughts on the advice page absolutely free; considering the length of time a well considered response takes to write, there must be an army of volunteer relief workers out there who have earned some brownie points in the hereafter. Although there are always (perversely) some people who log on to forums to spread doom and misery (for reasons that perpetually escape me), almost every correspondent to the web forum is guaranteed a variety of helpful ideas to grease the axles of their teaching days. Anonymous angels like *teachur, garyconyers, coolasacucumber, oldandrew, e1whittaker*, and many others, I salute you.

Most of this book is made up of the answers I wrote to correspondents on the TES website. I've rewritten the questions to avoid hijacking someone else's problem or copyright, but I've kept the content the same. In many cases I've expanded upon my original answer, in order to make the replies more suitable for a more general reader, while hopefully keeping the response specific to that situation. My success in this endeavour can only be judged by your good self.

Good luck, in all things.

Introduction

If you asked me for directions to the S Club 7 reunion at Wembley Arena and I replied with a lecture on Newton's Laws of Motion, then I might reasonably expect a sore face. You want directions, not a PhD. So why is behaviour management training for teachers in the UK like that? The thing that sticks out for me is something that I would like to describe as the elephant in the room, wearing hob nail boots, goose-stepping over a floor covered in champagne glasses. In a lift.

I've spoken and written to teachers everywhere in the UK about getting pupils to behave, and I found the same problem kept recurring: most new teachers don't know how to control classes. Why should they? *They were never trained to do it.* One of the axioms of this book is that behaviour management is fundamental to good teaching. If you can't control them you can't teach them. It's that important, in the sense that having water is fundamental to a decent bath. It just won't happen without it. So why, I ask the silent sky, would such a skill be so carelessly delivered to an entire profession?

Either the panjandrums of teaching believe that everything is hunky-dory with teacher training (it's not), or they think that schools aren't that challenging (many are). But with one in three teachers leaving the profession within 5 years of starting[1] (and half of them citing bad behaviour as the main reason), then the real world situation is much grimmer than the adverts portray. Clearly the way teachers are trained to handle pupils isn't working.

And that, my dear Watson, is the problem. Controlling other people isn't a fact, or a collection of facts. It's not a theory, or a set of rules. Hell, it isn't even a book on behaviour management. It's a skill – a doing activity, an active verb. It's a skill that requires the confluence of two parts of a person – the mind and the body: the mind, because you have to train your brain into thinking a certain way automatically, whatever the circumstances, and your body, because you need to get used to acting in a certain way, even controlling your physical reactions to certain situations until they, too, become automatic.

Controlling a class is like driving a car; at first you are so conscious about what you're doing that you can't think of anything else other than *is my foot on the right pedal?*, and *am I going to die today?*, etc. Gradually that all starts to fall into the background, as your mind and body get into step with each other and it all becomes automatic; soon you're on your mobile phone while you paint your nails on the motorway like everyone else. Teaching is a habit, and like any habit you want to acquire, it must be repeated until it becomes second nature. If you're into Aristotle (and I am; but relax, this isn't *that* book) you would say that teaching is a virtue of character not intellect. But Aristotle never had a whiny child in front of him saying that you violated his human rights by taking his iPod off him.

Right now, the way we train can be brilliant, and it can be awful, and that's the damning thing about it – it's maddeningly variable, dependent on chance as much as intent. If you're lucky you get placed with a teacher who really *gets* behaviour management, knows how to teach it to you, and has enough professionalism to stay in the damn room until you can take your first steps, and then knows when to back off, and how far. That's too many variables. For a profession that's obsessed with perfecting the science of imparting information and skills, we're pretty lousy at teaching our own teachers.

But until that changes, we play the hand we're dealt. The principles and advice in this book work. What they *aren't* is foolproof, or effective without exception. That's the point: there *are* no rules to behaviour management, only principles. Take them and use them in a way that fits how you teach, and use them in sync with your own behaviour management techniques. You're the boss.

Good luck.

Note

1. *BBC News- Education 7ᵗʰ January 2003 'Third of teachers plan to quit'.*

1 | What you need to know

The theory behind the advice

The first thing you need to know is that you can skip this chapter and go straight to the questions and answers. Actually you knew that already because you have free will to do whatever the hell you want with this book. I just needed to know that I'd told you, because if there's one thing about a plain answer to a simple question, it is that it shouldn't need a John Grisham-sized back story to explain it.

What this chapter will do is tell you (in terms even I understand) how people interact with each other. These are the premises by which I operate in the classroom, and they work for me. There's not a thing in this you couldn't contest, not a single proposition that you couldn't dissect and disagree with. Men and women far more learned than myself in the field of psychology have my blessing to snort coffee through their nostrils in disgust and derision. I'm sure that I contradict myself beautifully on many points. I care not a jot; nay, nor even a tittle.

Why? Because these techniques work. They have observable effects in the classroom, and that's all I care about, and what I suspect you care about too, because you're reading past the introduction (unless the book fell open here, in imitation of a well thumbed bonkbuster). I'm not as stupid as I undoubtedly look; I'm aware that my view of human nature, psychology and interpersonal skills are guaranteed not to be the whole story, or indeed even the last word when it comes to those grand subjects; but they work. Most of the theory I've read about behaviour management has been by non-teachers. How nuts is that?

Newton's physics explained the movement of the planets, but they weren't the whole story. Einsteinian relativity improved upon Newton. Then Planck and his buddies came up with quantum physics. Perhaps one of your pupils will knock that on its ass too and invent their own branch of science. Perhaps I can train a monkey to tap dance. Who knows? The point is that Newtonian physics still works perfectly fine, as long as you are talking about observable bodies at the human level, in speeds and conditions that could reasonably be called everyday.

And that's what my methods and strategies are based on: everyday teaching, with kids that are less than perfect and more than worthless. By my reckoning, that's most of them, and that'll do for me. Sure, there are kids out there with extreme behaviour so far off the spectrum it could reasonably be described as ultraviolet, but that's when teaching starts to intersect with the role of educational psychologist, and anyone that's expected to deal with that kind of situation routinely needs to consider their position. Later on, in Chapter 6 I talk about dealing with extreme behaviour – because meet it you will, unless you privately tutor savant twins in a Swiss finishing school. Maybe even then. Part of your role in that situation will be to identify when someone in your charge is beyond any reasonable expectation that you could meet their needs.

But I reiterate: the vast majority of problems you will face can be resolved. (And they *are* problems; when did it become the norm to call difficult situations 'challenges'? You open your door on a Sunday morning to a naked skinhead carrying a chainsaw: that's a *problem*. Someone smacks your cheek with a glove and says that you and your house are varlets: that's a *challenge*. I have a similar problem with describing all low-achieving students as 'weak' – what, are they tired? Perhaps they should 'work out' until they get a bit 'stronger'. But I digress).

So what's the simplest way to explain the way pupils behave?

What are you, an animal?

Actually, yes. Conventional wisdom believed for centuries that we were fundamentally different from the beasts of the field. The basis for this was primarily spiritual; in Christian traditions we were made in the image of God. Alone among the creatures in the Universe we had the capacity for salvation, atonement, and eternal life with the Father. It was a non-materialist view of something *we* had that other organisms didn't: a soul.

Given that I can neither prove nor disprove that view, I remain respectfully silent. But one thing I will contend is that we also, indisputably, share many, many features of animals: physical ones, and more importantly for this book, mental ones too. Now to many people that doesn't seem particularly ground-breaking. They sleep, we sleep. They eat, we eat. They carefully bury their faeces under a pile of twigs, we ... you get the idea. We all have similar circulatory systems, operated by something that looks remarkably like a heart in almost all of us. We have skin, eyes, ears, senses that connect us to the outside world, tongues and tear ducts, pain and fear, upset stomachs and full bellies. In fact, the list of what we have in common with animals is so extensive that it's easier to ask 'what *haven't* we got in common with them?'

This horrifies some people. It's as if they're terrified that we're no better than them. Unlike some of the more colourful letters I have had sent to me, I don't agree that it means anything of the sort.

The Ghost in the Machine

Of course, we may very well be spiritual beings, as much composed of spirit as clay, as the Greeks thought. That doesn't alter my theory one eyelash. We are *profoundly* like them; we have so much in common with them that a Martian would think we all swapped presents at Christmas. And that apparently uncontroversial belief is my starting point. What I'm about to say builds on that assumption. If it is wrong, then everything I say afterwards is probably wrong too. But I don't think so.

We have a lot of data on animals. We should do: they're kind enough to let us do whatever the Hell we want to them. We've dressed them in clown suits, strapped them in rockets and casseroled every inch of every one of them. God said to Adam, 'I give you dominion over the fish of the sea, and over the fowl of the air, and over the cattle ... and over every creeping thing that creepeth upon the earth,' and Adam rubbed his hands together and thought, 'Oh boy, hot dogs.'

The study of human behaviour had a late start: it was the realm of the occasional philosopher until the nineteenth century, and didn't turn into a self-help industry until much later. This was nothing new in the animal kingdom, of course; people had been studying them for centuries, usually in the interests of people, of course. It was useful to know how horses, dogs and cattle behaved, so that their actions could be predicted and their utility improved in relation to what we needed them for. Human anthropology started, unsurprisingly, on a very delicate basis. It was primarily the study of foreigners in their kraals, tepees and caves, and an exploration of their funny little customs that made them so frightfully uncivilized. It was of course the study of indigenous cultures by a vastly smug and imperialist scientific community. The cultural assumptions governing it were obvious to the contemporary observer: they (the foreigners) weren't entirely human, so they could be studied like animals in a zoo. Look! That one's got a bone through his nose!

It wasn't until the twentieth century that scientists stopped looking over their shoulders and started making serious anthropological studies of human beings in their natural habitats closer to home. Such pioneers as Desmond Morris, with his famous *The Naked Ape* (later ghoulishly parodied by that gurning cockney cartoon character Jamie Oliver in his *Naked Chef* series of seasonal gift-dominating confections) wrote devastating essays on what motivated human behaviour, explaining the basic biological premises behind such human perennials as laughter, child rearing, monogamy, smiling, getting angry at other drivers but not doing anything about it, even why we wear clothes when we have no need to do so (apart from, say, Scotland, where failure to dress sensibly would have resulted in the Earth being ruled by enormous reptiles with tiny forearms, crunching Prozac nervously as they worried about who to invite over for dinner, and could red wine go with monkey meat?).

And the amazing thing is that almost everything in our behaviour could be in some way correlated with a basic biological need, or a primitive cultural factor with origins so ancient that we could scarcely see why they still existed. Like male nipples, it seems we had inherited a lot of behaviour patterns that had their origins in our prehistory. And they're still there.

Animals on the Dance Floor

What has this got to do with our behaviour? I first became interested in this field when I ran nightclubs in Soho, which was a natural first step towards becoming a philosophy teacher. I spent a lot of time sober, watching the behaviour of others in an environment of heaving, drunken human beasts who were letting off steam and generally letting their guard down. (Among other things. Our lost property box looked like a knicker drawer). It was important to try to anticipate how to deal with crowds, to know what would keep large groups of people happy, and what would panic them. And because of the need to keep large, angry drunks from head-butting the sheet-glass windows, I needed to develop simple control techniques that would work on drunken belligerents – not physical restraint, of course, but ways of talking down a fight, or stopping one about to happen. We dealt with hookers, drunks, thieves, police, angry Kiwi juggernauts, and writhing twenty-stone debutantes, off their nuts on cheeky-girl talcum powder. It took a lot more than muscle to keep that lot in line.

Most fights are about face. Confrontation between animals usually results in one or both of the animals getting hurt a lot. Now this isn't a win/win situation, because any injury in the wild can be potentially fatal when you factor in infection, recovery time, and reduced hunting capability. So it stands to reason that most animals will avoid a fight if they can at all help it, unless there's little chance of injury. But of course there will be situations where an animal can't avoid a bust up with another one – he might have to defend a mate, territory, meat, whatever presses his buttons. What to do then? Fight?

Not always. Animals have developed a complex way of settling a fight without a single hairy punch being thrown: posturing. There are many examples of this in the animal kingdom: cats rearing up, fanning their tails; lions roaring wildly; dogs circling each other, baring their teeth and growling; insects puffing out every wing and piece of armour they can to appear twice the size. The point of all these displays is to convince the potential aggressor that if he wants to pick a fight, then he'd better make sure he has some bandages in his back pocket. In other words, it is a non-verbal display designed to intimidate an aggressor without actually fighting. 'Think again,' it warns. 'I'll bite you on the arse. Possibly.'

And that's the key element to this: *face*. This idea resonates in every culture – the idea that you have pride in who you are, and in how others estimate you. In China, for example, it was considered very poor form to show anger, fear, or even excessive happiness in public; it was a sign that you couldn't control your emotions, and therefore a loss of face. Your face was the public picture you presented to the outside world, quite separate from your internal world. Face was a contrived illusion, designed to show you at your best.

And in night clubs? Same thing. Most fights I saw were started over something completely trivial: the ubiquitous spilled pint, an imagined nudge on the dance floor, the dirty look (the preferred weapon of choice among female brawlers). And when the two antagonists square up to each other (puffing out their chests) it's amazing how little gusto their actions have compared to the language they use. It's all, 'I'm going to f*** you up, small fry' stuff, while their feet remain firmly where they are. Almost all of them don't want to fight – in fact they're desperate to avoid it.

I saw some real fights; situations where somebody really had it in for someone else. You know what they did? They just marched up to the object of their ire and *BANG!* smacked them on the nose without a word. No posturing, just a bunch of fives in the kisser when they weren't looking. You better *believe* that's a real fight. Everything else is about face, and the fear of losing it. In fact, in my experience the vast majority of fights were caused because neither of the antagonists could see a way to back out of the situation without looking like a big jessie. The moral? If you want to stop a face-off from becoming a fight, give both parties a way to bow out gracefully without looking stupid.

What's your status?

Something closely connected to face is status – what position do you hold in the hierarchy of your peers? Some people are all about status – they have to have the best car, house, fridge, or they are constant social climbers. Some people seem unconcerned about power, position and esteem. But humans belong to a class of animals that are very social, and where we are in relation to others is extremely important to us. We congregate together naturally, and even the most solitary of us feel the need for company, relationships and contact. True hermits are rare enough to be considered remarkable, and one of the biggest digs that anyone can make about you is that you're a loner (one letter away from 'loser'. And two letters away from 'laser'. Spooky). It suggests inadequacy, an inability to form bonds with others.

As social animals, our self-image and self-esteem are closely tied to the way others see us. *Sure*, you might say, *but I'm a strong-willed, self-confident big banana; I don't need others to approve of me!* Oh really? Even people so centred and balanced you could hang a plumb line off their egos; even *they* look subtly to others for reassurance. They might not seek the approval of the herd, but they look for it from smaller groups of selected people that *they* trust and respect.

In clubs I used to see this play out all the time. Large groups of men display it most obviously; you can read them like dogs, if dogs wore *Fahrenheit* and shopped at *Top Man*. In fact, the comparison with dogs is unusually illuminating because they display many similarities to people. Anyone familiar with their pet pup should know that dogs naturally congregate in packs, and pay particular attention to who's in charge. Dogs will inevitably establish a pecking order (without beaks, naturally. See? I could do nature shows). Sledge drivers know this; their dogs will have an alpha male, who simply *has* to go at the front of the gang or they'll be going in circles all the way across Lapland. The ones behind are the heirs apparent, the ones behind them are their successors, and so on, until you get to the back, where you find the huskies wearing glasses who never get picked for the football team. And they're delighted with this, as long as they all know who's in charge.

This is what is called dominance, and it's something that we show as well. Men who work together are often heavily motivated by this principle – as long as they know who's in charge they can pretty much get on with things. But if the boss is weak they'll nip at his heels (bitching, undermining) until he takes charge of them, or until the sleigh tips over, whichever comes first. One of my first bouncers agreed with this: he said that whenever a man walks in a room, he scans the crowd with two questions in mind – can I beat any man in this room, and what women am I attracted to? I'll side step an angry mob of righteous complaints by saying I don't entirely agree with this principle, but I think he's got something, at least at a subconscious level. We size people up instantly, and make judgements about them that take milliseconds to form, and weeks to contradict. In the animal kingdom, dominance is easy to judge – usually it's the bigger animal that could rip your ears off, so everyone knows who's in charge.

In the human kingdom, however, power over others is a lot more to do with social status and influence. We rarely settle disputes any more by punching each other on the nose, so who controls whom is dictated by other things: rank, age, looks, job, income, various indicators of how far you've come. But one of the biggest factors is how you carry yourself, your manner, your facial expressions, even the way you walk into a room. Did you ever see someone and just know that they're shy and retiring? Or see someone walk into a room as if they owned it? That's dominance.

Depending on how confident you feel about yourself, you'll react and respond to it in a variety of ways. If you feel nervous or unconfident about where you stand (a new job, a new group of friends) it's possible that you'll react submissively to the person. Or if you feel like a pretty swell kind of guy, you might ask yourself, who the hell *is* this prat?

Who's in charge of the room?

How do we express submissiveness? On some levels, it's incredibly simple to demonstrate. An old salesman trick is to go up to a prospective client/dupe and drop something: if they pick it up for you, then they're naturally submissive to others, and you can sell them real estate on the Moon. If they wait for you to pick it up, then you've got a tough crowd. Of course, this doesn't factor in such things as compassion, manners and customs, but it makes a point. If someone bumps into you in a crowd, do you say sorry first? Are you British, by any chance? If you find a fingernail in your Happy

Meal, do you apologise to the charming teenager for pointing it out? Do you laugh at your boss's jokes, despite the fact that they make you want to jump off something high? These are all displays of low dominance (perhaps a better term than submissiveness, which has very negative overtones). There's nothing intrinsically wrong with these behaviour patterns; they help hold society together – if an enormous Viking in a pub tells you that your drink would be more appropriate for a ten-year-old girl, your split second estimation of his ability to take you apart like a mosquito will probably save you a sore face. If a five-year-old points his finger at you and tells you to hand over all the money, you'll look a mug if you give him your cash point number.

We all judge each other, almost instantly, by the things we do, the things we say, and the things we don't do or say. I'll develop this more in the classroom section.

So there you have it. People are fallible, conscientious, cooperative, cruel, primitive, sophisticated biological organisms, animals that may or may not have a higher essence, but if they do it certainly doesn't impact a great deal on how they behave. Now we can move on to some more stuff.

How does any of this relate to the classroom?

Issues of dominance, status and self-image are crucial in the classroom context. Why? Because you as the teacher are going to have to get them to do your bidding, to exert some kind of control over them, in order to get any teaching done. If you're not comfortable with that statement, then maybe teaching isn't for you. Seriously. I wouldn't kid about this kind of stuff. I have genuinely seen teachers who think that getting the class to do what they want isn't part of what they signed up for, and they're not prepared to do it. Really? Perhaps my bin man should protest that collecting rubbish isn't really his cup of tea, and is there any way he could be a bin man and just, I don't know, *look* at rubbish or something? This is the job, and this is your role. And if you aren't prepared to put the spade work into your teaching then why the hell are you doing it?

Teaching isn't a job; it's a vocation, it's a calling. It's also a hell of a responsibility – after all, you're going to make a difference to their lives, whether you like it or not. If you're rubbish at the job then you'll make one kind of difference to them. If you're not rubbish then you might make a better kind of difference to them. This is other people's lives we're talking about here, and they don't have another one spare for you to waste or take lightly. So it's not only a vocation, but one of the biggest responsibilities you're ever likely to face bar parenthood.

If you're not comfortable with controlling others, then leave the room, the book shop, whatever. Put this book down. If you bought it, I'll refund you. In fact, no I won't, because you made the stupid decision to come into teaching. If you feel that the little darlings will come round to you eventually if you let them express themselves as they see fit, then run, I said *run*, don't walk, out of education, because you're not safe with kids. Honestly, have some yourself if you like, and screw those ones up, but don't you dare play loony teacher with someone else's children because I will personally come round and chin you, you vile reptile.

I presume now that they've gone and taken their sanctimonious odour with them that I can talk to an audience of adults who are prepared to accept that they are going to have to exert their will over others. How does it happen?

Dominance over others is a subtle art. It happens because of a huge variety of reasons, but fortunately the major ones can be described quite easily and certainly in terms that we can quickly take on board as teachers. It used to be said that kids had more respect for authority figures back in the good old days (that's probably true to some extent, although I'm always dubious about reference to the good old days. Which good old days are we referring to here? The ones where kids were sent to get shot at by Jerry in the mouldering trenches? Or the ones where limp, pneumonia-ridden urchins were sent up chimneys or sold in Victorian gentlemen's flesh pots? Which good old days are these? If there was a split second where the world resembled Narnia then I must have blinked and missed it, because things have seemed to be perpetually pretty *challenging* from where I stand).

It is probably true to say that children deferred more to elders – teachers, coppers and clergy – thirty or so years ago. My grand-mother's entire street would rustle like an enormous lace sail as a row of curtains twitched simultaneously as the priest glided along from teapot to teapot. Tellies would dim as his footsteps came up the path, so that the poor man must have thought that TVs were some kind of occult Ottoman in everyone's front room.

Even when I was at school I could never have conceived of anyone, not even the *mental* kids, saying half the stuff to teachers that we routinely get these days. In my first year I took a young charmer outside a lesson to have 'a talk' with her, and she screeched, 'Who the hell do you think you are taking me outside?'

'I'm your teacher and an adult.' 'So?' she responded. You know the kind of thing. It's probably why you're reading this.

Deference is not what it used to be. Dominance cannot be assumed any more simply by virtue of your position, experience, qualifications, age or assumed wisdom. I mean, what use are all *those* things anyway? Did Chantelle win *Celebrity Big Brother* because she had a degree? Did Paris Hilton get where she is because she worked hard? Of course not. They had the X Factor! Later on I'll discuss some of the possible reasons for this change in attitude but for now it's enough to acknowledge that it is true; it is existent; it is a very live parrot. This doesn't mean that it has declined universally, or in the same levels everywhere, just that it cannot be assumed. Play the cards you're dealt.

What are you going to do about it? Dominate in other ways. I've been on dozens of courses for behaviour management, for NLP, the power of the voice, body language, how to win friends and influence people. I've read scores and scores (and, possibly, scores) of books on this subject, from loony mystics to big business self help gurus (I was going through a phase, I confess. They had names like *Who moved my Cheese?* and *The Seven Habits of Effective Inquisitors*. I managed to pull myself out of it. It didn't take a book).

The net result of this voyage through the seedy back alleys of self-realization can be summed up quite neatly: good behaviour management is mostly just common sense. Everything I learned (that made sense or seemed useful in any way) I had already seen displayed by people in nightclubs, by good parents, policemen, by bouncers, by good entertainers, good teachers I already knew. They did it automatically, without even thinking about it. And if you asked most of them to explain how come they could hold an audience/get their kids to put their socks on/leave a club quietly, they wouldn't have the foggiest. Here's the simplest summary I can do for you. You're welcome.

1. It's what you do, not what you say

When you watch a politician make an election promise during an election campaign, do you go, 'Oh boy! Free ice cream for *everyone*? Zero crime by *next year*? He's the man for me!'? Or do you go, 'show me'? When the *Reader's Digest* lets you know that you have been *specially* selected (by a *computer*, no less) to win £1 million, do you weep hysterically and book yourself into a suite at the Playboy Mansion, or do you wait for the Great Satans of RD to show you the money?

If you answered 'option a' for either of these, then have I mentioned that I have some magic beans that I could sell you? Everyone else who breathes oxygen knows that talk is cheap, and that threats are cheques that are easy to write and hard to cash. The first time you say something, and then don't do it, you let the other party know exactly what you really meant in the first place. Actions speak louder than words. An empty threat is simply a lie, and liars never prosper. See how many aphorisms I could squeeze in?

If an animal was confronting a rival by standing up tall and banging its chest (curiously, gorillas actually do this. I thought it was just in Tarzan movies), but then scattered like smoke at the first sight of trouble, the second gorilla wouldn't take his threats seriously twice. So don't make the same mistake (and certainly don't bang your chest) by talking big to the kids and then acting small.

2. Act tough

Did you know that 80 per cent of our communication is non-verbal? How did we get to that figure? It sounds awfully precise to me. But then social scientists always get a bit funny with the idea that their subject might not be as scientifically solid as, say, gravity or the workings of a car engine. I don't really care, because it's plain that whether it's 80 per cent, 60 per cent or 99 per cent, the answer is 'a lot'. Following on from the idea that we should do as we say, it becomes clear that what we do is a way of saying something. If I tell you *I love you* (I do, I really do) while holding your nose in a vice, what message do you take? Unless you exist in a peculiar subculture that equates aggression with affection (or Glasgow) then you'll be confused and probably a bit offended. If a waiter walks past you in a crowded busy restaurant and says 'I'll be right with you,' as they rush away, eyes to the kitchen, face drawn with sweat and tension, how sincere do you think they're being? 80 per cent?

If I tell a class of rioting children that their parents will all be called if they don't behave, but I'm screaming it at one pupil, or whispering it softly to the wall, how credible is my message? What am I really communicating to them?

3. Talk like you expect to be heard

Speak softly and carry a big stick. This is a bit like 'say what you mean'. You should almost never scream at kids. Almost never. The few sole exceptions I make are for when the class genuinely can't hear you, and you need to exceed their volume to get them to hear you. Or if Ludwig van Beethoven is sat at the back of your class. Otherwise I wouldn't bother. Keep your voice just above conversational level, and keep the words slow and even. Speak as if what you say has authority. It does. You're the teacher, for God's sake.

Hurried, rushed language, a high pitched tone, stumbling over words – all these suggest insecurity, uncertainty and exhibit the fear that you won't be listened to. If you talk quickly it can suggest that you are worried empty air will be filled with someone else interrupting you. Let some air creep into the way you speak. It lends presence to what you say, and frames your words with an aura of authority. 'Look at my splendid words!' it seems to say. 'Kneel, worms!'

Practise this at home. Alone.

4. Think about how you move

Walk tall. Your body is speaking before you do, so pay attention to what it's saying. When you talk to the students do you face them and speak to them straight? Or are you turned away, or worse, moving at the same time? Like speech, movement requires gravity; considered, slow gestures, and restraint. Don't pace up and down like Johnny Ball, plant your feet on the ground like an oak and put your shoulders back. Head up. If you don't know what to do with your hands, hold a book, or keep them to your sides. But don't move about as if you're nervous, because that's what it looks like. A lion holds its ground.

5. It's your room

Set boundaries. Animals do this by peeing at strategic points. DFE guidelines probably prohibit this (probably; I haven't checked. They do like their guidelines, though) so best not to. But you can still make it crystal clear to your charges that they are in your space, not the other way about. How many times have you been worried about going into 'that' classroom with 'that' class? Think how absurd that this is – you are a grown up, a subject expert with a lifetime of experience. You can vote, drive a car, make a baby, join the army, buy fags, whatever. Some of them couldn't even get into a cinema to see *Spy Kids 4* without a grown up.

How do you make it your space? Put things the way you want it. You don't like the chairs and tables in rows? Move them. You want them sitting on the floor in a circle? Do it. Be there before they get there if at all possible and put things out the way you want. Set the board up, get the books out, do anything you fancy that says, 'I am here, I am ready, you tiny monkeys. Dance, monkeys, dance!' Throw your weight around in a way that immediately tells them, 'Me Tarzan.' Give them a seating plan. Get them all to take their caps off. Do it, anything you like, as long as you think it is conducive to a safe and ordered learning environment. There's a wonderful line in the *Watchmen* novel/film, where the captured vigilante Rorschach is put in prison along with scores of villains he himself put away. They think it's Christmas because they can settle old scores; but he just hospitalizes anyone that comes near him, and screams at the terrified room of criminals, 'you don't understand! *I'm* not locked up in here with *you*! *You're* locked up in here with *me*!' I couldn't put it better so I won't try. It's your room, not theirs.

6. Don't blow your top

Keep your cool. One of the best ways you can show that you're in charge is to show that you're in charge of yourself. Try to avoid losing your temper at all costs; don't raise your voice much, and show emotion sparingly. This is all an act, of course – you'll no doubt be boiling or wilting inside, but have some control. You're a professional. If you react emotionally to something that they do, then they can see that they've got under your skin, and that they can take little piranha-sized bites out of your ass. So if somebody refuses to follow an instruction, don't blow your top. Just take the name, issue the detention and follow up, nice and quietly.

When you speak and react to them, do it impassively, whether it's a positive or negative thing. The best advice I was ever given about tone of voice was to imagine I was buying a pound of potatoes in a greengrocer (if you were born after 1985 try to imagine a very tiny Tesco, with no car park. And human beings behind the counter). You wouldn't snarl at the counter assistant, would you? No. You'd talk to them as if what you were saying was reasonable and natural. Pound of carrots, please. No debate expected. Dominance is a funny thing. If you speak to someone as if they're a piece of dog dirt, then all that they'll hear is, 'I'm important and you're nothing.' Bad outcome, because automatically you've set yourself up against them, and anything you might have asked them will be forgotten, which isn't exactly the result you want (I once watched a bouncer as he walked over to a table of perfectly reasonable ladies and said, 'Are you going to f***ing drink up and go, then?' Funnily enough, they didn't really hear anything after the fifth word.)

At the other extreme, if you are too ingratiating with them (i.e. display very low dominance), they'll assume you're weak, and subconsciously what they'll hear is, 'I am pathetic, nothing I say is valuable. You are far more important.' So please, please don't say to a room of belligerent pupils who view you with disdain, 'Please class, I'd love it if you did some work, it would be really good of you.' Begging is awful; it's like, man, who farted?

No, best you go with the assertive, neutral tone, posture and character when you start with a class. It carries a lot more weight than wheedling, or barking at them. It suggests that they are simply one thing on your busy schedule that you have to deal with, and you won't brook any interference with your agenda.

Punishment and Rewards

Here is a basic piece of human psychology: people like things they enjoy, and dislike things they don't. Did I go too fast for you? Go back and read it again. I apologize. Now I'm going to build on that premise: people will do things to avoid things they dislike, and do things to get things they like. You can relax now, that's as far in as I go (insert joke. I can't be bothered). Of course, you knew that, it's the very basis of punishment and reward: you punish behaviour you disapprove of and reward behaviour you like. In a classroom (and, I think, in life) this one thing is true: people will do a helluva lot more to avoid punishment than they will to gain a reward. It's true; the threat of an immediate punishment is a far more powerful influence over behaviour than a promise of an equivalent benefit. The stick is far mightier than the carrot.

I know that where this is going makes some people feel uneasy: congratulations if it does. The desire to inflict pain or punishment on another must surely rank among the least lovely of aspects of the human psyche. It seems sadistic. It is. But that alone doesn't affect the truth of it either way. We are far more influenced by the fear of pain than we are by the promise of pleasure. Slaps win over doggie treats every time. That's why behaviour management systems in classes entirely devised around rewards are well intentioned, but doomed to failure overall: because some pupils (Many? Most? Enough to ruin it for everyone else, certainly) just won't be bothered to chase the carrots you dangle. But everyone (nearly; a tiny minority won't, but you'll have personalized strategies for them) flinches at the thought of punishment.

It's perhaps not the most edifying portrait of the human animal, but still true: we like to be comfy. We'll shift endlessly in our sofas to get to a point where we're *not uncomfortable*, but often do little actually to improve our lives significantly.

And in the classroom? Same principle. Of course you have to reward good behaviour (and any other aspect of their education like, oh I don't know, academic progress and effort). But if you don't have a system of sanctions in place then eventually your wagon wheels come off. Some teachers never use sanctions and still get good behaviour. How? Because they've been doing it for long enough for the kids to know that they will be punished if they cross the line – in other words, the sanctions were there in the first place, and now the children have been habituated to good behaviour, so that nobody needs to be punished.

If there's no threat of reprisal, they'll do whatever they want. Why shouldn't they? Innate goodness? I've covered that already: even if it were true, it wouldn't, it *couldn't* apply to every one of them – there would still be a minority of chair chuckers to ruin it all. It only takes a few naughty kids to make a class go sour.

So whatever you do in a classroom, for God's sake, have a system of punishment. Make sure it is *consistent, fair* and *proportional*. If it's not consistent, then all you teach them is that *sometimes* they can get away with it, so they'll keep doing it (whatever it is). If it's not fair then they will loathe you at a level approaching the supernatural. Cue: accusations of racism, sizeism, favouritism, and charming phone calls from parents accusing you of 'picking on' their unlovely offspring. And if you're not proportional, then you'll get a reputation for being nasty, and they'll probably be right. If a kid forgets his pencil once, don't blow the roof off in your mighty wrath.

Basically, you punish them when they do something you don't like, and reward them when they do something you do. But you should be doing a lot more of the former and less of the latter, at least initially. If you reward them too much they'll think that you're a rosy-cheeked Santa Claus, not the pillar of destiny and authority you need to be. If you're too nice to them (and yes, you can be too nice) they won't respect you, sad but true. They'll think you're a pushover, and you will be, and they'll have no hesitation before committing an endless stream of miserable misbehaviours. Also, be *very* careful when you reward someone, and for *what*. If a class has been bloody awful (or some individual has been shrieking like a moron throughout the lesson) please, please (and I'm begging you here) don't say 'thank you' to them at the end, or something insane like, 'you weren't too bad there,' because they shut the hell up for thirty seconds at the end to stuff some Skittles in their gob. It's really important that we praise positive behaviour, but if you only do that then all they hear is sweetness and light. Sorry, but you don't have the time for that in a room full of twenty or so kids, all of whom deserve an education. You've let them down by indulging the selfishness of one. That tactic might work in a one-to-one environment, or a PRU, or a booster group. It doesn't work in a class.

Show them you've got teeth; the only way to do that is to bite them. I'm not suggesting you just sink your teeth in randomly but make sure that they know exactly where you stand on behaviour. Draw your line(s) in the sand. Then, if anyone crosses it, imagine you set a wolf trap on it. SNAP! The sanctions apply. Someone else does it? SNAP! Off goes another trap (you've got plenty, don't worry). And so on. SNAP! SNAP! The first time somebody crosses one of your lines and nothing happens, they learn that they can cross that line, even if it's only sometimes. So they'll rush over your line and see what other lines they can cross. In other words, imagine you're in Jurassic Park. You've got the electric fences to keep them out, right? Lots of signs that say *No Entry. You are approaching a Forbidden Zone.* The kids are the raptors (like the comparison?), racing along your fence to see if there's a section where the fence is down, or the current isn't on. As soon as they find it, they're through, and looking for the next fence to jump over.

All this happens very quickly, usually by the end of the first few lessons, certainly by the end of the first few weeks. They'll behave reasonably for a while, sniffing around the fences, padding innocently about, but when they start crossing lines (or fences) they won't stop until *they* feel like it, or *you* do something about it. Remember: fences; electricity. You have the juice. They are the raptors. How far will you let them get?

Never Give Up

This is the simplest advice I can give, because it draws on all the other aspects I've mentioned so far. Kids believe what you do more than what you say (oh, untrustworthy children) because in our more cynical age, we believe the evidence of our eyes more than our hearts. So if you set a detention, then it must happen. If someone doesn't show then as far as they are concerned, if nothing happens to them, then you might as well not have set it. Pouf! It's gone, like magic. So never give up. Keep your admin on detentions and phone calls home tight; that means write it down, alas, and cross off pupils as they attend your sanctions, or otherwise. Keep times, dates and details of incidents, so that when they challenge you (and they will, they will) you have the ammunition to settle the matter. For every time they ignore a detention, a meeting, a deadline etc., then escalate the sanction so that they regret calling you on it.

Remember, if we assume the animal paradigm I'm suggesting, you should only have to do this a few times before you have trained them into a certain pattern of behaviour and responses. It may not be pleasant to smack a pup when it leaves a turd on your rug, but would you prefer you were hand washing excrement out of wool until your pooch expires in fifteen years, or would you rather train it into a more agreeable behaviour pattern of laying its canine eggs in the garden? That one was rhetorical. Pursue them across the endless wastes of time. You are the Terminator. Did Arnie give up? No. The matter is settled.

We are teaching these kids to behave, not because we get kicks out of controlling people, not because you never had any friends at school, but because you care about them. You care about them so much that you want them to do well. Because you want them to do well, you will insist that they obey your rules, because they are the basis of a good educational environment. That, after all, is the big picture. It might hurt them a little; the rules might pinch a few. It might even bore them. But you are the grown up, and you have their interests at heart – more importantly, you know what's good for them, in the same way that a healthy diet might not be as exciting as Lobster Thermidor with chips, but it'll help you live a lot longer.

In some ways, your behaviour management rules are like Bran Flakes, or exercise – sometimes depressingly wholesome, but vital nonetheless. You're not doing this job because you want them to like you (if it happens it's nice. But seriously, who has 12-year-old friends, apart from Jonathan King? I like *loads* of my kids; maybe they like me, but none of them are my friends. I don't set detentions for my friends, or chew them out when they forget their pens ten times in a row. I have drinks with my friends, and allow them to criticize my self-destructive lifestyle choices. I swear with them, and take their life advice seriously). You're doing it because they *need* you. They need you to be an adult, to take charge, to be in control. As a wise old owl of a colleague once said to me, 'Kids are funny. They resent authority, and they crave it at the same time.' True, brother. Ask any kid what makes a good teacher, and alongside all the usual red herrings of *funny, makes us laugh* and the like, you'll invariably see them say *can control a class.* It's universal. Kids respect you if you show that you are worthy of respect. They will damn you if you are weak. It might not be pretty, but it's true.

Let's not forget what kids are doing: they're learning to be people. They have rights, of course they do, loads of them. They may even have something worth saying at times. But never lose sight of the fact that we are here to guide them through and into adult life. We are not there simply to impart pages of information at them. We never were. We're teaching them to be people. That means we have to face up to our responsibilities as teachers and acknowledge that we are in charge. I think that's one of the most damaging things I've seen in the profession since even *I* started: the almost craven uncertainty some of us have as to how much power and control we do or should have. Or 'do we have the right to set rules for them?' At its worst, this uncertainty has led to pathetic attempts to placate the egos of children, to negotiate rules with them, and to try to *convince* them that they should do as they are told.

To hell with all that. If a four-year-old wants to touch a burning coal, do I negotiate with her, patiently explaining *why* she mustn't do it? Of course not. I just tell her she mustn't. If I'm wise I'll explain why, but fundamentally she should follow my instructions because I said so. Now, as the four-year-old grows up, she is perfectly entitled to start questioning the way things are, and maybe start thinking of the ways things should be (and good for them – that's what growing up is all about). But she has to earn the right to make the rules, like I did. And until then, she'll follow the rules set because older, wiser people than her have said that they are just, fair and correct.

For example, as a teacher of philosophy, I'm aware that many things in life are neither right or wrong, but somewhere in the middle. Is it ever right to kill, for instance? Maybe … In war, possibly. In self defence, possibly. You get the drift. But I'll tell a child that killing is wrong, and lying is wrong, and stealing is wrong, even though I know full well it isn't as simple as that. Why? So that she gets the idea and as she grows up she can learn the subtleties of the argument. But it's too much to expect a four-year-old to appreciate the finer points of ethics, of the complexities of life, so I won't burden her with them.

Similarly, it's too much responsibility to give most teenagers the right to make the rules for themselves, because they just aren't there yet, they're just not ready. Many of them are in a psychological phase that could be described as 'up their own asses', i.e. they are self-obsessed in a way that they are likely never to be again. Many of them find it difficult to empathize with the needs of others. Many of them are focused on questions of identity to the exclusion of the rights of people around them. In a word, they're a bit selfish. But that's OK: it's to be expected. I was a bit like that too; I didn't know any better. What I didn't need was some well meaning DFE gonk telling me how 'valuable' my thoughts and feelings were, and that if I wanted to misbehave I was simply 'communicating a need'. Give me strength. Children are instructed by adults, until they become adults themselves, and then we'll let them do what they see fit – as long as they can take the consequences. They can shut the hell up and listen to us until that point.

We are the adults. We are the teachers. They are the children, and it is our duty (and honour) to help them do what we have already done, to match and sometimes exceed us. That is why our job is so important, and if we are going to do it properly, then we're going to have to teach them how to behave.

'Who the Hell do you think you are?'

I'm your Teacher.

2 | Dealing with low-level disruption

A stream cuts a score down a mountain until it becomes a ravine, and then a valley. It doesn't do this because it's powerful. It succeeds by persistence and patience, using the same weapon with which a weed splits a paving slab: time. A student can do the same to your lesson, and eventually your sanity, if they are allowed to drip, drip, drip away at you. Low level disruption is what teachers face most of all, and most often. You can forget the staffroom stories of deodorant-can flamethrowers and chairs thrown across windows (actually don't forget about them: see Chapter 6), because the reality of the job is a playful brook (not a torrent) of niggly, annoying behaviours that will wear you down in a thousand cuts.

Low level disruption appears, in isolation, like nothing at all. It's hardly worth even mentioning to your non-teaching pals when you emerge from your educational cocoon at the weekend and pretend to have a normal life. But when you combine the cumulative effects of all those tiny, persistent little goblins chattering away around you, it adds up to an ocean of misery, a long night of the soul that stretches out forever. Low level disruption is kryptonite for the well planned lesson.

What qualifies as low-level disruption? I can offer two answers: a definition, and examples. Examples are easier to start with: chair rocking, pen tapping, chatting over others, chatting over you, passing notes, passing wind, entering late, chewing gum, texting, drawing in their book, poking their partners ... in fact maybe it isn't so easy to categorize exhaustively. Let's define it instead: anything that undermines the flow of your lesson without actually blowing it out the water. I usually define it as 'anything that annoys me', although that might not be very useful to you, not being me and all. It's the little stuff, the wriggly, niggly behaviour that pupils do instead of learning, when they don't dare to tell you to stick your lesson where even OfSTED won't go.

And that's why it's so corrosive; because of all the things you'll have to handle as a teacher this stuff will be constantly with you, looking over your shoulder like Long John Silver's parrot, pooping gaily on you as you take the register, and laughing. It's an inevitable part of teaching, like barnacles on a boat. Because it seems so minor, it feels like it should be easy to handle: and so it is – in isolation. Any teacher who can manage to inhale and exhale successfully can deal with a lone pupil clicking the lid of his biro a couple of times. But a whole class doing it, intermittently, while others make sinister humming noises at the same time as the whole back row are placing bets on when your stack will blow, for how long, and how high … now *that's* hard.

If you're a member of the human race you have a limit on your patience. You will also have a limited number of things that you can focus on before you feel as though you are surrounded by a room of breakdancing oompa loompas. It is amazing how it only takes a few annoyances to drive you insane. Two things to remember:

1. It happens a lot
2. It's hard to put out a dozen fires at once

Pupils know all this stuff already. They know that they can put the mercury of your blood pressure through the rafters like a fairground try-your-strength . Most pupils don't have the guts to stand up to you directly – believe it or not, they are only kids, and despite the reputation some have for torching orphanages and selling their grannies on eBay, most are still pretty intimidated by grown-ups. So instead of standing up in your lesson and pirouetting through the class, most will amuse themselves with the time-honoured pastime of teacher-baiting. Unlike bear-baiting, this is still legal. Understand that the motives for this kind of behaviour fall broadly, into three categories:

1. To watch you change colour
2. To distract you and themselves from a fascinating lesson on Jewish food law.
3. Because they've switched off so much they are trying to occupy themselves. Poor loves. What on earth is there for them to do in a classroom? Oh yes …

Most teachers (especially new ones) are very switched on to bad behaviour – it leaps out at them, begging to be squashed. So when several things happen at once, or something happens repetitively, it gets extremely stressful, extremely quickly. The most important thing to try to do is not to let it disturb you, or get under you skin. Yeah, I know – easy right? But most of this disruption is aimed at entertaining themselves, pure and simple. If they see you having an aneurysm, there's nothing more guaranteed to get them to repeat the behaviour. If they see that you aren't bothered by their low level japes, then they will soon get bored and look for something else to do. With luck, it'll be your lesson.

How do you keep your temper? In chapter 8 I look at managing the stress of being a teacher, inside and out of the classroom, but for now it's sufficient to say that it involves a change in your attitude. You have to not care so much about it. You have to realize that it's not personal (they don't know you) and that you're doing a job, not raising your children. And you absolutely have to know, deep down in your giblets, that any misbehaviour will be punished – if not in the classroom, then hereafter (and I don't mean in Heaven.). The simple knowledge of this – and I mean you have to *know* it – will give you the satisfaction of keeping your cool when even Fonzie would be spitting feathers.

Low-level behaviour of this sort is also a way of keeping themselves occupied in other ways, because quite simply they're often just bored, their attention wandering all over the archipelago of your educational voyage. This book looks specifically at behaviour, so I won't dwell on the necessity of keeping lesson pace brisk and interesting – mainly because all the bells and whistles in a lesson won't get them motivated if the teacher can't deal with the behaviour. If George Bush were a teacher (rather than a clownish nightmare) he would have said 'It's the behaviour, stupid.' So how do you deal with the actual behaviour itself?

Apart from pretending that you don't actually want to burst the miscreants like balloons, the main processes that need to happen are **name taking** and **ass kicking**. That's it. There is no way to get around it – this is what you have to do to be a teacher in an even remotely challenging school. A bin man has to lift rubbish; a tailor sews seams; a lawyer will … well, do whatever lawyers do that requires me to mortgage my soul every time I need one. You're not a failure if you have to do this stuff. You're a success. You're a professional. You're doing your job right. You'll do it for as long as you teach. Never ask, 'When will I be able to stop telling them off?' Because the answer, Grasshopper, is 'maybe never'.

As you can see in the questions and answers that follow, the procedures for handling the small stuff is easy in theory and tiresome in practice. It is entirely a war of attrition, and the key thing is for you to win. You mustn't flinch, or blink, or break eye contact. Do that and you'll win. Don't do it, and you'll be fighting the same battle for as long as you teach.

So what do you want to do?

Hypochondriacs and how to cure them

Dear Tom

I've just started on my PGCE in Year 4, and it's going OK except for one thing: my class seems to be afflicted by a plague of sniffles, headaches, sore tummies and runny noses. The kids constantly come to me and say they're not feeling well, and they want to blow their nose/see the nurse/go home/eat McNuggets all the time. I don't overfuss with them, and I treat it seriously but efficiently every time. But it's all the time! Sometimes I have my hands tied for about twenty minutes dealing with it all! Of course I can't ignore it either, in case they really are ill. What do I do? I'm a teacher, not a paramedic!

For suspected hypochondriacs it can be useful to meet their complaint with firm, serious concern and say something like, 'Hmm, I see. Well, sit quietly until break/lunch etc and we'll see how you feel then.' Then soon after, instigate a lively or fun activity that requires active participation. If the complainant appears to be joining in boots first, then you know they were exaggerating their illness; if not then they may be genuine. If their eyes start rolling back, they probably needed a hankie. Or *Holby City* has lost a midget.

Her sick mum means I can't call home

Hi Tom

I've got a difficult Year 8 class, but I pretty much have most of them where I need them. But there's one girl who's a real problem – and when I spoke to the Head of Year, she said she couldn't do much because the pupil's mum had just had a stroke. Plus her brother has mental issues, and tries to kick her door in at home.

I really feel for her; her home life sounds dreadful, but I can't take her aggressive behaviour. I don't feel that I can phone home either. How do I get past this?

This pupil needs clear rules and firm boundaries possibly *more* now than before because of the turmoil and anxiety in her home life. I imagine her mother would be terrified that her present condition would in any way contribute to her daughter's education suffering. If I were her I would be hoping that other responsible adults in her daughter's life would support her as much as they could.

You don't say if this girl is looking after her mother, or is looked after herself, or another parent/guardian is involved. If there is another adult presence in her life, then get in touch with this person and explain the need for school sanctions to apply to all pupils, no matter what their situation. Compliance to the values of a community is an expectation that the community can make of us, and this girl needs to know it. Her mother is going through one of the most challenging times of her life. In a sense, harsh as it may sound, how *dare* her daughter use that as an excuse to treat others and you rudely? Her mother needs support, not the worry that her daughter is going off the rails.

OK, that's the tough talking she needs to hear if she tries to play the 'you can't talk to me, my mother's sick,' card. If her mother is well enough to communicate with the school then you should do so. Otherwise speak to other adults in her life that have influence. If she has to go home straight after school to assist her mother, then other sanctions/times must be sought. If she doesn't, and she still fails to attend school detentions, then regular procedures and sanctions should apply, up to and including exclusion.

Life's tragedies don't justify selfishness. They might explain it, or provide reasons, but not justifications or excuses. (I once had a pupil in Year 10 who lost her mother, and then actually came *in person* to explain to her teachers that she'd need some time off school and that she'd catch up in a few weeks. I was devastated by this level of maturity.) She needs a lot of love, and certainly you need to speak to her in a sympathetic and understanding way. Explain that you appreciate how difficult things are for her and her mum. But she also needs boundaries, and that's something we *can* provide.

She pretends to be deaf

Dear Tom

I teach a little madam in Year 10 who undermines me constantly. She pretends not to hear me, gets me to repeat everything, and then smirks at her friends afterwards about it. She butts in when I'm telling others off, and tuts at them; also she laughs her head off at any stupid, silly thing. And her Mum's a teacher! We've done detentions, and she gets better for a bit, but she always goes back to 'normal'. Any ideas?

This is the kind of behaviour that makes you want to poke your eyeballs out with wooden spoons, so frustrating and annoying it is (to borrow Yoda's sentence construction).

First of all the main controlling device for this behaviour will always be sanctions; ruthlesslessly, rigorously applied. *Every* time they laugh out loud, make snide comments etc, then the normal disciplinary cogs start to turn. Calmly, without fuss, inform them they have a detention/school sanction. Prior to this make sure you have clearly explained the following: laughing out loud = shouting out; tutting etc. during a telling off = talking over the teacher. All of these low level disruptive 'disguises' are weak attempts to wriggle out of being punished. It's deliberately sneaky, because the pupil is consciously attempting to insult you, but cloaking it in a secondary behaviour that they can complain was relatively innocent. If that's what they think, then as long as you've explained to them *once* that you consider that misbehaviour, then no matter how much they protest, they have to accept your definition, and if they repeat the behaviour then they've had fair warning.

So make sure that if it's every lesson they're pulling off this kind of stunt, then *every* lesson they get a smack on the nose with the discipline stick. If they fail to attend, then escalate all the way up until they get temporarily excluded if need be. *They* are bringing the escalation upon themselves, not you.

It sounds as if there might be a relationship issue (understatement, possibly) – does the pupil seem to dislike you? That underlies some misbehaviour, even if it's just because you're the only one who disciplines them properly. If you can, have a chat with them in which you (good cop) say that you really want them to do well and you think they could if they tried, but the reason that they're getting the detentions (bad cop) is because they keep breaking the rules of the class. You might be able to slip a little flattery into the conversation, on the basis that no one ever thinks they're a bad person, and their behaviour is always excusable in some way. In order to persuade them, you need to establish a common ground, some mutually agreeable territory that leads them to believe that you don't actually come from Mars, and that what you have to say might be valuable.

Lastly, try at all costs not to react to her/his petty behaviour, at least not in any way that gives them satisfaction – just tell them later about the punishment they're getting. If you don't rise to it they often drop it. They're doing it to annoy you, the little darlings.

They're not scared of me any more

Dear Tom

I'm beginning to doubt myself as a teacher – I've been one for years, and had a career break. Now that I'm back part time I find it very difficult, and the school isn't great anymore. Usually I teach small classes and things are at least OK.

When I do cover lessons (a lot), the class just won't do a thing I say. The lessons aren't of great quality, and the kids do just enough not to get me calling in the SLT, but they never really learn anything because I'm constantly fire-fighting for the whole lesson. That's not good enough for me. I love this job (loved?) but if I can't actually teach them then I wonder if I'm cut out for it any more. I feel as if all my classroom management strategies have vanished. I need some advice before I start to think about quitting. I used to be known as a fearsome dragon, but one that was nice once you got to know her.

We can't win every battle. Your ambition is laudable and professional. Covering strange classes is a test at the limits of every teacher's toolbox. It makes you realise that the best body language or presence in the world can't compete with the benefits of familiarity and clear codes of conduct, reinforced by repetition, sanctions and consistency.

If you really mean what you say, and you want to get to the bottom of this, then you're going to have to *commit* to generating a new reputation. Follow up on every misdemeanour in your covers – if you don't know their names then visit them in form rooms and get their teacher to identify them. Then follow the sanction/escalation route so beloved of teachers. And do this every time. It will take an almost heartbreaking level of commitment and time. It will seem as if nothing is working for a long time before your activities bed in. You will gnash and wail at the dawn like Job. Eventually you will have presence with them. 'She's the one that never gives up,' they will whisper to each other. Have you got the chops for that?

The alternative is perfectly reasonable. Bend when you need to in order not to be the reed that breaks. Build up your reputation slowly (much more slowly, given your part time status) and eventually they will acknowledge your authority. You will be the Dragon Lady again!

Can I save them from the gangs?

Dear Tom

I teach some extremely disaffected boys and have done for almost a year; most of them are in gangs, many of them take drugs (soft, I hope), and it is impossible to get them to engage with education for any reason. They just don't care about it at all, and can't see the point of it. They don't have anything like a life plan, and say that they only turn up to get their EMA allowances. I teach a practical workshop, and they only signed up for it because they thought it led to a job – but they don't even bother with it anyway! Surely there's some way of pulling these boys from the brink? I've tried everything I can think of. I've worked in some of the hardest schools in the East End of London, but I'm at a loss as to what to do next. Help!

Grim. If this is 6th form, then they need a behaviour and academic contract drawn up between them and the school. If they fail to comply, then some people need to be shown the door. That might give the others a practical incentive to buck up and start seeing sense.

A lot of arrogance and indifference in young men is a front – they say they don't care but many do. They care about what they'll do later in life; they care about living on the dole, etc. The other side of the coin is that they desire things – there are always things in life that people want, no matter how amoeba-like they seem. Even if it's money, phones and trainers, they aren't too stupid to see that all these things take cash, and cash takes graft. Read *Freakonomics* (see: **Further Reading**, at the end of this book) to understand how almost every member of a gang dealing drugs earns less than working in KFC, and with more danger, and no perks and benefits. So many young men imagine they'll get by in life by 'hustling', although they have little idea what that would look like as a lifestyle. Get some people from the outside to talk to them about how hard it is on the dole.

They also need to learn to believe in themselves – that's a *huge* task. Tell them stories about men and women that are inspirational, about people who came from poverty and made it in some way. If they *are* in sixth form then many of them are probably beyond your ability to help – but not all. Purge the worst offenders, putting pressure on those that remain. Then work with them to show them strategies that will take them places. Perhaps a few of them only need the idea, or to know that someone believes in them, or that the world can be better or that they too can be better people.

The one who does nothing

Dear Tom

One pupil is causing me a headache. Without my constant presence and pressure, he does ... well, nothing. He's quiet, unobtrusive, and lives in his head, it seems. Getting the title, aim and date out of him is a daily mission. I checked the medical and additional support needs (ASN) files and there's nothing about him. I spoke to him about his work and he agreed to try harder and when I asked if there was anything I could change that would help him, he said no. His Mum is onboard, but even other veteran teachers can't get much from him. But at the rate he's going, he'll fail the course (he's Year 10 – it's not too late). But he also sees himself as thick because some of the kids in the class are quite able. Where do I go with him?

This is the other side of behaviour – a pupil who isn't disruptive but is 'behaving' in a way you can see will lead to massive underachievement.

Threats and punishments will only go so far with this boy – he *might* be encouraged to do a bit more if only to avoid the drudgery of detentions. But he will only do the bare minimum in order to avoid incurring your wrath, which doesn't feel like much of a solution. Besides, it will take mountains of sweat on your part to generate a sparrow fart of work. Hardly inspiring.

What's the home background like? Is education of little account there? If family don't support and endorse the school, then the child probably won't either. But most parents (even those who dodged the system in their own youth) are smart enough to value learning for the sake of the pupil's future. Have you had a chat with them yet? Pressure from their end is worth a hundred detentions.

Fear of failure is indeed a potential obstacle – in which case give him loads of praise for anything positive. I recommend doing this in comment on his homework, as it becomes very personal and powerful. Note that 'anything' can (and should) include pastoral achievements: kindness, politeness etc.

This might be an extremely high mountain to climb – potentially a lifetime of discouragement and low self-esteem. So don't expect miracles, and don't feel a failure if progress is slow/non existent. Even if you never see the difference, he'll remember the effort you put in for the rest of his life, so even if you don't get him through the exam, you might just give him the memory of someone that believed in him. And that's something that might just be very valuable.

Pupils claim their behaviour is my fault

Dear Tom

I teach a girl in top set Year 10. She's sharp as a knife but gives me a lot of grief. Here's a typical example: "You're teaching's rubbish, and if I fail it's your fault." I started to write a detention note for her and she walked over to me and looked at what I was doing, then complained about how unfair I am, and I can't do that. Then she said that she was going to complain about me because I pick on her. Then she stole my board marker and eraser.

If she's bright then maybe you can surprise her by showing an interest in her intellect – it's possible (and common enough) for a G&T pupil to react to low challenge with misbehaviour; it's a method of displaying contempt. This in itself needs to be combated, but it's useful if you can tell her you know she's really bright and wonder if you can set her work that really challenges her. This appeal to her ego can also work wonders.

Despite this caveat, she needs to be brought down to earth, hard and fast. She sounds like a behaviour trendsetter, and if you don't crack down on her then she'll rule the class. She's a ringleader, and others will take their cues from her, so deal with it, otherwise she'll wreck the room for you (as you know). Apply your school behaviour sanctions with all the tenacity and force you can muster. If this girl isn't excluded or given a huge detention for stealing your board marker then the school needs to have a serious look at its policies, and how it supports its staff.

When Brainiacs attack: the bright kids terrorize me

Dear Tom

My school has lots of gifted and talented pupils, and although I really enjoy the challenge this provides for me as a subject expert, I've got some bright sparks that obviously try to 'catch me out'. When I say that I (sometimes) don't know the answer, they look smug and I overhear them say, "He doesn't know – again," or similar. I think they're trying to make me look stupid. What should I do – ignore it? Maybe they're just showing interest.

This is a dark side of the G&T equation: arrogance. It's far from interest, apart from their interest in being smug. A few suggestions:
Seat them apart from each other – you can re-jig the entire class so

they don't feel victimized. Or just move them. Who cares what they think? That way, if they need to make comments then they'll have to be audible ones ...

... which they seem to be already. In which case you have a clear case of rudeness to the teacher, which in my book suggests punishment. Say nothing in the class, and then keep them behind after the lesson (no explanation, to avoid confrontation in the classroom). Have 'the chat', which should cover rudeness and manners as key topics. Follow 'the chat' with 'the detention.' They clearly understand that making derogatory remarks about you is out of order, and the longer you ignore it, the longer you allow them to undermine you. This will reinforce their confidence, and lead them to greater heights of scorn. Worse, it could encourage others to do the same, given that you haven't crushed the cheeky blighters already.

Seriously, nail this behaviour now, or your class discipline will suffer – children can smell weakness, and respect strength in a teacher. They know that you know. So let them know something else, i.e. 'cross me and you'll regret it.'

The chattering classes: widespread talking in my set

Dear Tom

I've got several large classes of over 26 pupils classes, and a few of them are giving me severe problems. In each class there will be around seven or so students who chatter so much that it actually becomes impossible to teach. I set detentionsfor them but the next lesson they still continue to do the same thing. My lessons are being hijacked as each time I have them I know I can't send them all out. If I even draw breath they're off again, and I can't remember a moment of silence in the room with them. What do I do?

An aggravating situation to be sure. How long have you had them? If all year, then you need to look at what they are doing in detentions – is it severe enough to act as a deterrent? Make sure that they are doing *work*, and don't accept it from them if it's not completed to your satisfaction.

Are the detentions long enough? If you only give them five minutes or so then it's not enough (see: deterrent, above). Half an hour at least for disrupting a lesson, in silence, with work, or you escalate. Half an hour becomes an hour, becomes two, becomes a Head of Year detention, or a Saturday detention, or an internal exclusion (I refer you to your school behaviour policy). Make sure they escalate. Frankly, if a pupil was to get a detention every lesson, week after week, then I would automatically escalate the sanction, on the grounds that their disruption was persistent and wilful. Oh yeah.

Who's involved? This sounds as if other colleagues (senior to you) need to get involved. Get the parents in for a chat, and use home discipline as an extension of your discipline. Where are they in the class? Isolate them geographically. Give them no one to talk to.

Reiterate your behaviour policy to them, and apply sanctions *every* time they transgress. *Never* give up and *always* set (and attend) detentions fairly and evenly. With consistency you will find that all but the toughest nuts respond to treatment. Then you get the nutcrackers out.

You don't really.

How do I harpoon the big-mouths?

Dear Tom

My class is great, except for two boys. Separately they're fine. Together ...
I'm gonna do time for them. The first one is a big gob on legs – all attitude, late, lazy. The second one is just silly, but follows the first one like a puppy and does what he does. They're bright, but of work there is nowt. The whole class detests the first boy, and I know he doesn't mind being sent out into the next class all the time. They think it's my bad teaching but it's him – he's an arrogant sod. He's just set himself against me – he never listens when I talk to him, and never makes the improvements he says he will.

They banned kids up chimneys, right? OK, plan B. The thing that jumped out at me was 'bright' (actually 'nowt' jumped out too). I deal with a lot of bright kids who exhibit behavioural problems (OfSTED-speak for cheeky) – arrogant, rude, lazy, contemptuous of lesser mortals, that sort of thing. There are two varieties:

1. The manic loner. The gifted kid who one day will have a nervous breakdown, screaming that we're all 'Worms' etc. See: Nietzsche, James Bond villains, etc.
2. The pair. Feeding off each other's arrogance, they magnify their self-esteem by fondling their partner's ego with secret handshakes, in-jokes, rolled eyeballs and telepathy.

You might have the latter. They've banded together and decided that your lesson is disposable, so they're going to wipe their feet on it. It's a competition between them as to who can be the most disrespectful. At the end of the day they swop stories and hug each other, teary-eyed. Perhaps I exaggerate. But the fact remains that together, these boys is moider. Can you separate them permanently? That should resolve the unpleasant dimension of their unhealthy dynamic. If this isn't an option then do the following: seat them apart (of course); punish them separately. Never allow them to sit detentions together. Get the parents in.

Appeal to their vanity while simultaneously differentiating appropriately – give them more challenging tasks. Perhaps they're bored, or feel the subject is easy. Make it hard. Easiest way of differentiating upwards? Give them work suitable for the year above, in design or structure or skill, while keeping the content similar/syllabus related. Perhaps if you can tackle the work while tackling the behaviour you might win them over at the same time as showing them who's boss. (Incidentally, the word 'moider' should be pronounced with a Jimmy Cagney accent.)

Too many SEN for me to deal with

Dear Tom

I'm training to teach English to Year 7s and 8s (my previous school was posh, this one less so). The reading age of the class averages seven years old. We have seventeen SEN kids in one class! Basically, I feel totally unprepared I never experienced this in my last school, and I am finding the kids' behaviour extremely difficult now – I can't get them quiet at all. I do firm but fair, but they only shut up for senior staff, which just makes me feel rubbish.

I'm trying to get them to be quieter, and try to copy experienced teachers but when they do it, it works, when I try it, it flops.

Another reminder, if we needed any, that good behaviour is axiomatic to good learning, and that no amount of teaching skills will make a significant impact until the class is listening and appropriately attentive.

You *are* unprepared, because the current British PGCE/teaching route is insufficiently focused on behaviour management. Sometimes you get lucky and can work with an expert, who guides you slowly through the process, sometimes not. Problem is, this process isn't rigorous or consistent. This, coupled with the general dislocation our society has experienced from traditional hierarchal structures (for good or bad), means that your job is much harder. I say this so that you don't blame yourself for being unable to meet your other targets. Of course, it might not be your *fault*, but it is your *responsibility* to do something about it if you want to get somewhere.

The senior staff have built up a relationship with the kids that you can't imitate immediately. What you can do is work on the structures and routines that the senior staff will have built their presence around, and that means good old-fashioned detentions, sanctions etc. Follow the school behaviour policy to a T, even if it means detentions every lunch-time, break and after school. Take names of non-attendees and follow up every time, escalating the sanction and calling home etc. Soon, the classes will see that you mean business, and all but the toughest nuts will fall into line.

Of course this assumes that you have good support from your line manager, one who is prepared to escalate the sanction for you. I suggest you observe some teachers you know who are great at controlling the kids and see how they conduct themselves, how they hold themselves etc. Remember that when you do observe someone, you might not be able to see how they control the class, simply because so much of what they do is behind the scenes, or has been done in the past, and the classes are trained into good behaviour already. But you can pick up very useful 'tone and style' tips.

Make sure your mentor is aware that the behaviour issue is impeding your progress in other areas, so that you are not judged harshly if you don't meet other goals.

I'm not even sure if she's breathing: the child who does nothing

Dear Tom

I have a child in Year 2 who almost never does any work at all. She's not rude, but just so easily distracted that virtually nothing goes in her book. I've tried praise, small goals, paired-ability work groups, coaching, coaxing and nagging, moving seats. I even got cross with her once. Nothing! Mum says she writes little stories by herself (I saw one and praised it a lot). What next to get her to work? Without work to assess she won't even get a level 2. Please help.

In a sense, there is work to assess, potentially: the child's stories. This single fact confirms that she can work and she does produce something. And stories mean creativity, independent effort etc. So this could the way in, the access to her education that you need.

Get her to write her stories in class, even at the expense of the regular work, but try to put a bit of a spin on the story work so that it links to the regular class work. Praise anything praiseworthy about the stories, especially if it does link to the syllabus. Then gradually try to move the emphasis of the tasks towards the work that *you* need her to do, while perhaps simultaneously keeping the story tasks going. After all, this could be her primary talent that would flourish under encouragement. For some kids, it's difficult to see things like maths and so on as important, especially if they interpret or understand the world artistically. Obviously she needs to learn the joys of algebra too, but try to engage her using what she enjoys and it might just pay off.

Punishing with rewards: how much praise should I give them?

Hi Tom

I have a new class, almost all boys, in Year 9. A large chunk of them are low ability. They squabble a lot when they work on computers in my ICT class. I'd love them to be more engaged with the lesson. I've heard that I should reward and praise them for even tiny achievements. So do you have any ideas for being more positive with them?

One part of the problem will inevitably be weak students sharing a computer. If they must share, then make sure they don't pair themselves off. Couple pupils who don't know each other, and mix up genders, ethnicities and peer groups. Try to pair more able with less able (which as a strategy can also be beneficial to more able students if it allows them to peer-teach).

In the absence of one computer per student, give a section of the class a non-computer task that needs to be completed in order to complete the next, computer-based task. Then reverse it. That way they can all be occupied individually (and managed in a similar fashion), and they learn that computer time is a privilege earned through preparation. Many weak students don't work well in groups (although some do), I have found, possibly because this may make it easier to fall into an anti-academic attitude.

If communication is an issue in the classroom, then make sure that you mark their homework diligently; this is an excellent opportunity to praise them for whatever positive behaviour you choose, without embarrassing them in front of their mates. It can have profound effects on their self-esteem, especially when it's clear that you've put time and effort into thinking specifically about them and their work.

Finally, a word on positivity; it's one of the best ways of raising success, but it mustn't be used in isolation from solid discipline. Always let them know when they've fluffed it. Otherwise we as teachers can be led into the trap of feeling that everything is permissible; the pupils sense this and discipline decays.

Jokers laugh at me – how can I make them take me seriously?

Dear Tom

My Year 6 class has a variety of issues – almost no girls and 11 pupils with SEN. My behaviour management is good, incidentally; I'm a deputy head at a primary.

I have a small group of boys who won't take any discipline seriously – they just giggle when someone tells them off, even the Head. This is driving some of my teachers up the wall. I can usually bring them down a peg when I get there, but it's exhausting for me. Any advice please, as I think they'll just keep doing it as time goes by.

Gigglers deserve their own circle of Dante's Hell. There are at least two significant factors here. Giggling is a classic ruse for getting a rise out of authority figures; they can always justify their behaviour by saying, 'We were only laughing!' (See also *sneezing/coughing/clearing throats*). This is of course, merely a feint – it's exactly the same as shouting out in a lesson or throwing bits of rubber (or any one of a seemingly infinite variety of depressing strategies for being a pain in the neck).

It also gets the desired effect – like a tiny fire ant burrowing under your cuticles. They can see it works with a broad spectrum of teachers, and as Darwin never said but probably thought: what works, wins.

One fit of giggles could be excused (few things are harder than suppressing a bout – in fact, it seems to exacerbate the depth of the hilarity) but repetition signifies defiance, or perhaps mental issues, but as it seems to be a group problem then I think we can rule out airborne mania.

Sounds like you have the right strategies in place – firm, but … what was the other bit again? I always forget. As long as *they* know that *you* know that it's a deliberate act of rudeness then they can't cry foul when you sanction them. Every outburst gets the punishment, every time. Try not to let them do detentions together, because one of the functions of this behaviour is to express camaraderie between the members of their little tribe, to signify the 'us-ness' of the group and the 'them-ness' of the square teachers. Shouting at them is exactly what they want, to get a rise out of the teachers and show their pals they can get to you.

Consequently show *no* emotion when they do it. Mark their cards with dignity, and carry out the punishment as coolly as if you were frying some onions. Never feed their appetite for disruption with the bread of your discomfort and they'll soon lose the stomach for nibbling at the table of … well, you get the idea.

The Joy of Text: mobile phones constantly interrupt my teaching

Dear Tom

Loads of my Year 10 boys spend all lesson with their hands under the desks, and looking down. I'm sure they're texting. How do I stop them without being too confrontational?

God, I hope they are texting, otherwise that's a whole other problem. If you want to keep it discreet then simply move the suspected texters close to you so that if they still want to chat compulsively about *The Apprentice's Big Brother; Uncovered* or whatever via the miracle of the mobile, you can spot them easily. In my school we reserve the right to confiscate any visible phone. But if you don't want to do that then simply seeing it is justification for a detention, nice and quiet.

Of course, I also recommend getting the iron hand/velvet glove combo out: 'Either I get the phone or it goes out of sight, Smiggins,' (accompanied by a dry, pained smile). You've shown a bit of humanity but reiterated the rules in a way that allows them to withdraw without losing face. If they say, 'What phone?' then you can keep the smile up and say, 'Ah good, then we don't have a problem if there isn't a phone.' They know. You know. Their mates know. Everyone's happy. Possibly.

Why's monkeys – Stopping kids who taunt you with questions

Dear Tom

Here's some pathetic behaviour that makes me potty; you ask a pupil to step aside for a quick word, and they explode with, "Why!? Why? What have I done? God!" It's so immature, and it's boys and girls that do it. They do it when you bend down next to them in a lesson too. However discreet you try to be, they howl about the invasion of their space. Usually it then degenerates into a huge row and a headache that lasts all day – how can I keep this kind of histrionic behaviour to a minimum?

We have to set the agenda. The more we respond to their behavioural cues, the more they are effectively controlling us. So in order to reverse this position, we have to set the agenda for behaviour. Respond as little as possible to their groans and grunts, unless it's to issue sanctions and warnings. If you engage with their line of enquiry, then they are leading you down a path. It's a bit like getting asked a really distracting, pointless (but possibly interesting) question during a lesson – it's so tempting to start talking about it, but then you know the kids have got you, deliberately distracting you from the aim of the lesson (and usually, them working).

If a kid shouts, *Why?* or indeed anything else, then that's shouting in a lesson – as far as I'm concerned, that's an automatic punishment, detention, whatever. They have to be trained in appropriate behaviour, so make it unpleasant for them when they cross the line. Think of it as an electric buzzer attached to their chairs; whenever they misbehave, you flip the switch :-)

I'm kidding. Don't wire them up.

They call me mate, they call me rude boy. Pupils who get too familiar

Dear Tom

I'm in my second year of teaching in a difficult inner-city secondary school; my problem: lots of students call me 'mate', or 'blood' in the corridor – and always when there are loads of students around, never when we're alone, which makes me think they are extracting the p**. Now there's a development – some of them call me by my surname, as in, "Alright, Bradburn!?" It's not just the same kids – it's loads of them, and to different teachers. It really makes me lose my cool because it's quite a humiliating and demeaning feeling. Are there any solutions to this? I find it hard to try to follow up on it all. Thanks.

I find that the best approach is to ignore them completely. If they see it gets your goat then they will repeat the process until you go bonkers. But if you don't feed their pleasure then they'll quickly tire.

If we respond to their comments then we've allowed them to set the agenda – but if we can manage the seemingly impossible task of forcing them to respond to us then we show that we are in control. It's the same principle that leads us to ignore questions without hands up – eventually they learn that no hands = no response. Otherwise, we train them into bad behaviour.

Of course, if the rudeness gets extreme, and the comments become unbearable then take the culprits aside, one by one, and explain to them that you find it inappropriate, and any reccurrence will result in a punishment. And yes, it does take time to follow up on all that. But if the name calling persists beyond another few days, then it's something you'll just have to do. Alright, mate?

I am doing it! God! Kids who overreact to instructions

Dear Tom

There's a worrying trend in my KS4 English class: whenever I try gently to put them back on task, or remind them of work set, they shout back angrily, "I'm doing it!" Of course I understand that they don't like to be told what to do, but it feels like they're just doing it to undermine me. Are there any simple preventative strategies that will reduce or stop this irritating habit of theirs?

Prevention rather than cure; as you walk around the class look at what they are doing and quietly suggest where they need to be ('Good start but you're tailing off a bit. You need to be at question 10 soon,' etc). They can't argue with your instructions if there is no disputing the factual content of it – namely, they can hardly claim they're doing it when you've seen they aren't.

Tone is important here. I find that a neutral, authoritative blend is best, as unhurried as if you were ordering a pizza over the phone, but as certain as if you were telling someone the time. Try it. Alone preferably. It's a tone that suggests stating a fact rather than confronting or pleading. It neutralizes most aggression because it offers none.

If you're supervising from the front (being a desk general) you can simply ask them what question they are on. Start by asking a polite, non-confrontational student, then move on to the offenders, who can hardly cry foul at you when you're asking others. You're simply asking for a fact, not checking them. Of course, you can then ascertain if they're telling the truth shortly after by wandering over around the desks … And in my book, finding out a kid has lied to you is always a good reason to detain them after school for some extra work. Do that a few times and you'll cut down on lying, kicking off, or indeed tardiness.

The Lollipop of the Lesson: using treats to get good behaviour

Dear Tom

My school would probably be called a 'sink' school by politicians – loads of ASBOs, high rate of Special Needs, high truancy, etc. But I like this type of school – it suits me.

One of my main strategies is something I call the 'Lollipop of the lesson' – I give out lollipops to kids when they do something extremely good. This has led to a marked reduction in misbehaviour, and a huge increase in attendance and effort. I recommend this to anyone. Surely this should be a part of mainstream practice?

Hmm, not unless you believe the claims of Mars bars and Ribena that they are 'part of a nutritionally balanced diet.' In much the same way that arsonists are part of a thermally diverse landscape.

One of my colleagues (let's call him Tim) wishes we could hand out lollipops to everyone *except* the really annoying ones – a bit like giving out the dunces' caps without actually giving anything out. I told him that this was very negative thinking, and packed him off on an INSET: 'Aspects of SEAL and the student voice – giving your inner child a hug.'

Problems with form groups

Dear Tom

In my Year 8 form there's a new boy who answers me back whenever he feels like it. Detentions don't really work with him, and the school tends not to support phoning the parents because they tend to support the kids. Problem is, I started friendly and have now turned up the heat, but it feels a bit late. When I shout it just sounds wrong and it doesn't have any effect. My form moan that everything is boring (maybe I've spent too much of my focus on my subject teaching). I try to plan some fun things for them, though. My classroom teaching is good, but I know my behaviour management isn't so hot.

Frankly if you're getting results from your classes in other areas of the school, I'm tempted to say that you already know what you should be doing because you're developing success in the classroom.

Forms are a bit different of course: many pupils think, 'What has he got to do with me? He's not my teacher – he just takes my name!' etc. Genuinely, the best way to get round that is to treat your form time as a mini lesson – anyone who acts out of line gets detentions, just like normal. You say that phoning home isn't the done thing – try it, and see. Instead of telling the parents how rubbish their kids are, start off with something positive like, 'Listen, Danny's been doing great in Art, etc, but he's letting himself down when I need to tell him things. Can you help?'

I know that some parents are tiresome and unhelpful, but the vast majority want what *you* want – their child's success. If you can show them this common ground then they'll agree with you, back you up, and you'll have the kid by the nostril hairs. Figuratively.

Take a lesson to explain your rules, or simply give them out, and warn them that, starting tomorrow, if they break them they'll do time. Have faith in yourself. Form time is *your* time, and they'll damn well do what you want or they get punished. Once they settle down a bit then you can let them chat a bit ... if *you* want them to. They'll appreciate it if you reward them for good behaviour. But I would can the parties in the mean time – they're being foul, so why reward them? Or reward the good kids *only* somehow- merits, cards, postcards, etc. Show them that rewards *mean* something.

Finally, you need to obliterate the prime trouble maker. Go the whole hog with the school behavioural procedures, with both barrels. Make him regret his conception.

Symbolically.

Turning them on when you can't find the switch: motivating the lacklustre

Dear Tom

There is a boy in my Year 7 group who is totally disengaged from lessons. He couldn't care less about school whatsoever. Because he doesn't care he breaks all the rules and he doesn't give a rat's ass about consequences, detentions, or whatever. Nothing seems to work; mentoring, sports, nothing.

His family are supportive, but his older brothers were the same about school. I think maybe education isn't valued in his house, so what do I do to reverse this? Thank you!

Tricky: this one goes to the heart of the matter – why do kids switch off from school? Why do some switch *on*?

Kids (and people) engage with things that they get some kind of reward from, and disengage from activities that make them feel bad (the utilitarian model of human behaviour). Although this is processed in complex ways, I think that these axioms are pretty sturdy.

What do pupils get rewards from? Two categories of experience (at school anyway): either they enjoy the activity/subject itself, or they enjoy the secondary result of doing the activity. For example, one pupil might love PE because they love football. Or another might love PE, not because they love football, but because they love being on a winning side, or the praise they get from the teacher, or even the health benefits of exercise. I don't enjoy lifting weights, but I'll endure the gym in order to avoid my abdominal muscles disappearing in an avalanche of Galaxy Truffle.

Similarly, what do they disengage from? Activities they actively don't enjoy, or ones in which they don't enjoy the secondary results. One kid hates maths because he finds numbers difficult and he doesn't want to appear stupid (although he'd happily do maths if he was in a similar ability group), and another hates maths because she just finds it really boring, even though she can do it well enough.

I would add that we tend to enjoy activities we are good at, and tend not to enjoy ones at which we are not: it's a combination of primary and secondary enjoyment. We might like doing the activity, and also like the esteem that doing it brings us.

How is this relevant? Because there is something inside this young man that tells him 'Nothing matters at school – there's nothing here for me.' You're absolutely right to be looking at the family environment – is education valued at home? Did the elder sibling set/ do they set a good example? You've answered some of these already. Perhaps the elders only learned this attitude of hopelessness as time went on, and now they've simply communicated it to junior. Worse, do they actively discourage him in some way from doing well? It could be that they are the reason he has fast-forwarded into fatalism. He will undoubtedly model behaviour from them. Could you get them on side too?

Ways forward? Find out what he likes to do – *anything*. Devise some way of integrating this into his curriculum (assuming that it can be translated into a discrete academic area) and have a talk with his teacher in this area. Make sure that his teachers praise any achievement, however minor (without over-praising mediocrity, of course) so that he learns to associate school with good feelings, and links it overall to achievement. It could be that he doesn't get a lot of warm, fuzzy feelings at home, so try to make sure that he does at school.

Every punishment he gets will reinforce his belief that school is the 'place-he-doesn't-want-to-be'. He still needs to be punished for misbehaviour, but if you emphasize praise too then it won't be so one-sided.

Show this kid that you care about how well he does, and even praise him just for doing something nice, like passing a pen, whatever. In conversation with him reinforce an image of himself that you want him to have – tell him, 'you're a nice guy, and I know that you want to be successful; I think you're actually quite bright, and sometimes you can't see the point of school.'

Achtung, baby: getting and holding attention with the younger ones

Dear Tom

I'm doing a lot of Key Stage 1 supply, and I have big problems getting and holding attention. As soon as I start teaching them anything, they're wriggling, rolling and tapping. It's very frustrating; I even keep carpet time short, but I need at least 15 minutes to do any phonics with them! Maybe I talk too much. Any advice would be gratefully received.

Hmm, I wouldn't automatically start thinking you were the cause – wriggly primary kids are an occupational hazard. Of course, there are always things you can do to improve your charisma with classes (and all of them are acquirable through instruction) but given that you work on supply I would be inclined to think that at least some of your troubles come from the embryonic nature of your relationship, and the fact that some of the less compliant ones will find it difficult to acknowledge you as an authority as quickly as some of their classmates.

Apply the sanctions that you normally would to the instigators of the bad behaviour, and make sure the other pupils see this too. Despite the fact that it feels counter-intuitive to do so, even the little ones need to fear your wrath somewhat, until they automatically shy away from incurring it and self-modify their behaviour. Possibly they still see school as extended playtime. They need clear, simple explanations of the behaviour expectations, and the cold water of punishment if they transgress. Repeat until the desired level of compliance is achieved.

Some pupils are naturally active, energetic and mobile. Despite the current vogue to describe such behaviour as predestined and inevitable, most of it can be controlled through the exercise of a faculty called 'willpower', which is in itself stirred into action by another faculty called 'choosing to do so.' But help these pupils, too, with combating their pesky natural urges. You could give them a stress ball to play with while sitting, which might divert their energy into something involving their hands and not their fists, feet and fidgety faces.

PS There are some excellent workshops out there run by actors for people who want to improve their storytelling skills, something I think we neglect too much as teachers.

Chatty boy drives me batty

Dear Tom

My Year 5 class are lovely, but now a new boy has joined our class with a reputation as a hard nut, although I think he's just a sad, lonely and insecure little boy who needs boundaries. He mutters to himself on the floor and chats to anyone, no matter who they are. I feel sorry that he's so needy, but the constant chatting has to stop. Others tell me he can be abusive to them, so maybe I'm lucky. But he's clever, and I don't just want him quiet, I want him to succeed.

Sounds like you're on the right track with this boy; after all, he's new to the class, and is probably working things out right now as much as you are.

He also sounds like he might be a bit special – and I don't mean that in an ASBO way. He might very well be quite bright indeed (*scuffing sound as he mounts his G&T soap box*) and be in need of some G&T hugs. One thing I've consistently found with badly behaved, bright children is that they don't like tackling the work the same way as the others, so it might be worthwhile thinking of some other activities he could be doing. And sometimes this means that he might be allowed *not* to participate in what everyone else is doing; think of unusual and challenging ways he can approach the same tasks as the others with extra challenge built in.

If he chats with *everyone* then he's being very needy (not to say indiscriminate), so keep reassuring him that he is valued. This can be for pastoral and academic tasks, so praise him for being kind, polite or thoughtful. But there's a reason he's 'only' chatty with you and not disruptive as in other lessons – he has a connection with you. What is it? Personality? Do you make him feel safe (and I mean the OED definition, not the ghetto version)? Do you treat him respectfully, or presume he is intelligent when no one else does?

Whatever it is, you're doing it. Have you had a serious chat with him? Why not tell him you know he's very bright, and ask him if he sometimes finds the work easy? If he says yes, then nail his ego by telling him you know, and that you know that he could do loads more and be really great, etc. If he's like 99 per cent of other isolated underachieving G&T kids I've worked with, it'll be like rainwater to his thirsty self-esteem.

Taking names and kicking ass: using names on the board to keep them in line

Dear Tom

I usually use the 'names on the board' technique; if they get three ticks next to their name, they're in trouble. It usually works as kids don't like having their names on the board.

Until now. My Year 7s have started to caper about when the names go up, mocking each other and shouting, 'Oi John, you're on the board!' with glee. Big laughs from all the class. If I stop the lesson do they win? It is so very annoying. Or should I just carry on? I tried to write names on a piece of paper on my desk but then they just squeal, "Am I in your book?" at me. Sounds silly, but I'm wondering what to do.

Of course, half the usefulness of the 'names on the board' technique is the public shaming it entails. If there's a group of pupils using it to bait each other (boys, it's always boys …) then you might want to try the other technique. Ticks on a sheet, your planner etc. That way they don't see who's going down on the naughty list, and you just clobber them at the end. It hits them like a brick.

Of course, this loses you the 'threat' value of the sanction, and takes you right into 'punishment' mode, but I once found this valuable with a class who behaved in exactly the way you suggested. Overall though, I'd persevere with your current strategy – it sounds like it only needs time to break them …

He's just a big baby: pupils who act like toddlers

Dear Tom

There's a boy in my reception class who throws tantrums that look exactly like he's still two years old. We are all working hard to figure out ways of keeping him calm; but how do we teach anger management to a five year old boy?

Anger in children is based on frustration; in my experience it's a conditioned response that has been learned as a coping mechanism with situations that they feel unable or unwilling to respond to. Essentially it's an overreaction to circumstances that others would deal with much more lightly, and as such could be viewed as a statistical deviation from behavioural norms. It's vitally important to be aware of the triggers that anticipate these overreactions and attempt to throw water on the powder before it catches.

Alongside this, the child needs to be able to tackle the over reaction itself; difficult when the subject is so young, and probably has difficulty articulating feelings and being self-critical.

If you discover the triggers, you could attempt to re-condition the pupil to react appropriately to these triggers; present him with minor versions of the triggers in a controlled environment where he can safely learn ways to deal with the situation without getting the red mist. This is a time-consuming strategy, and would need an expert to really pull it off, although you can help by doing it in a minor way. I find that angry people can be distracted by things that have nothing to do with their present problem, in the same way that a crying baby can stop crying instantly if you show him a rattle. Ask them what time it is, or get them to nip out and get you something, *before* they kick off. *During* is too late. I've found that this strategy works with angry drunks as much as angry kids (who are in many respects identical to drunks in their behaviour, as far as I can see).

It's good to talk: dealing with mobile phones

Dear Tom

Even though my school bans mobiles they still get into my class, and my pupils sneakily text each other. How do I react to this?

Any law that attempts to prohibit behaviour that people habitually exhibit is destined to have a rough ride, particularly when the perpetrators don't see the activity as immoral or harmful. This applies particularly to mobile phones, as they are so ubiquitous these days that pupils see no more harm in popping them out than wearing a watch.

Unfortunately, as they are still relatively new in society, and are so damn useful, we haven't had time as a society to develop clear etiquette that governs their use, which is why you see so many people using them in buses etc. in a manner that they wouldn't think of repeating in a face-to-face encounter (loud shouting etc.), or leaving them on during meetings, in church etc.

Banning them is one solution. At least it's clear, but you will inevitably run into the problem outlined above: you create a rule that will habitually be broken, so you either police it like Judge Dredd (with all the concomitant headaches of time and labour) or you turn a blind eye, in which case you crode your authority by looking weak.

Simple classroom control usually eradicates most phone usage. No bags allowed on desks, no jackets on, all mobile phones must be turned off and stored in bags etc. Any mobile phone visible in any way is liable for confiscation. All confiscated property only to be returned with the parent's permission, or something suitably annoying for the pupil.

It's impossible to *stop* them being brought in (without metal detectors and gate frisking), so devise a clear policy that the pupils can understand easily. Explain it to your classes, either at the start of Year 7, or as desired. Send letters home to parents explaining the reasons for this policy. Pupils are easier to control if they know that *you* know that *they* know the rules.

He's given up: what do I do now?

Dear Tom

One of my boys has given up completely. I think it's because his parents put a lot of pressure on him to succeed, and he doesn't live up to their expectations. He's a big lump when it comes to listening, although he'll do some pretty-rushed work.

Now he's turned into the class joker, throwing pens, flicking ears, distracting others around him. It's textbook attention seeking (he's Year 4)

How do I respond to this? Do I punish it? Do I turn a blind eye? Do I shower him in love? I've tried them all. I have little hair left from tearing it out by now …

There are two approaches (at least) to this problem:

1. External. His behaviour is unsatisfactory, and without trying to understand it you need to come down on him every time he misbehaves, until he associates clowning around with punishment, and alters his beaviour. That means, of course, sanctions *every* time he misbehaves, and a follow-up and escalation for every time he fails to attend or comply. If he's nice then there's no need to come down like a ton of bricks, just be consistent and fair.

2. Internal. What's really going on in his head? Have you really talked to him? He might not be able to assess his own mental state as clearly as you would wish, so interpret the conversation in the context of what you know about him and the parents. Still, he may be able to give you some useful pointers as to how he reacts to the world.

But your opinion is more relevant here, and he needs to realize that his behaviour is damaging his education and that of others around him. If he's overreacting to pushy parents then you need to try to make him feel that school isn't home. Praise him whenever he does something right, and that especially includes pastoral and social activities. He needs to see that he's valued for being a person, not just a learning machine.

Losing my religion: the kids don't like my subject

Dear Tom

I'm covering maternity leave mid-term, and I've had to take over some Year 11 classes. With the younger years, I can use rewards and stickers to influence them easily. Funnily enough, the Year 11s aren't so motivated by them. I teach RE and loads of the kids don't care for the subject, so I spend a lot of time telling them why it's important.

One teacher told me to tell the disruptive ones to sit quietly and do work for other subjects they like while the others do the RE work, but unless I occupy them with work in the first place they'll just muck about, and they claim they don't have work to do for other subjects ... So what carrots and sticks can I use for the older kids

Fellow RS teacher I salute you. You will endure years of this complaint – 'Why are we teaching RS?' Don't worry – they're not really complaining about the subject as such, it's just a bit of an easy target because its aims are famously misunderstood. Presumably these same pupils can see the point of reading Shakespeare or working out calculus. They scorn RS because they've been brought up to believe it's a low status subject. So you need to bang the drum for your subject. I tell my kids I think it's the most important lesson in the curriculum, and not because I'm recruiting for a Jesuit Mission or anything, but because it talks about real issues in life, and meaning, and purpose.

But that doesn't really matter anyway. They do it because they have to: because they're at school, because they're in a class, and because they don't have a say in the matter. Harsh, but true. If you go soft with them, they'll simply see it as low status. If they complain, give them a detention. And if they don't come, phone home and escalate the sanction. And keep escalating, enlisting HODs, SLT etc. until they get the message. The key word here is consistency. *Never* give up. *Always* punish people that disrupt lessons or fail to do as much work as you'd like (expectations vary). *Don't* let them do other subjects in your class; you teach them not to value your time, and the lesson just becomes playtime for them.

These kids need some punishment in their lives. It will take time, effort and resolve on your part. You'll feel like giving up. You won't see results quickly. But the miracle happens, it really does. Even for kids so near their exams; if they realize you can make their last few months very uncomfortable for them, then they'll buckle down a bit, at least enough for a lesson to proceed properly. Think of all the good you can do the ones that really *want* to learn. And some of the rebels might be surprised to find that their Ds have turned into Cs with your support; after all, so much of the GCSE is content that cramming in the last few months can have a profound effect on grades.

Surface dwellers, beware! Pupils who hide under tables

Dear Tom

There is a group of boys in my Year 3 class who sulk under tables when they don't get what they want; one boy started doing it and the others copied. It is, as you can imagine, hugely annoying, and stops the lesson dead. Although I tried to praise them, ignore them, and so on, they still do it. The current strategy is to for them to lose playtime if they don't manage to keep good behaviour cards.

This can't be ignored or tolerated; as you have witnessed, children take their boundary cues from the behaviours that they are permitted to enact. They also have a vicious sense of justice and fairness, and if they see one pupil getting away with high jinks, they'll replicate it. If you're not careful, you'll all be under the desks soon.

The first boy needs the focus; the SENCO needs to be involved with him, as his behaviour could be a symptom of a range of issues from abuse to neglect. Or it could be simple attention seeking. Either way it is the epicentre of your behaviour earthquake. The other boys need to see you getting tough with them. Every time they do it, they get a sanction and one that hurts, like a detention where they do something hard.

Walk into class tomorrow. The next time someone acts like this, say that you won't accept it any more and have them either removed (make an issue of this with senior management or teachers – you need this support) or tolerated but then punished severely.

Punishing children isn't pleasant, but if you don't then you allow them to develop behaviour patterns that can stay with them and damage their development.

In the company of boys: teaching an all male group

Dear Tom

My school is a mixed comprehensive with two single sex forms, and I've got an all-boy class in Year 8 for History (I'm an NQT). One by one they're lovel; as a group, a mob. They're whiny, picky, rude, lazy and competitive, like unpleasant Disney dwarves. By now I just don't want them near me because they're so unpleasant. I've tried competitions with them (you'd think this would be a winner) but half of them (the losers) are just awful. I'd love the lessons to be little more peaceful and enjoyable, but my class has too much testosterone to allow it, it seems.

There's one thing that boys respect and appreciate more than anything else: strength. The male ego is particularly receptive to concepts of hierarchy and dominance, and you need to be the alpha male in the room.

It sounds like you have tried a range of strategies to see what works best. My advice would be to stick to one main strategy, i.e. 'don't you bloody dare talk over me, and I want your work done in silence' and then ensure that you apply sanctions against them whenever they break it. Always follow up with what you promise, as children (and people) learn quickly that what you do is more important than what you say. If they smell even a whiff of inconsistency from you then you teach them that your rules can be broken ... sometimes. So they will spend all their efforts finding out when, until you feel exhausted. Better by far to: remind them thoroughly of what you expect; take down the names of anyone who offends; nail them to the ground for it. *Every* time.

Only the hardest nutters will resist this strategy, I promise you. It's when we become in any way inconsistent that it seems like it all doesn't work. Sometimes it takes longer with some groups than with others, but it works with all but the maddest and baddest.

Kill the praise a bit; if they hear that they're doing really well all the time when they're being a bit silly, then they know where the behaviour goalposts are. Make praise quiet and serious. Many boys hate it publicly, while loving it privately, so praise privately at times. With difficult classes, it's not about how OfSTED-friendly the lessons are at first, it's all about control. Then, once reasonable control is achieved, you can enhance the structure and content of the lesson to address the individuals, but you have to get the group first. So put most of your effort into behaviour management (paperwork, phone calls etc.) and let interactive lessons of joy and wonder take a back seat for a little while. Once you have one, the other can follow naturally.

What's the point of school?

Dear Tom

I am Principal of a secondary school in Burkina Faso, West Africa. How do I cope with my pupils' changing attitudes, particularly the teenagers? Pupils aged 13–15 have poor school results because of their attitudes. They lack the actual eagerness to work hard at school. Despite the measures taken to urge them to work, they still have the same attitudes.

I would be grateful to you for your invaluable pieces of advice.

Yours, etc

That's a very broad topic, so I will make some general suggestions, and hope that some of them may be of use.

Teenagers famously rebel at this age, as part of their maturation. They find it far easier to reject and condemn what they *don't* like than to embrace things that they *do* like. They also lack the adult ability to perceive long term goals, and often prefer to find acceptance and self-esteem in the admiration of their peers rather than in the respect of their elders.

So praise is a *huge* part of the education process. Give them comments that make them feel good about themselves, and always link them to desirable behaviour, whether connected to their education or their conduct. Boys can be particularly competitive, so establish league tables, giving them points to reward good achievement, and deduct them for bad behaviour. At the end of each month, these points can be exchanged for benefits – rewards, trips, exemption from small duties, giving them privileges for a day – whatever works for you and them.

Keep in constant contact with parents, particularly the parents of children who are underachieving academically or socially. Arrange meetings between teachers, parents and pupils, and discuss ways that situations can improve. Speak positively at all times, even when admonishing pupils: focus on what they should be doing, rather than what they shouldn't (i.e. 'I would like to see your son improve his behaviour,' rather than, 'your son's behaviour is terrible.') and link the conversations to explaining the benefits of behaving and learning well. Depending on the financial contribution that parents make to their children's education, it is possible to make them consider how much time and money is being wasted on the privilege of education.

The Invisible Bully: dealing with low-level intimidation

Hi Tom

Everyone thinks behaviour in sixth form is perfect; well, it isn't. In one of my classes, some pupils gang up on some of the others, but in really subtle ways; talking about them but not naming them, for instance.

Any time you call them out on it, they deny all knowledge of what you're talking about, so the best I can do is give them general advice on how to talk about people. Apart from this they work quite well, but the atmosphere is poisonous at times, and I'm worried about the pupils that are the butt of this very low-level bullying.

This is tricky: mostly because both the offending behaviour itself is hard to identify, and also because the effect of the offence is hard to substantiate beyond that the students are upset. If they won't make a complaint then you have a practically invisible, unprovable crime.

We can't govern their behaviour outside of lessons, merely influence it inside your room, and one of the best things you can do is always to provide a good role model of behaviour, being polite and kind yourself. People parrot the behaviour of others around them, so sometimes a strong personality can influence them subtly. Mind you, I wouldn't hold your breath.

Of course, if there is ever anything overtly rude, then make sure you stamp on it; keep them behind after class, hand out detentions, or call home, just as you would at KS1-4. Make people realise that the room is a safe environment, not a playground.

But as I say, speak to them individually. And make sure you *are* sure of your facts before anyone gets accused; even bullies deserve a fair hearing, and the only way to get through to them is if they see that you are being fair. It's funny how the most unfair pupils I have dealt with have been the most concerned with the even distribution of justice when it's being meted out to them.

Finally, have you made a seating plan? It could help if you mix up the groups a bit. If they're behaving immaturely, then treat them accordingly: no talking, heads down, hands up, that sort of back to basics. Then they won't have an opportunity to slander each other.

My bright spark is a live wire: bright kids that keep shouting out

Dear Tom

My reception class has got a very smart boy who can't stop shouting out questions and answers. The trouble is that what he says is brilliant, and just what I'd want from a pupil ... only with hands up. How can I encourage him to keep thinking and asking, and still discourage him from shouting out?

These pupils are like stealth bombs, destroying the attention of the class. The bigger problem is that other students start to follow their cues, and imitate their disruptive behaviour patterns, especially if they get away with it.

The simplest advice I can give is to turn off the oxygen of attention. If pupils call out, *ignore* them, completely. Instead, take a question from another pupil. This is a lot tougher than it sounds. Literally ignore them. Only engage with pupils who put their hands up. Pretend they haven't shouted out at all. Don't respond on any level at all, not even to rebuke them – that comes after the lesson, when you say, 'Gerald can I speak to you about your behaviour?'. It doesn't matter if his comments are intelligent or not – they destroy your focus and your authority, so they are a Trojan Horse for the lesson.

Train him into compliance this way and I guarantee he will improve. The students often follow our cues and if you respond to his shouting, then why does he need to bother putting his hand up?

No-smirking zone: the Hell of a pupil grinning at you when you're serious

Dear Tom

Can you suggest how to handle a child who just stands and smiles at you when you're telling them off? It sound absurdly trivial, but it gets under my skin so much I feel like chinning him. It is SO annoying!

I totally understand – and there's a reason why the smirkers get under our skins so much; because it's incredibly rude. We get so used to watching what we say to people with our mouths that we forget something that everyone already knows: body language is far more powerful than words. Think of the different ways we can say 'I love you' with different emphasis, and you get the idea (cheeky, tender, sarcastic, etc). The context of the words (tone, register, posture, eye contact, etc.) transforms the meaning of the content.

What this means is that pupils should be made aware that you're not only looking for polite words/silence, but polite body language. If somebody uses a funny voice, smirks, shuffles, plays with their pen, sighs, etc. then they are just as guilty of being rude to you as if they said, 'stick it up your pipe, Grandpa,' or whatever they say these days (who can keep up with their transient, fragile jargon?).

So treat it accordingly: if a pupil smirks when you're talking to him, apply/threaten a further discipline if they don't stop. You don't need to get too technical with them ('I can see that your non-verbal body language is at odds with the verbal content of your communication'), just say what parents have said to rude kids for centuries – 'How *dare* you talk to me/look at me/speak to me with that tone!' You don't actually need to say, 'Wipe that smile off your face!' but don't be afraid to. After all, they're doing it to be rude, so don't be afraid to react assertively just because it's not something that can be recorded in words.

I usually say something along the lines of, 'your smirk makes me think you don't realise how much trouble you're in. Treat me with more respect or I'll assume you want to be rude.' Don't blow a gasket, even though it's incredibly annoying. This is just what they want. Speak softly and carry an enormous naughty stick.

3 | Behaviour for new teachers

I remember when I was training to be a teacher; I sat with my fellow RS hopefuls in the ubiquitous, utilitarian brown-walled conference room that characterized the modern college, and we were asked if anything in teaching still concerned us. It was unanimous. Everybody wanted to ask about behaviour.

'What happens if they start chucking chairs?' said one.

'What happens if they ...,' dramatic pause, 'if they ... *refuse to do what we tell them to do?*' A silent room; everyone relieved that someone had said what was on all of their minds.

To be honest I can't remember the answer. Whatever it was, it didn't help me. Neither did the solitary earnest lecture dished out by our college (or 'professional qualification delivery provider' as I imagine they are called by now). And to be honest, neither did two months in a hellish sink school, followed by two months in a pretty well-behaved school. But it's the thing that terrifies beginning teachers more than anything. Yet somehow the gap between the skills training we need and the skills training we get is frightening. If you're a new teacher, and you're struggling with behaviour control, relax. What you're going through isn't just common; it's bloody well to be expected. You are not alone, and you are almost certainly not to blame.

What's the reason for this chasm of disparity? There are several. One of the main ones is that, to be honest, most people are pretty uncomfortable with telling people what to do. It's not something we experience much in our daily lives; hell, I have enough trouble making decisions for *me*, let alone taking on the responsibility for others. In fact I'm rather relieved that it comes so haltingly to us; the arrogance and manipulativeness required to feel that you somehow have the moral right or practical experience necessary to run others' lives is a kind of defining characteristic of the megalomaniac. It's certainly a prerequisite to become a local councillor. Luckily, we're not naturally disposed to be Little Hitlers. We may be judgemental sods, but when it comes to the crunch, most of us would rather someone else stepped up to the decision lever.

Good news for democracy, bad news for teachers. Power is thrust upon us. And yet, what inspired us to go into teaching in the first place? Was it the desire to dominate children? Anyone that answered 'yes' to that question should get their coats now. Seriously, don't look back or I'll brain you. So what was it? The desire to work with children? Hopefully. Love of your subject? That would be lovely. A wish to impart knowledge to others? Step this way. So far so good.

Let's look now at the selection process. What are Teacher Training Providers looking for? I remember an application process that looked for basic qualifications and some (any?) experience with youngsters: one week shadowing a primary teacher wasn't hard to arrange. And then an interview. Not much there about controlling a class, is there? And as we've just seen, not a lot in the training process either. So, really, you start you first job without a tool in your kit. Of course, if your employer was careful they'd have made you teach a sample lesson, with two senior teachers observing you, cowing a class that, by their very nature, are less likely to act up until they know who you are. By the time they've sniffed you out, you're gone, like Keyser Söze.

So the absurdity of the situation is that you can get through the whole process and still know bugger all about handling tough classes, rude kids and teenage hell. But remember when I said that most new teachers panic about bad behaviour? That's because they are spot on: it *is* the biggest challenge they will face. Not subject knowledge (tricky, but come *on* – how hard *is* Year 8 geography?), not marking and assessment (boring, but merely irksome, like washing a dog), certainly not remembering all their faces (if you don't have a seating plan then you're a masochist, but at least you picked the right job). No, it's all about behaviour. It's all about you walking into a room full of strangers who don't trust you (with good reason – they know why you're there, and frankly, they don't like it) and who would rather be buzzing Pritt Sticks round the room or swapping ring tones than listen to you (they presume) drone on about the causes of the Spanish Civil War. Oh, the horror. It's you and them. Locked in a room for an hour; and your job is to form order from the formless void, and their job is ... well, they don't really have one, that's the point – they *are* the formless void. No wonder we struggle.

Every new teacher has problems with behaviour. The harder the kids the more problems you will face. The less disposed you are to telling other people what to do, the harder you will find it. The less self-assured you are, the harder you will find it. The kinder you are, the harder you will find it. That's a lot of factors. There are dozens more. It is a long and troublesome path to good behaviour. Take it from me: I'd run nightclubs in Soho for years; I'd worked on the door of one of the busiest places in the West End on the busiest nights. I'd bartended all over Britain and bounced out hundreds of drunks and talked down hundreds more. I was, I suspected, a bit tasty with crowd control. Maybe I was. But faced with my first year's classes, I went to pieces like a glass sledgehammer. I suffered every indignity heaped upon man; I was Job, with elbow patches. I made just about every mistake I could make trying to get them to behave.

And I'd rather it didn't happen to anyone else. Not because I think that reading a book can solve the problems. Quite the opposite – one of my reasons for writing this is because there's too much emphasis on theory, and not enough on action – but because there are things that we can share as teachers that could at least make it easier for beginning teachers to adjust to the new situation that they find themselves in.

That's another reason why teachers begin teaching so fatally underprovided with behaviour chops: because it's far easier to talk about managing behaviour than doing anything about it. I have no idea what my training told me about behaviour control, honestly. How *could* it mean anything to someone that isn't embedded in teaching yet? Teaching – and particularly controlling a class – is a doing activity, not a chattering, philosophizing one. Oh sure, there are philosophies that underpin it (I bored you with my paltry theories in chapter one) but if we leave it at that we may as well be talking about who would win in a fight between Superman and the Incredible Hulk. Fun, but not very helpful.

To learn about behaviour, to get really good at it, you have to *do* it. It's a skill, a craft, and sometimes an art, but what it isn't is an abstract belief. You have to watch brilliant teachers and see how they speak, how they act, what they do and what they don't do. The best time to do this is when they take over a new class for the first time, because that's when the skeleton of their control techniques is laid bare; after that it's less valuable, because by then they have socialized their classes into their ways, and what they do at that point is often merely oiling the mechanism, giving the odd reminder of how to behave. You can still get a lot out it, but the prime time to get the good stuff is right at the beginning of the teacher/class relationship.

This is why a lot of Teacher Placements in the PGCE year are well meaning but ineffective at teaching behaviour management. At that point teachers are so blinded by every other aspect of the craft that they are panicked into forgetting more than they learn. It's hard to be a reflective practitioner when *you don't know what you don't know yet*. And it's equally hard to know what you should be looking out for on your puny observation schedule. Perhaps you got lucky; perhaps you observed a real master at their craft, and perhaps you were luckier still because they had the self-awareness to understand what they were doing, and luckier still if they could take the time to relate it to you in a meaningful way, coaching you on behaviour techniques and giving you feedback every step of the way.

Was that your experience of the training process? No? Then read on. Beginning teachers, I salute you; roll up your sleeves, gird your loins and get ready to kick ass. Walk tall and own the room. And never give up.

The trouble with girls: coping when girls gang up on you

Dear Tom

I'm a male NQT struggling with his girls; I just don't seem to be able to reach them at all, and other pupils are now copying their bad behaviour. Last week I made a joking sarcastic comment to a girl who's normally on my side, and she really had the hump with me. I apologized loads, but she obviously still hasn't forgiven me. Now she just answers me with total malice and disrespect, and other girls are now copying her rudeness. I thought she would respect my honesty and my apology.

It really doesn't matter if they like you or not, at least not in a professional sense. It matters of course if they *dislike* you, but only because it creates its own problems, as you have found. But frankly, I don't give a damn if my kids like me or not. It's a job, we're professionals and adults, and our job is to provide them with the best education we can to prepare them to succeed in life. Liking me is incidental, and delightful when it happens. And you know what? If you treat them with respect, give them firm boundaries, create an ordered classroom and work your hardest to be a human being, probably almost every one of them will like you a bit, or at least enough for the class to proceed, and that, after all, is goal number one.

Don't crack any more funnies, not until you *know* that the class relationship is there. But really, I'm not sure that this was the problem: I think it sounds as if a spiteful girl took the opportunity to make you wriggle a little, because she knew she could take advantage of your generosity of spirit. Besides, if you're going through the difficult first year when many kids naturally distrust you, then the last thing on earth she needs is for you to make a little joke in front of her friends; it would be *desperately* uncool for her to be nice back to you in case her friends think she's a kiss-up. Far better (and far more social capital to be had) for her to torture you with your niceness. Next time (if there is one) ask yourself if she is overreacting (which I suspect she would have been) about the level of hurt inflicted, and if you think she's taking the Mickey then just say, 'stop being silly, we're trying to get on with lessons here – don't overreact,' etc. You gave her the power to roast you, and the apology you made increased that power. Apologies need to be short, sincere and singular. Anything more and you weaken yourself.

Next time she or any other pupil speaks to you in a way you don't like, keep them behind and apply sanctions. We accept far, far too much ridicule and abuse as a profession, and the children will only do it as long as you let them. It sounds like you're suffering from all the normal doubts and worries about competency and doing a good job that all virtuous teachers experience in their first year. Try not to let them cripple you. You're the grown-up, and you're in charge.

The journey of a thousand miles: making a start with a new class

Dear Tom

I'm going to my first school soon on a part-time basis and I'm worried about my behaviour management; the school isn't big on discipline, and I'm not sure if I'll be good enough to control the kids. I'm OK in general, and I try not to shout, but I still have to wait ages to get them quiet. I also find it hard to get them to line up. I've tried putting names on the board, but I lose track of who I gave them to, and how often. I use praise, golden time, but still have trouble keeping classes in order sometimes. I think they think I'm a bit wishy-washy.

There are a lot of natural factors (some beyond your immediate control) that will conspire to make behaviour management more difficult for you. Your relative newness, for a start. One of the best tools you can have to control a class is the relationship you develop with them, and although some aspects of that can be instantaneous, as with any relationship, most aspects of it are developed over time and can't be rushed. Like wine. Even the best teachers don't walk into a room of strangers and get perfect behaviour.

Your part-time status also affects things. This is linked to the previous point, in that the less time they see you, the less opportunity you have to develop the bond of trust and presence that familiarity and good routine can provide.

Names on the board is normally a good tactic, and a core activity for classic Assertive Discipline (as it used to be called). It sounds as though you already have some good systems: taking names, recording escalation of misbehaviour, and punishing the unrighteous. However, it sounds like you have run into a key snag with this system: the practicality of taking names, turning to the board, keeping track etc.

The best advice I can give to this is: don't let the system defeat the *object* of the system. If taking names is confusing, then simply dismiss the pupils that you feel deserve to be dismissed, and detain the rest. Or go by faces alone. Or trust your instinct to an extent. If recording names causes you to turn around, then record the names on your mark book, and never let them out of your sight. Don't be afraid to escalate straight to detentions if you feel that a consequence code system is confusing you. It's not the Old Bailey, and you only need probable cause to justify punishing a pupil. The bottom line is: if you feel that they've disrupted your teaching *or* pupils' learning, then they deserve some punitive feedback.

Wishy-washy? Let others be the judge of that. Essentially kids need two things from us: discipline and love. Both work in tandem. We discipline them because we care about them. We show love by giving them a safe environment of rules. Give them rewards, by all means, but let them see you've got teeth. Take some time to go over the rules with them again. Make them stick them in their books, sign them, put a poster up – anything to remind them that you have boundaries, and so do they.

If the school is weak on discipline, then you will be handicapped in your behaviour management. The pupils (and staff) need to know that if behaviour problems escalate beyond their powers, then someone else will intervene for the good of the community. If SLT wash their hands of this responsibility then you're much more on your own, and reliant on your own charisma, presence and routine.

I want to drop my form

Hi Tom

I'm an NQT. I've managed to get my Year 10 lesson class in some kind of order! I've also picked up a Year 10 form group, and to be honest, I'm not all that taken with them. It's probably fair to say that we won't be sending Christmas cards to each other in the future. Is it wrong of me to ask to give them up and ask for another form group? And would the school disapprove?

The short answer is, yes, it probably would reflect badly on you; simply put, a teacher is expected to take what he or she is given, within reason. There really needs to be an extremely good reason for a teacher to change form groups. The point of the pastoral role is to develop relationships, and like it or not, you will have some sort of a relationship with the form group. You are, despite your misgivings, an adult of some familiarity to these children, and that can be very valuable, especially to children who may face inconstancy in their home lives.

With perseverance you will make inroads with parts of this group. Start by thinking about the ones that you do gel with; I bet there's more of them than the ones that don't. But above all remember that we're not there to be their mates (God forbid) but to be their teacher, and whether we like them (or they like us) is of secondary importance. What they need is a grown-up, a professional, and a regular face that they learn to trust. Give it time.

I go to pieces under the microscope: coping with observations

Dear Tom

I've been to various interviews for teaching posts, but whenever I'm observed on my trial lesson, I always seem to get hard classes and the behaviour goes to pieces. I find it so difficult in these situations, where the students know there won't be any follow up if they misbehave. How do I get past this?

A school is unwise to field a tough class to an interviewee; it's not a genuine reflection of teaching ability, when so much of behaviour management is connected with familiarity and consequences. In an interview class you need to make a short, sudden impact. Lose the smile, the gold stars and the cookie jar, and get serious, sound serious and speak slowly.

Tell them it's a pleasure to be there, perhaps, but don't overegg the praise. In this context it's better to be feared than loved. At the same time find a balance; be stern enough to show them you mean business, but don't sound like you hate them. Tough classes take an instant dislike to new teachers who try to throw their weight around, but they don't respect teachers that sound too kind it looks weak, like it or not.

They shouldn't get too out of hand with a familiar teacher at the back, unless you're giving them a reason to act up. Do you think you come across as uncertain (they'll pounce on it) unprepared (they'll slaughter you for it) or mean (they'll resent you for it)? Is it possible for you to get feedback from your unsuccessful observations to find out why *they* think it didn't go as well as you would have liked? I'm sure you'll get there in the end. You have merely, as they say, not succeeded yet.

Getting control back once it's flown the coop

Dear Tom

I just had a demo lesson for a Year 5 class in a tough school. It didn't go well.

My starter dragged, and the kids started getting bored; soon it was really hard to stop the rising tide of low-level misbehaviour; I tried to be positive, but it was all slipping way quickly, even when I moved the ones that misbehaved on the carpet.

Disaster – a fight started between two boys and other teachers had to intervene. Then the class hamster woke up and it was game over for me and my bloody lesson. Once it's been lost, how do you get 'it' back? I didn't get the job, funnily enough; the Head was kind when he gave me feedback, but he said I needed a broader range of strategies to deal with bad behaviour. What might they look like? Cheers.

The Gods are fickle. I sympathize – one teacher might get lucky with an obedient class and get the post, while another faces a mob on a stormy night and gets pasted.

A good observer/interviewer will be aware of a class's disruptive potential, and will be watching you not merely to see if they behave immaculately, but how you handle the situation if it turns challenging. I think that's what they may mean by having a repertoire of teaching skills. Lessons go belly up for scores of reasons (bumble bees, eclipses, gas, royal weddings, equinoxes) and we have to learn to deal with that. And that means getting flexible. If the kids are getting restless because they're bored, tighten up and move on. If they start to act up, address it, there and then.

Your mission isn't to deliver *everything* you've prepared *exactly* as you imagined it. Your mission is for the pupils to learn what you want to teach them. Some lesson plans just have to go out of the window (and not just after OfSTED either). This is a skill learned with experience and practice; it can't be imparted by books, behaviour forums or lectures. But you can be open to the idea that teaching is a dynamic activity. The plate spinning metaphor will serve here, hoary and cobwebbed though it is. You are the plate spinner in the classroom; some plates wobble before others and must be attended to. Some plates can hit the ground for the good of the others. And some plates can't fall! (Is that cryptic enough?). Behaviour is one of the 'can't fall' plates. Ploughing through to the end of a starter is one of the former. Control isn't something you 'have'. It's not a possession or even a state; it's a process, a continuous activity. Good news then – you can never 'lose' it. You just get it started again.

Start off with a brief reminder of your expectations. Then mean it: as soon as someone crosses the line you set, do something about it. Every time, until the end of time. They'll get the message. And if the disruption is threatening to swamp the class, then make sure the on-task kids have something to do (if you can) and *then* roll up your sleeves and get to work on the wrong 'uns. That way you're dealing with the class, and not simply individuals.

You sound like you have the makings of an extremely professional teacher, given your attitude, your concern and your desire to do well.

Top sets terrorize me

Dear Tom

Okay. This is an odd one; I teach classes in a real sink school, and I can handle the Year 7s, even though everyone says they're the worst ones in the school. But weirdly enough, I freak out when I get my top set Year 8s. I stutter, trip over my words and generally act completely embarrassed. Seriously, I just lose it completely with them and I dread getting them again. Any ideas?

Don't sweat it, and don't dread it. No matter how lousy you felt about the last lesson, it's in the past. It's gone, dead, buried. It no longer exists unless you remember it. The next lesson might as well be your first one. Maybe you feel more comfortable when you're constantly active, constantly batting bad behaviour back over the net? Then, if you're presented with a class that is supposed to be well-behaved and bright, you wonder what your strategy should be because you're outside of your comfort zone? The answer then is to plan a fast-paced lesson with loads of challenge. And don't be afraid to let them do most of the work, perhaps some collaborative learning, peer work etc. Maybe try giving them work more suitable for Year 9s, and watch them try to rise to the challenge. See your G&T Lead Teacher for help here.

Also don't worry about the flustered feeling; we all get it. But they are 13 years old and you are not. They are children, and they need you. They need you to be the adult. Forget about the last lesson.

This reminds me of a story: two Buddhist monks are travelling together when they come to a river's edge. An old woman asks if one of them can carry her across the rapids. Now, monks aren't supposed to touch women, so the first guy refuses. But the second picks her up, carries her across and sets her down on the other side.

Two hours later the two monks are still walking along. The first monk is fizzing with anger until he can't keep his mouth shut anymore. 'I can't believe it!' he says, 'How could you touch that woman?!' Second monk answers, 'I left the woman on the bank of the river. But you are still carrying her.'

Ditch the old lady.

Alien versus Predators: when a bully gets bullied

Dear Tom

I'm going into teacher training soon, and I'm observing at a school to get some experience. In my first class, there's a kid who has the same name as a cartoon character, and the kids all shout it at him. They sing the theme tune and do all his catchphrases, the whole thing. He was walking with me to the study centre, and all the other kids just ganged up on him, until he told them all to f*** off, and made sexual comments about their mothers. So of course I had to get him in trouble for that, and he got more upset, teary and tried to hide from me.

I found out that some of the kids have asked to be moved out of his class because they say he's horrible to them. To me he seems just a normal kid (he's 9) who gets wound up easily, but he lets them get to him. How do I stop the kids picking on him, or how do I get him to stop over reacting?

If ever a kid needed an intervention, it's this one. Without some assistance, this boy could start to form destructive habits of lashing out when provoked, which could persist beyond instances of provocation, He could become aggressive and argumentative *whatever* the circumstance. Kids, as we all know, can be extremely nasty (that's what we're there for – to bring out the love) and love to stir up people who are easily provoked. They *really* love it; it's like telly for them, and never mind the damage it causes the antagonist/victim.

Show this boy that he is valued and cared for. Give him some extra time; and make sure that the right adults crack down *hard* whenever someone provokes him. I can hardly blame him for lashing out at continual provocation (without condoning it). Would any of us cope with repeated humiliation and bullying any better? These are formative times for this boy. Name calling sounds harmless to an adult, but persistent, relentless bullying could make this boy feel as if he's in Hell. I think he might need you quite a lot right now, if only because you care, and you noticed.

Looking for a Rainbow: panicking about being graded badly

Dear Tom

I'm an NQT going through his second term. So far so good, but now I'm worried about passing this term. The behaviour in one particular class is killing the teaching and learning, and it's all down to five players in a class of thirty. One kid snapped his fingers in my face and he touched my face while he did it. He's still in school; all he got was a talk from the Head of Year. I don't have a HOD because she's just left to have a baby, and no one's covering her.

I've asked for guidance, especially with this class – I don't want them to give me a lousy grade when I'm observed. I adore teaching, and I know I can be good, but this class is becoming a nightmare for me. I told the school I'm applying for jobs around the borough and I'm concerned they'll hold it against me that I'm moving on. But I have to – my peace of mind is in tatters with stress over these kids. What should I do in this situation?

Before your observation, it is essential that you tackle these key players – take out the head and body falls. Most kids don't have the heart to be genuine troublemakers, so if you polish them off, you know your life will be easier. Tackling them is initially simply a case of enduring one more difficult lesson with them, recording all the bad behaviour, then clearly giving them a sanction for it. If they don't show, then you escalate, and keep proceeding on this basis.

If you are a HOD short of a department then the school hierarchy must allow for this and there will be someone else you can refer to for support, presumably your HOD's line manager. It is their *duty* (and therefore your right) to support you with behaviour. If they don't, then your life is made impossible, and no observation could ever be a true reflection of your professional mettle. Speak to your school mentor and explain this clearly to them.

It may be that you have to do some 'managing upwards' in this case, i.e. making people above you do what you need them to do; this is necessary simply because it's easy to lose sight of how others (particularly new staff) are doing if you take your eye off the ball. Or sometimes they're just not doing their job properly.

Remember, these kids are just kids – they don't know you, and they don't worry about what you think about them. If they misbehave, they get punished, simple as that. If you're worried they won't listen to you, just keep the admonition simple and polite in class, don't lose your cool, and move on. A lot of behaviour management is performed outside the classroom. I would also advise you to have some 'plug and play' lesson worksheets for the rest of the class if these kids are making it impossible actually to teach a lesson; that way, the lesson proceeds despite them, albeit somewhat boringly. Of course, if they are persistently disruptive during lessons then most schools provide you with the right to remove them to an internal exclusion area; usually SLT does this. So don't be afraid of getting tough with them – and that doesn't mean shouting. It just means showing them that you mean business, and that you care about *everyone's* education in the room … even if they don't.

PS If you've indicated that you're moving on, the school might very well be tempted to mark you as 'low' priority; don't let them. Keep bugging the people above you to do their jobs. Eventually they will realize it's easier to support you than to ignore you. Unfortunately we sometimes have to manage the behaviour of our managers. Who watches the watchmen? You do.

Ground away to a greasy spot: what are my job prospects if I've quit?

Dear Tom

I'm having a heart attack because I think I'll fail this year. I started trying to be tough, but got too friendly, too quickly. Now ALL my classes take advantage of me, even top sets. I've tried to follow all the textbook advice but they're still riding me like a donkey on Blackpool Beach. I have observed other members of staff and while they also have problem,s it is nothing compared to the treatment I receive.

After being assaulted (and not supported by the school), I resigned. I can't do it anymore, and I don't want to fail my NQT year. But will another school even sniff at me after this fiasco? My confidence is in pieces.

It really sounds like you've followed procedures well with your pupils. If the school isn't prepared to back you on the discipline then you have a mountain to move; after all, if pupils think that they can ignore punishments because nothing will happen, then why would they behave? If you're new then you especially need the support that comes from teamwork, and it sounds like you've had precious little of it.

If you've resigned then it's time for a fresh start. May I recommend applying to schools where behaviour is demonstrably better? Much better chance for you to pass your NQT year that way. Or at least apply to a school where the behavioural procedures are tight (although the two categories usually go hand-in-hand). These are the sorts of questions you need answered *before* you apply, and certainly by the time you get to interview. (Ever wondered what questions to ask at interview? *There's* a great one – 'How does the school address behavioural issues?' etc).

Given air like I'm not there: being ignored

Dear Tom

I have a Year 10 boy who totally humiliates me by ignoring me. Even when I'm a few inches away from him he turns his back and chats to his mates. Worse still, it's damaging the respect the rest of the class has for me. What do I do next?

Oiky behaviour – warning – punishment. In that order. And sometimes I just go straight to punishment. There's no clever way of dealing with this – it's just rude, and as such you need to stand up for yourself and demand better. Tell him not to ignore you, issue a detention, savour him ignoring you for the last time, and then wait to see if he turns up. If he does all is well. If he doesn't, phone home, escalate the punishment and then involve senior staff. See how long he has the stamina to resist constant sanctions. The thing is, you have to set them – and mean them. Wear them down, wear them down.

Herding cats: getting them to listen to me

Dear Tom

I'm a PGCE student in a mixed Year 1 and 2 class. I'm very concerned about getting the best from them, and I don't want to become a nag. How do I get and keep the attention of students this small? The biggest worry is that there is a group of children who would always rather be playing with their hair and each other than listening to the teacher. I gather that it's good not to keep talking if they are, but to stop and wait for them to finish. But is this expecting too much from very small children?

The younger the child, the more often you need to repeat your expectations. As adults, we are used to hearing something once and getting on with it, and it's hard to keep doing it ourselves because we are worried about boring others with repetition. But the little ones have the attention of tiny flies, with very varying levels of understanding concerning responsibility and duty, so it's our job constantly to remind them. They are very sensitive to body language too, just as we are, so act in a stern authoritative way: stand, sound and look like someone who means business. Imagine a person who, in your eyes, commands respect, and copy their body cues. Act it out, by all means. After all, you have a teacher persona who is not you, or at least not entirely; it's the tough you, the stern you, the *tough love* you. Imagine yourself to be that person until you really feel it.

And of course, remember it always takes time with any group, so don't feel a failure every time they fail to listen, just like a mountaineer doesn't feel like a failure if he isn't at the top after a few feet.

Carpet bombing – how can I make carpet time more organized?

Dear Tom

I'm a trainee on final placement in a Year 1 class. Behaviour in my class is awful – only 15 kids but it feels like a lot more! Carpet times are the worst. There is one boy in particular who won't do anything he's told, and once one of them gets going the rest copy and join in. Listening lasts about ten seconds, then some of them get up and walk around, and I am completely ignored. Tidying up is non-existent and nobody will share anything, unless they're throwing it at each other. Then they have a good old time rolling around the carpet.

I use traffic lights; I use 'star of the day'; put names on the board; I use stickers; I use raffles; I tell them why they need to behave. Nothing, not a bit of an effect.

Ouch, sounds like a world of pain. A few things in your question struck me as significant. First, it sounds like you're doing lots right; they're still relatively new to you, they're certainly still quite new to each other, they're obviously young, so there's bound to be issues. Of course you would hope that at this stage most of them would have settled in. Try to remember that (I imagine) most of them behave most of the time, on a minute-by minute basis, and that if you were honest you could probably see that the majority are OK. I am of course massively guessing here! But I've found that it's rare for an entire class to present behavioural problems all the time simultaneously (he said, optimistically).

Don't bother explaining the rules to them anymore. Don't bother having conversations with them about their behaviour, and giving feedback of any complexity. If they can't understand what good behaviour is already, then they need an Educational Psychologist. They are choosing to ignore the commands because they don't care about you enough to stop, or enough about your sanctions. If we continually 'discuss' the pupil's behaviour with them they start to see it as something removed from themselves. They need to start *feeling* like they've done something bad, not just *know* it.

Which leads me on to sanctions. You say that some of the pupils aren't bothered about the detentions, and I think that's a key problem. If punishment doesn't hurt then it's not worth doing; they may as well watch cartoons and eat sweets. Make detentions/sanctions *bite*. Give them hard work to do, sitting in silence, separated from each other. Make them work individually during class time when others work in groups. Make them do boring activities, removed from their peers, whenever the rest of the class is doing something fun (keeping them in the class while everyone gets to go outside to play games is a winner) – anything, so long as it makes them uncomfortable. Get the parents in to discuss their child's behaviour – home discipline on *your* side is like having superpowers in the classroom.

Are they quite a weak group ('they want spoon-feeding')? This could mean that their tasks are too hard and it causes them to disengage, but even the weakest pupil can understand 'sit still and shush!'

Get tough with them. Can the stickers and stars for a little while (unless you are extremely mean with them and give them out for Olympian feats of generosity or achievement). Get out 'cross teacher' for a while and don't be terribly nice, no matter how counter-intuitive it feels. No smiling, no laughing with them. They need discipline first, then the love. Take the love away for a while, and they'll start to miss it. If the class can't behave, then they can't learn, and that is our first priority and duty to them.

Can I lasso a runner? Catching the kids that leg it

Dear Tom

I'm on student placement and my Year 5s are giving me trouble with low-level disruption all the time. They get loads of detentions. But some of them are tough nuts who just give you a mouthful of abuse if you tell them off. One even does a runner when he gets isolated. I then got stick for letting him run off! Not really sure how I could have stopped him; not sure how anyone could have. It really makes me down, because I don't want to fail because of this.

How on earth are you supposed to stop a kid running off? Unless of course you rugby tackle them. I would ask the experts at your school to give clear examples of what they would have done in your situation. After all, if you're on placement then you can't be expected to have built up much of a relationship with them.

How consistent are you with your sanctions, and are you giving enough out? Often the problem is just not being tough enough with them. Detentions should mean detentions, and if they no-show then phone the parents. It's tough work getting behaviour right on placements, but the hard work you put in now will pay off later in spades.

Have you done enough observations with more experienced teachers? Have they observed you? You are entitled to regular and thorough feedback in order for you to learn. If they have thrown you in the deep end then you have the right to demand that they don't, otherwise you can complain to the establishment that sent you. Don't sign any of their observations unless you can clearly put your concerns in writing on the observation.

But do make sure you've got a healthy dialogue with your mentors. Talk to them about ways to improve, have them observe you doing it, and then see where you need to go from there.

Driven round the bend and I can't see an end: when nothing you try works

Dear Tom

I want to be better at behaviour management, but I don't know where I am going wrong or where to start in order to fix it. I've been teaching for seven years in various ways, and now I'm an NQT. But it's never been like this. I try everything: altering voice tone, detentions, consistency, warnings, warnings, warnings … they just carry on talking and talking! Aaaaaargh!!!

Why can't I do this?

Now others want to observe me more as I may fail this term. Some classes (not all) I just can't get on task quickly enough, and trying to change direction or activity is a mission. If I don't improve I'll fail … but no one wants to help me.

What can I do? I feel like I am banging my head against a brick wall. I had two days off work last week because of stress. I used to love teaching, now I am starting to hate it. WAAAAAAAAAHHHHHH!

You are not alone (as the King of Pop said in his usual creepy, messianic way). Follow these four commandments:

1. I always bang on about this, but it has to be said: *consistency.*
2. *Always* do what you say you will.
3. *Always* follow up.
4. Set *clear* guidelines. Of *course* they know that chatting etc. is wrong; they need to hear it from you, so tell them exactly what you expect from them.

If you can follow these guidelines (and they are easy to do but a real slog to keep doing) then they will come around to you in a manner not unlike a cruise liner turning around, i.e. slowly but surely.

Try not to get stressed in the classroom (yeah, I know, easy, right?). Here's how: once you've communicated the rules to them (by lecture, PowerPoint or sticky labels,) then simply record the names of everyone that breaks the rules. And then give out sanctions to everyone on your list at the end. Don't get upset by it, don't shout at them, don't even blink. Take the names like you're train spotting, and let them know about their punishment as if you were telling them the time. You are.

If they fuss and mug, ignore it. See who turns up for their detentions, and anyone that doesn't, gets an escalated punishment (an hour's detention, etc) and the involvement of a more senior teacher (presuming your HOD starts to get involved at this point). *Always* follow up. Phone home in a sympathetic way ('Little Johnny is normally great but I'm afraid today he let himself down a little bit and I need your help to make sure he manages to reach his great potential ...'), send letters. But be consistent. If they fail to turn up to that one, escalate again. Get the HOY/ HOL involved. You're entitled to these support mechanisms when pupils don't turn up, or the school behavioural system ain't worth spit, and you can legitimately cry foul if they barrack you for poor behaviour.

Time to behave: does the time of day affect their behaviour?

Dear Tom

I need some advice on planning lessons for different times throughout the day. I had a Year 10 class at the end of the day, who totally ignored me, and chatted throughout, despite warnings. The same class in the first period were angels – perfect behaviour and loads of work. It seems like the good work yesterday was a fluke. The 'fun' lesson I planned as a reward fell apart as soon as I entered. Lesson over.

How do I get their behaviour to be more even? I refuse to accept that I should just accept this. I feel so deflated.

Don't be deflated. We need all the air we can get. Most of us forget exactly what it's like to be in a pupil's position, mainly, I think, because we're doing such a different job to them, we are (a) adults, probably a bit more responsible and driven by duty and responsibility (I said probably), (b) prone to eat more sensibly and not stay up till three in the morning finishing the thirtieth level of *Grand Theft Shoot My Hooker Up On Zombie Planet III* (or whatever) on their Playstation 5, while catching up with ten mates on Twitter, (c) somewhat more into our subjects than they are and, most importantly, (d) paid to be there.

Have you ever been on a rubbish INSET (hard though it may be to imagine), where you sit at a desk all day and get lectured at, or worse, asked to discuss/feedback etc? Six hours of that has me thumbing out my eyeballs in desperation, so I can only imagine how hard it is to be one of a generation of kids that gets the news from *The Hits Channel*. Frankly I wouldn't feel like learning about Hindu funeral rites either, and I'm *interested* in them.

Best thing I do for my Friday period 6 bunch is to produce a slightly didactic, teacher-led lesson with an emphasis on factual content, recall and comprehension (if you're fond of Bloom's Taxonomy as a teaching tool) and a series of tasks or questions that follow on easily from each other. Something that wouldn't put a smile on any OfSTED inspector's face basically, but then they never make me smile so why should I worry about them? The kids will thank you for it, albeit subconsciously and in another life. They usually respond with gratitude, knowing that for them, Blue Peter is only an hour away … (Or *Hostel VIII*).

Never accept bad behaviour though, no matter what time. In fact, you're in a brilliant position simply to keep the offenders in immediately after the lesson. Indeed, that's when I set all my one hour detentions, precisely because they hate it so much.

Go it alone or ask for help?

Dear Tom

I'm an NQT on a long-term supply placement. What do you think of this? I've finally got a class under control, sort of, by involving the HOD. A few of them are still obnoxious, and I'm wondering what my next move is. I want to get them all marching the same way, but I'm worried if I ask for more help it'll look like I can't do it without assistance. Is it OK to do this or not? Thanks.

We work in packs, not alone, so not only should you ask for help, but you must. It's great that you've enrolled other staff, because by leaning on existing members of staff you reinforce the notion that the teaching staff is a monolithic unit, which in turn emphasizes the idea that they can't win! Hooray!

Don't say that you can't cope (no one can cope entirely alone) but instead tell your line managers that you want support in order to raise standards and improve behaviour management. If you struggle on by yourself you *could* get there in the end, but with other teachers backing you up you'll get there in a fraction of the time, and probably save your sanity and self-esteem in the process.

If your superiors are worth their salt, then not only will they *not* think you can't cope but they'll appreciate you for your professionalism. Besides, if kids think you're working alone then they'll pounce on you like wolves. Unfortunately when it comes to the teenage pack mentality, animal metaphors come far too easily. Put them on a leash.

From peripatetic to teacher: making a transition between roles

Dear Tom

I've worked in 20 schools in ten years in a variety of music training roles, but now I'm in my NQT year. Behaviour management wasn't an issue before, but now I'm a full teacher, it is. And I've had problems from day one

Some of my lessons have terrible levels of misbehaviour – talking, rudeness to me personally, not finishing work. Detentions, consistency, withdrawals – nothing has worked, at least not more than a bit. My mentor and I don't get along, but that's not important.

Someone told me to vary my voice tone – I have! I am at the end of my rope, and I've started to get migraines. I think I need someone to work with me, not just talk to me about what I should do. I asked for someone to observe my lesson to see how awful the kids were, and it somehow became a formal observation graded unsatisfactory! It's being held against me, I'm sure.

Now I feel so depressed. I don't want my career to end ... what should I do?

First of all, how long have you been teaching there? Since the start of the academic year? If so, then you can de-stress a few grades: most teachers in their first year experience this kind of syndrome. In fact there should be a chat room for teachers who have sailed through their first years, and I bet it would be blank. Trust me, there's no one who doesn't have tough classes (at least one or two) all year long in the first year, despite good intentions and high hopes. You're not alone.

Secondly, one of your entitlements at school is support. There are things you can do in order to make this happen and be proactive. You can (and should) ask some exemplary teachers in behaviour management to allow you to observe them, and really make the observation count by focusing on nothing but behaviour: what do they do, how do they stand, etc. Perhaps you could ask some of the SLT to show you how they do it (but avoid holding your breath). Then you should ask a non-SLT teacher who knows about behaviour to observe you informally and they can feed back to you in a non-judgemental way.

Finally, why do you think they're using it against you? What do you mean? Do you think they want to dismiss you? Unless all your lessons are falling apart, it's unlikely; they have to show that they have offered you every support to improve, especially in the NQT year, otherwise any dismissal would be wide open to charges of unfairness, and be struck off at tribunal. But I'm sure it's not as bad as all that. It sounds like they've cut you loose a bit. Time to get on their backs and ask what *they* are going to do to support *you*, instead of what *you* have to do to please *them*. You've got enough pressure!

A whole class with nothing to lose: when they know they're going to fail

Dear Tom

I'm currently a student Maths teacher (PGCE) on my second placement. The first place was easy. On this second placement, one of my classes is a trial: a Year 10 group will constantly inform their teacher that they, 'Ain't f*cking bothered'. They get up and wander around, showing texts and hitting each other. Their predicted grades are G-U. They know it, and can't be bothered to try.

They also know the school is 'all-Inclusive', meaning that whatever they do, they won't get kicked out. They just laugh at detentions, literally, and those that set them. I'm supposed to be observed by an Assistant Head with them next week.

They actually make me dread going in to school and I'm just counting off the days until I can escape to a real job.

It's always tough being on PGCE placement, and being in a challenging school multiplies that. Don't blame yourself, and certainly don't think that it makes you somehow a bad teacher. There are many kids who simply won't behave for you if they sense in any way that you're unsure of yourself, which is absolutely normal when training as a teacher. You have no existing relationship with them, and whereas many pupils automatically defer to authority figures, many others don't have this conditioning, and will only defer to you once you have established yourself with them. So the best advice is achieving that relationship ASAP.

No matter how chaotic it gets, always remind yourself that you are the authority in the room. Just because they don't acknowledge it doesn't mean you're not. Every time someone breaks a rule (which I imagine is frequently at this stage) then take names (so learn them) and make sure they turn up to detentions you give out. If they don't attend, escalate the sanction, and follow that up too. This will be exhausting. It is also essential, and every drop of sweat you put into it will be repaid in this life, not in the next. It takes time and Herculean effort.

Never blow your cool. Keep your temper, and try never to shout. If they see you react to them, then they instantly know they have power over you. Don't allow them this power. If they misbehave, just calmly remind them of the consequences, then move on ... and make sure the consequences happen. Feel like a punch bag in the classroom? Fine. You'll feel much better when you make their lives unpleasant afterwards. Not vindictively, but from a sense of natural justice. We don't win by being ruder or nastier than them. We win by being fair, consistent and relentless. They just can't compete with this.

Even if your school runs a no-exclusion policy (which is like an army having a 'no-bullets' policy. Bravo to the committee of soulless robots that approved that little gem) then you still have powers that finish before that. Meetings with parents etc. are all suitably unpopular with your average pupil to be effective.

How on earth do they know their predicted grades? What is a school doing telling pupils they are expected to get a U? That's crazy to the power of crazy. *Every* pupil should be expected to do well in some way, and every teacher should communicate this expectation to the students. So I advise you to do the same. Tell them that they can all do well, and that they don't have to believe anyone that tells them otherwise. We become the person we perceive ourselves to be. Tell them that you expect them to do well relative to their ability if you must, but tell them you believe in them.

Your SLT should support you, not undermine you, so ask for behaviour guidance, and observe other teachers working who can control these classes. And demand that SLT/HODs follow up with sanctions if yours are ignored. If they're not doing this then they have no right to criticise you.

Not all schools are like this, and teaching these kids might just be a tremendous learning experience for you ... even if it feels like Hell right now. Time spent in the wilderness can seem like time well spent when you get a perspective on it.

Nasty girls who don't get it: when pupils turn on you and complain

Dear Tom

I started a new school in January, and I have a class of Year 10s where the girls are really nasty to me. 'sir, you aren't explaining it properly', and, 'sir, you aren't teaching us properly,' are just the kinds of things they keep saying to me.

At the beginning I believed them and gave them lots of time with my explanations of the subject, but now I suspect that they are just doing it to avoid working; plus it's kind of mocking me.

Worse, like a pack they complained to my HOD .. and he believed them. I know how convincing they can be. If I try to discipline them, they just complain that I'm not teaching them properly, or that I'm picking on them. These girls are bullying me, and I'm the one being blamed now.

How can I deal with this?

This sounds to me like fairly standard 'new teacher' baiting. Put a shot across their bows by making sure you have your differentiated activities ready to roll for them every time you teach them – that way they can't complain that the work is too hard.

Apart from that, bad behaviour should always be treated as bad behaviour whatever the origin or reason. So if they're shouting out, if they're talking over you, if they're refusing to work, then apply sanctions against them. Pupils hate change – they're horribly resistant to new teachers and howl at the injustice of having to meet someone new, the poor wee lambs. Don't tolerate it. They're just using it as an excuse to have a dig at you, pure and simple, so don't entertain any sympathy for them.

The third issue is the lack of support from SLT and the HOD. It's time for you to turn the tables around on them; stop running from them in fear and take the fight back at them. Tell them (don't ask – say you need this) that you want an observation from SLT or the HOD, or both, with a focus on T&L, specifically Pupil Challenge. Then show them a lesson with well-prepared resources etc. Two things happen – either they see your class working well and they find out that the girls are lying, or they see a class behaving badly despite your good preparation. Either way you have absolved yourself of blame in this matter, and can use the observation as evidence of professional credibility if any student makes another bogus claim.

Any HOD or SLT worth their salt should gather evidence before accepting a claim against a teacher, and their natural instinct should really be to err on the side of supporting the teacher. It makes me angry to think that senior leaders would be weak enough to support a group of apparently vindictive teenagers. But then, it's easier to be sympathetic than have the guts to face them down.

The power of one: when you feel all alone with your classes

Dear Tom

NQT sending a distress flare up. My Year 9s were appalling – in a 40-minute lesson they still couldn't line up or let me talk for ten seconds ... even though the HOD was there! The class has lots of EBD problems; I try to be consistent and fair, but so far I haven't got anything from them.

Some members of SLT are supportive and help when I ask, but none of their solutions fix the problem. The Heads of Learning are supposed to support me, but they don't seem too effective.

Worse, the current head leaves soon, and OFSTED will be here next term.

Is it all hopeless? Can I make any changes to a class's behaviour on my own?

Tough one. Without support from above, then you've lost a lot of power over them. After all, if the senior team don't act when situations escalate, then the behaviour policies are toothless. It's like having a society without prisons – all the police in the world can't keep the streets safe.

But make sure you are using the systems correctly. Are you giving detentions consistently? Do you apply behaviour policies fairly and evenly, and at all times? Do you make phone calls home for pupils who fail to attend detentions? Do you pass on the details of any that don't to the relevant bodies? Do you press senior teachers all the time to support you, and not just sometimes?

If you can say *yes* to these questions, then you're doing your job properly, and they aren't. You can't change the behaviour of your pupils if the behaviour of your SLT isn't supportive. It's not a one-man show: teachers are unbeatable when they work in teams; alone they only have their personalities to make a difference, and even sparkling behaviour management skills can only go so far.

Keep it in your mind that you can leave, tough out your NQT year, and make a decision then.

Gang rules: groups of pupils who misbehave as a group

Dear Tom

My Year 5 class has a group (about a third) who won't go along with anything; they refuse to work, hide under tables, climb over tables, ignore me, distract others and generally do what they can to ruin my lesson. It's not a class – it's a club for them, being there. I use sanctions of course, and SMT have supported me, and I have someone from the borough coming in to advise me. But it's not working, and as an NQT, if I can't provide a safe space for them to learn then I could fail my year. Please, please, help me.

Controlling a class can be broken into two parts: your conduct in the classroom – your presence, your body language, the way you give out sanctions; and your conduct outside the classroom. Do you attend all detentions, are they followed up, are they escalated if ignored, etc.? This is where SLT come in.

I would ask you to make sure that your sanctions are always consistently applied (do you *always* give them, or just when you have the energy?) and are ruthless (slightly scary in their severity: they have to be tough enough to be meaningful). When they attend detentions do they get to play in the sandpit, chat to each other, run around the room? Or do they have to sit and do hard work in silence, otherwise their punishment escalates? If they can doss about in detentions then they cease to be scary.

Make sure you give out lots of detentions, and do it as soon as they start mucking about. They don't need warnings any more, they know they're being bad.

I would also take the better part of half an hour talking to them about acceptable behaviour. Make them write the rules out in their books, and explain why each one is there, and the consequences of the rule breaking. I wouldn't bother much at this stage about getting them to write their own rules or 'agree to a set of rules'. You're the boss. You make the rules. The day I let kids make up rules in the classroom is the day they teach me Plato.

If this structural part of your behaviour management is OK, then it would be good to look at the way you communicate your presence. Kids read you much more effectively by how you act than by what you say. Observe other teachers that have great control. What are they doing? Watch *how* they say things, and *how* they stand, set work, etc. rather than the details of their instructions, although that will be useful too. Take notes, and think about ways you can imitate them.

Great control is a learnable skill that takes time. I think observations of your lessons are a great idea, and you should take interest in the feedback. Every NQT has teething problems, and in time yours will dwindle. Just don't give up. Sanctions take time to embed themselves in pupils, and new habits of behaviour also take time. For some of these kids, learning to behave with new teachers is like trying to quit smoking. Give them time to kick the habit, and don't stop your behaviour control until it's had time to start getting under their skin.

How long does it take to control a class?

Dear Tom

In an average comprehensive, where the behaviour is average, and you see the kids once a week, how long should it take before you have good control over a class? I realize this might be a question without an answer.

This question does the rounds every now and then. There are lots of variables that make this practically unanswerable, but it behoves me to try anyway.

Broadly speaking most teachers get a hard time for the first term. You are their punch bag, and even your sanctions are mocked.

After Christmas they realise you're not on supply and that you might be sticking around. Behaviour improves slightly, perhaps in a way that can only be measured using a microscope and a slow-motion camera.

If you are applying regular and consistent sanctions then by the end of the second term you should see a noticeable improvement. You may, for instance, no longer be called 'The Vegetable.'

By the end of your first year you should have reached a plateau. By the second year you can start to re-evaluate your expectations, your behaviour strategies, and what does and doesn't work in your classrooms.

If you make good use of parents' evening and report cards then you can accelerate this process. Phone calls home and school meetings will too.

Failing to apply sanctions consistently, freaking out at the class, getting into personal arguments with kids, being cruel, being unprepared for lessons, taking cheek – these will all slow the process down.

In honesty, there's no stage at which you will feel you've 'made it' – it's not like climbing a mountain. As you get better and better relationships with your classes, you'll see other improvements you would like to see, new summits to climb. Plus every class and school and subject is different. Plus every teacher learns about behaviour strategies at their own pace, so really, any attempt to set a benchmark period is a little hazardous and unfair to most teachers. Good behaviour isn't a goal, it's a process.

I hope that's made everything vastly more unclear. Glad to be of help.

They're using me for target practice: literally

Dear Tom

At my new school some Year 7 boys are throwing things at me, sweets and rubbers. Two were caught, and they were given one-day exclusions, but the matter was only dealt with by the Head of Year. Why do they do this to me? It's left me feeling broken; teaching was always my ambition, but this kind of behaviour makes me feel like throwing in the towel. Any advice? I try to make my lessons fun and interesting, but sometimes it happens in class too. I'm in my first year.

Early in my teaching career a pupil told me I was an f***ing b******. I reported it and the pupil was given an hour's detention. The next day another pupil made exactly the same comment to a senior teacher, and a ten-day exclusion resulted, so I know very well how it feels to realise that your position on the pyramid of power is at the bottom, pushing stones about for the Pharaoh.

You're feeling rubbish right now so I'll talk straight: you're not rubbish. You're an NQT, and as such, subject to levels of abuse that only young children can dream of. Right now they don't trust you, and they don't recognise you as an authority figure ... yet. But they will. Unfortunately in our society teachers are no longer automatically acknowledged as authorities. But it *will* come.

Secondly I need to point out that, no matter how victimized you feel, there will only ever be a small percentage, an absolute minority of pupils, treating you this way. It might seem like the 'school' is against you, but that just isn't true. The vast majority of pupils are on task, well-behaved and pretty good, actually.

I don't blame you for feeling put upon; it's much easier to see danger rather than calm in any situation; we're biologically disposed to pay attention to threats in case they are significant to our survival. But this is just a filter to the way we see a situation. Use a different filter. Make two lists: the first, all the rubbish you had to put up with in a day, the second all the times when a pupil was positive, or helpful, or friendly, or even just on task. Your second list will be *much* longer than your first list. Yet we spend all our time worrying about the latter.

Things *won't* get worse over time if you don't let them. Keep putting pressure on SLT to take this seriously. Enlist your HOD, your mentor, your faculty manager, your Head of Year – *anyone* who has the power to escalate sanctions. *Never* give up, and keep as much pressure on them as you do on the pupils. You *will* get them eventually, one by one they will learn that it isn't worth the pain and bother you will inflict.

This point is important: you're not trapped in there with *them*: they're trapped in school with *you*. You're learning something that experienced teachers know: yes, interesting lessons help with behaviour management, but behaviour management is prior to, and needs to happen before, sparkling, witty lessons designed to the last letter. It's horrible to see your evening's work thrown back in your face by a class of seemingly ungrateful wretches. It's because they're waiting for you to take charge.

So your focus needs to be on behaviour management, before any other pedagogic consideration. It makes me angry to see how little support NQTs receive from teacher training institutions and their placement schools on this issue. As you already know, it's a huge consideration, especially when you're starting out.

Every teacher I admire and respect went through the ordeal of feeling useless and disrespected in their first year. Every single one. I did too, and now *you* are.

But don't give up. If you've wanted to do this all your life, then grit your teeth, accept that you're going to have to work hard (but then you knew that) and you *will* make it.

Boys in the Hood, up to no good: young classes made up of boys

Dear Tom

I'm on my third placement and about to take over a Year 2 class that is almost all boys. I have no idea how to control them, because they are so, well, boisterous. Previously my classes have been a nice mix, but this one smells like a gym. What do boys respond to?

What, apart from *Zoo* and *Playstations*? Boys are pretty competitive (most of them) and thrive on the idea that they might in some way be beating someone else. Anthropologists would say that we have a pack mentality, like dogs – not a flattering comparison, but a useful one. The dog at the front of the sled team is the alpha dog, and the ones immediately below in the pecking order are always snapping at their heels to be in charge. So it makes sense to run with this inbuilt competitiveness and make it work for you.

Any games can do this job – I use *Blockbusters*, *Bingo*, *Taboo*, whatever – choose the one you enjoy and transplant it. One word of caution though; the problem with competitiveness is that some people lose, and you want to avoid a rump of kids who persistently end up feeling like failures, so engineer situations where they can feel proud of what they are good at, even if it's a little artificial. Primary years are where self-images are made, so tread lightly with these ones, and make sure that at some point everyone's a winner.

Angels and Demons: weeding out the minority who misbehave

Dear Tom

I've been an NQT since September, and my classes haven't settled down yet. Most kids have, in most classes, but in two or three classes there are always two or three kids … My Year 11 are fine, and my top set 7s and 8s are sweet as pie, but the Year 9 and 10 classes torture me.

My mentor has practically given up with me, because I can't handle them. When someone else is there, they're angels, but when they're not, anarchy is unleashed. I'm not following procedures with them because I'm so stressed out by them. Yes, I know I shouldn't say that.

This is one of the most common queries I get, but I have an unlimited tolerance for repetition when it concerns NQTs in Hell. I don't get out much.

Of course you shouldn't be on top of everything by now! Seriously, there can't be a teacher in any reasonably challenging school who doesn't struggle. I still fight tiny battles every day with some classes, and I'm sure I always will. That's the nature of the job: creating order from chaos. It never gets perfect, although it does get easier. If so many of your classes are being good for you then remember they are being good for *you*, so you must be doing a lot of things right.

You must follow behaviour policies as closely as you can. Being inconsistent is probably worse than not having a policy at all (and that's *plenty* bad enough). If I could give one piece of advice to all NQTs it would be this: never give up. At this point you're tired after your first term and by now you expected it to be easier. You've tried the policies but they aren't working for everyone. So you feel like giving up a bit.

Don't! This is precisely the time you need to pull strength from your happy place and keep going. This is exactly when NQTs make the killer mistake. If you keep going with the policies then it will work *eventually*. It may take a while; it may even take your whole first year – but badly behaved kids crumble when you *never* give up. It is a question of wearing down their will with yours. Now, some kids have got stronger wills than others, and more deeply learned responses, so you have to make sure that your will is made of diamond. Imagine yourself as a cliff made of granite, and their misbehaviour is a wave crashing futilely against it. (Terribly Oprah, I know, but I use it when I'm feeling a bit battered). You're granite! You're diamond! And you thought you were a teacher.

It's only a *few* kids in a *few* classes. By my calculations that means that in almost *all* of your lessons things are almost *all* good. Doesn't that sound like the definition of a great result? I think that as humans we are programmed to see the bad before the good; look at the average staffroom conversations. Not many people talking about quiet well-behaved pupils, are there? Yet if we're honest, that's what most pupils are like.

So be honest about how well you're doing, and take the advice of your mentor. NQT year is a safe ground to make mistakes as long as we learn from them.

And did I mention that you should never give up?

Time to change tack: when kids think you're a soft touch

Dear Tom

I'm doing my GTP; but the department head is very busy, so I've been teaching alone since day one. I coped pretty well, I think, with most pupils, but I'm starting to think that I started off a bit of a softy with my classes. Most pupils behave OK for me, but in every lesson there are some wandering around the room who won't do as they're told, although they're not hugely disruptive; but they don't work either.

I also get lots of kids coming into my room during lessons (God knows where from) to chat to friends; they say that they come in because I'm 'safe'. My HOD has become a lot more supportive now, and I realise that I need to start getting much tougher with these pupils. But how can I suddenly change gear with them now that I've settled into a pattern with them? I feel very nervous about getting tough with them. All I seem to be doing these days is dealing with behaviour, not teaching. Is this common?

More common than it should be. Most new teachers would say that at first all they seem to be doing is managing the behaviour of the whole class, and it's not until later that they start to feel that they are actually teaching, so you're not alone.

You can change your strategies as quickly as you like; simply walk into the class and start to behave as you want them to behave and accept nothing less than what you expect. The class, if it has learned a certain pattern of behaviour with you, will challenge this at first, but they will soon realise that your 'new' expectations are here to stay *if* you do, and if you punish and praise consistently according to your own guidelines. It doesn't require a big 'run up' – just start enforcing it from next lesson. Explain to them that you need them to improve so that they can learn better and reach their potential; I always try to make sure my students know that I'm being strict so that they benefit, not because I enjoy giving detentions.

All damage can be undone; pupils relearn behaviour as quickly as you teach them it. Just be a model of good practice yourself. As for the 'intruders', take names, and follow up at all times, let them know that they have intruded upon *your* space, and they are subject to your rules too. It's tiring, but if you want to improve your situation, it's going to require a bit of time and effort. Keep it up, and never give up. You will wear them down before they wear you out.

Shut up, please: why do they fall silent to everyone but me?

Dear Tom

I'm a first year student on a BA Primary Education course. I'm in my first week of a seven-week placement in a Year 1 class. It's going great in general, but I really want to know one thing: how do you get their attention, and then keep it? The teacher only has to flare his nostrils and they fall silent as stones. With me, I could put chloroform into their Nesquik and they'd still be jumping around like loonies. What's the trick?

My sensei told me this trick for getting attention from a class that's quick, easy and infallible. Unfortunately it's almost useless: he said, "Hold a pen up in front of your face and shout, 'Everyone! Look at the pen!'"

It works for exactly two seconds. Once.

This taught me a few things. One important lesson was that it's one thing to get their attention, and quite another to hold on to it. If you want to hold their attention then you should act as though you believed you deserved it. If I think of someone that I can listen to for a while, I imagine someone who acts confidently, speaks with a controlled measured tone, and who looks as if they are in control of what they are doing. Practically, this means slow and considered movements (which then give sudden gestures greater impact) and a thoughtful and calm voice (which also lends impact to a sudden escalation in volume). People who are uncertain about themselves gravitate and respond to people who look like they know what they're doing.

So it is essential to look as if you are in control. Avoid looking worried, or reacting quickly to behaviour (as if you are jumping around responding to them) because it looks to them as if you are following their agenda. You need to set your agenda and keep at it, acting as if you expect them to get on board with what *you* want. You need to act as though you are the boss of the room, and there's no question about it. Every teacher needs to have that as a mantra at the back of their minds, as it affects everything you do in the room, the way you speak, what you expect, etc.

I know these are mainly ideas for maintaining control, but people that are in charge get attention because they exude status. So for a new teacher, the simplest advice I can give is 'pretend to be confident' – even when you don't feel it. Or especially then!

Everyday behaviour management

Teaching is a job. Perhaps you noticed? The payslips give it away. But while you're washing your feet in Krug and shelling baby lobsters from the Caspian for your pet lynx, have a thought for how your salary is earned. There is an enormous amount of variety in the profession; every year a different set of kids, a new dynamic in the classes; each combination of pupil, room, subject, maturity level and teacher offering a range of possibilities matched only by a Rubik's Cube ten squares broad. But alongside this cornucopia of variety comes an inescapable fact: every job comes with a portion of monotony, repetition and dreariness, even if you're a Human Cannonball (I'm guessing here. Don't write in).

To complain is human, and we wouldn't be human if we didn't groan at the thought of yet another lesson on the same subject for the umpteenth year, or another detention for talking, another staff meeting, another initiative, another parents' evening, another 'talk' about homework. In fact, looked at from above, there is a huge amount of repetition and routine in the job, as in all jobs. That is why we don't call them 'funs', because often they aren't. So it won't surprise anyone to be confronted by this routine everyday. Strangely, some still complain about it, and wonder if teaching isn't for them because of it. Perhaps I missed the induction day when NQTs are promised a career of bohemian array, every day a Dolly Mixture of wonder and novelty.

Once a teacher has broken the seal on his or her career and no longer feels like they've just been plucked from the NQT cellophane, a whole new set of dilemmas starts to appear. OK, so the classes now grudgingly acknowledge that you're not going anywhere. Perhaps they don't openly refer to you as 'The Cabbage' any more (at least on their Public Profiles on Facebook). You have begun to see patterns in behaviour; you know approximately where the entrances and exits are; you are teaching. If they don't exactly sing your name in Psalms as you enter, at least they know that you work there. Now, secondary behaviours start to become important to you: are they bringing homework in? do they try their hardest? do they carry pens? You have gone past the battles to get them to enter and remain in your classroom. Now you have to learn to deal with everything else that they do. Or don't. Suddenly you're trying to deal with them all around the school, and in the classroom you're trying to get them to be more than merely docile, you're trying to get them to learn.

In the classroom this is going to involve stamina: to keep doing what you've already been doing, and to pursue the content of your desires with grim resolve. The pupils need to learn that you care so much about their educational and social well being that you are prepared to thwart their short-term goals for the improvement of their long-term ambitions, even the ones that they themselves don't realize yet, like life skills and exams. But that's what being a grown-up is all about, particularly if you are responsible for the futures of scores of pupils.

Teachers also confront the fact that they have to deal with behaviour every step they take in a school day. This means learning how to control yourself – your behaviour, your feelings, your reactions (see also Chapter 8). It also means opening your mind, and setting it free from the classroom. Pupils aren't only at school in your room, and you're not only a teacher when you're in the class with them. You're a teacher all day long, and the closer you get to the gates, the bigger your teacher boots get. Every action you make in their presence will be absorbed and added to their evaluation of you as a teacher overall. If you walk through a playground and ignore pupils gambling or bullying, then you have sent out a powerful message about your boundaries that you probably didn't want them to learn. And they'll take that learning into the classroom.

So open your mind. The corridor is your classroom. The playground is your classroom. So is everywhere else. Act in these areas like you would want a teacher to act. Conduct yourself in a way that you would want others to emulate. *Be* a teacher; don't *try* to be a teacher. Rest assured that the students will be students, whatever you do, effortlessly. Of course, it's impossible to follow up on every single bit of misbehaviour and less-than-perfect conduct that you will come across – you're not some hundred-handed Eastern deity – but you must be seen to be doing what you can. As soon as the pupils sniff that you'll let things slide outside the classroom, then their conduct around you will be as loose as they want it to be – after all, what will *you* do? But if they know that misbehaviour around you won't be tolerated wherever you are, not only will this support your classroom presence, but it will reduce the number of actual situations you have to deal with, because the pupils will be more amenable to your guidance with a quiet word or (and nothing beats this feeling) a look.

Does this sound tough? It is. But it isn't quantum physics either. It takes willpower – or the illusion of willpower. It takes you gritting your teeth and saying 'It's a job', at the same time that you remind yourself this is what the students *need* you to do. This is what the job requires, and this is what you're paid for. You can't do everything. You can't fix every problem. But you need to do your best to fix the problems right in front of you. And best of all, if you keep it up, you'll get better at it, and it gets easier, until you find that there are no more big surprises in teaching day-to-day, because you'll have dealt with everything that the profession throws at you, and you know how to (or how not to) handle them.

And when that happens, that feels great. You might even enjoy the grind.

Getting really motivated: making them want to learn

Dear Tom

I am a primary-trained teacher who in September will be with a Year 7 group. The school have tutor time for 30 minutes at the start of each day. I was wondering if you have some ideas for activities for this time that will motivate the boys and get them ready for their first lesson of the day. When I observed the current Y7 group recently, they very quickly became unsettled and then disruptive – then chaos reigned!!!

Motivating people is a notoriously difficult thing to do; it is a complex combination of connecting with people's values, the desire to change, and the knowledge that change is possible. Don't confuse it with exciting them – it's easy enough to get people excited – just do anything that raises the heartbeat and gets the blood pumping. Despite an entire self-help industry devoted to pretending that firing people up for five minutes is the same thing as motivating them, it isn't (I once worked in a franchise chain where the store managers would tell their staff that they had to 'get motivated' before the start of every shift, as if motivation was a decision, like scratching your nose, as opposed to a state of being.)

But of course that isn't the motivation we need in classrooms; in this context what we're trying to motivate them into doing is learning, growing as people and (let's be honest) behaving.

To create long-term motivation for any activity or pursuit the students must:

a) *understand* why the activity is valuable (what's in it for me?)
b) be *able* to do it, or learn to do it
c) derive some *satisfaction* from the activity, or the attempt.

Therefore why not get the students doing a show and tell about the things they are good at, or the things they would like to do in life? Ask them to present reasons to the class why educational is valuable. Tell them stories about inspirational people, and get them talking about why some people find them inspirational. Above all, help them to achieve some perspective about *why* they are in school, and *why* it is incredibly important to work hard, be kind to others, and focus on developing their talents.

To get them ready for the first lesson you need to take a different approach; this is essentially getting their heads into 'school' mode, rather than 'run around the room screaming about dinosaurs' mode. So really this needs to be something that will soothe them, bring their heartbeats down and get them thinking. There is a range of activities that promote this. My favourite is always telling them that they have to bring a reading book (or at least a newspaper) to read quietly – that's all. No noise, just silent reading. It's amazing how many pupils look forward to this quiet period where they are allowed to do nothing but read.

In my school we have experimented with meditation classes (non-denominational, secular meditation, in case you were worried) with small groups, although it takes time for all class members to play ball.

P4C (Philosophy for Children) is an excellent activity: short, fun and thought provoking, it costs nothing but helps train the kids to be real thinkers, not passive receptors. I can't recommend it enough as a teaching tool. There is not enough space for me to explain the particulars about this if you're not familiar with it, but I direct you to Dame Google as an easy way to find out more.

Does every child matter? When you have a bully in the room

Dear Tom

I have a student who is constantly being bullied by another student. The bullying is low key but persistent – flicking, name calling, pinching etc.

We've been told to seat them apart, and the Head of Year has told the parents that it's all being dealt with. But it's not. I saw the bully belt the kid again, and told SLT, who then said they were too busy to deal with it. Nothing's been done yet, days later, and it's driving me mad.

You might want to remind SLT that (apparently) Every Child Matters, and that the ECM strategy came about because of a lack of urgency (perceived or otherwise) in proactive interventions. In fact, this isn't even about being proactive – the bullying is an existing situation, so it's reactive. If the child being bullied belonged to one of the SLT, I wonder what action they would take then, hmm? Bullying scars for life. And if we teach the victims that nothing will be done then we also teach them *not* to ask for help, *not* to resolve things peacefully and *not* to trust adults.

Speak to the Child Protection Officer and the union rep, and write an email to the Head/SLT asking for a response. You might even want to speak to the parents and ask if they are aware of the situation, although I would check with the HOL/member of staff responsible for pastoral care first to check that no toes are stepped on.

I think this child needs you very much right now. Sometimes life presents us with situations where we are the only ones who can make a difference at that exact moment. This might be one of those times.

I have felt your presence: can I get them to behave when I'm not there?

Dear Tom

I have a great relationship with my Year 6 class; they work hard, have fun and do well. But every time they get another teacher or adult, they act up. It's never anything terrible, but I always get reports that they've let themselves down a bit. Everyone but me seems to have a problem with them. Now, I run my class on very strict guidelines, and all observations have agreed that this is the case. And I really follow up when I get negative feedback on them, and always set detentions etc. I see everything through. I've been teaching a while now, and my colleagues all respect my behaviour control. So how do I get them to behave for other people? I feel like they're letting me down.

This is the sort of problem that only occurs with teachers who are extremely good at managing behaviour; it's a sort of Zen Master dilemma, not 'how can I get them to behave?' but 'how can I get them to behave when I'm not there and someone else is teaching them?.' What you're looking for is a kind of remote control over two dozen independent young minds, and I wouldn't beat yourself up over not possessing that kind of Jedi mind trick.

It sounds like you're doing everything absolutely spot on in your space – the kids work hard and well. That's a testimony to your ability and their respect for you as a person. But you can't expect them to have that for everyone else; their behaviour when you're away is only fractionally a reflection on you and your teaching. The best you can do is to follow up on behaviour reports when you get back; possibly you could do a bit of coaching with the teachers that cover them; possibly you could give your class yet another 'talk' about behaving when you're gone.

But there's not much you can do telepathically! Some teachers have the ability to wind up classes; some pupils will only behave for teachers they know and trust. Some things are out of our hands to some extent, and may we have the good grace to accept the things we cannot change.

These aren't the droids you're looking for. *waves hand*

Public enemies; getting them to behave when they move around

Dear Tom

I was wondering what tactics you use to make sure classes move around the school quietly. I've got a P2 class, and recently they were so noisy that the head commented. I felt so embarrassed I wanted to vanish.

Hmm, I find that if I want to threaten pupils with a meaningful punishment, it has to be unpleasant enough to deter them, particularly for younger pupils. Find out if they are booked on any fun school trips or activities. If the misbehaviour is widespread enough, then one simple answer is to tell them that if they're not going to be polite enough to move around sensibly then they'll have to forget any activities that involve them moving anywhere, like trips, and return them to their desks for some nice sums or Apocrypha study. They will think you are strict and possibly horrible but it's a big warning to them not to do it again.

Try to be specific who you target; whole class punishments usually do more harm than good, having the subtlety of a carpet bomb, and causing the nicer kids to loathe you. Good luck.

My spider sense is tingling: they misbehave when I'm not looking

Dear Tom

Every teacher must get this, kids who throw paper balls at each other when you're helping someone or just looking the other way. Problem is that I don't want to be unfair and punish the wrong kids, and I do make everyone tidy up at the end, but that means there's no real punishment, and it's at the end of the lesson anyway. Short of growing a third eyeball what can I do?

Here's a short cut to becoming tri-ocular:

Bluff 'em, Danno. Act as though you are about to look away, but then don't, e.g. start to bend down obviously as if to help a student but then look up suddenly. These chaps aren't brain surgeons, and predictably fall for ruses.

Have two or three entire lessons spent at your desk/board with absolutely no activities where you leave your post. If they need watching all the time, maybe you should *give* them what they need. It could break the cycle of behaviour.

Webcam/CCTV etc. It's not illegal, and even the big unions accept it in classrooms as long as they aren't trained on the teacher, or used for 'lesson ob' purposes (might be the thin end of the wedge though).

And when you finally *do* get one of them, make sure the punishment counts. Five minutes at lunch time for 'the chat' isn't really what you're looking for. If you've repeatedly warned them, then an hour working after school should teach them how to behave.

Balancing firm and fair when you're a Head of Year

Dear Tom

I'm a new Head of Year at an all-boys' school, and I'm trying to be firm and fair (and sometimes struggling with both). There's one difficult kid who can't be bothered with school and therefore me, but I really want to get him on board; as the years pass I can imagine him getting more unruly, and I don't want that. I want a relationship with him now to stop that happening. I see that he does need discipline when he deserves it, but he won't turn up to detentions and is frequently in trouble.

All the other kids in my year fear/respect me, but not him. Parents are all right, but not really that involved with us. How can I punish him and get him on side?

Testing. Here's a boy who desperately needs boundaries. He's lucky to have a HOY like yourself who sincerely wants the best for him; obviously whether he appreciates that is another matter.

Despite your desire to build bridges with this student (or perhaps because of it), you must be dispassionate and clinical about the way you apply sanctions to him. If he crosses a line, then the sanctions should immediately snap into place. He must understand that there are consequences to his actions. Being too gentle with him will risk teaching him that rules don't matter that much, and that his education doesn't matter that much, because he can push the rules about and get away with it.

This certainly doesn't mean being cruel to him. Just treat him like every other student – set detentions, escalate if he doesn't attend, keep having meetings with the parents (perhaps they too need to realize that you're serious about helping this pupil). Show that you're prepared to dish out tough love because it's vital to his education as a student and as a human being that he learns to comply. If he doesn't learn this valuable life skill (i.e. getting along with other people and realizing that other people matter too) then he'll leave school unprepared for adult life. He could also learn to respect you, because you do what you say will. I remember one particularly amazing conversation where a student who was permanently excluded said to his former Head of Year, 'I never held it against you, getting me thrown out. Even then I knew I was being rude, and the way you treated me, you gave me more respect than I got anywhere else.' True story.

So when he does experience sanctions, they can be supportive and reasonable (for instance, you can use the time to get him to catch up with class/course work, or simply have a chat with him) but the sanctions must happen. He isn't on side right now; he's letting himself down. He might just need to be given clearer guidelines about what is required of him. Plus, of course, sometimes when we try too hard to keep them on side we risk placating them, and that is an inversion of the natural roles of teacher/student.

The Taming of the Crew: when is it time to give up with hard classes?

Dear Tom

I've recently started at a tough inner city school. I've set quite a few detentions for low-level disruption, and now I'm worried that I'll get a reputation for being a bad teacher for doing so. The kids I have are all low ability, and they've had supplies all year, so they're pretty wild right now. Should I keep on being tough with the detentions, or take a softer approach?

Trust me; you'll be struggling if you *don't* set the detentions. Keep it up; you're doing exactly what is required to get to the state where eventually you will hardly need to set any. Saying that only struggling teachers set detentions is like saying only bad schools exclude pupils. Sometimes, you gotta do what you gotta do.

Post natal blues: adjusting after maternity leave

Dear Tom

I've come back to teaching after maternity leave. I have a Year 9 group that makes me not want to go in to school. The kids know that I haven't taught for long anyway, so I'm following school policies to the letter. But will everyone think I'm cr** if I'm the one always setting detentions? I see others let them get away with loads in the lessons, but I won't put up with it. My line manager is great about it, but I'm worried my reputation will suffer – even though I don't want the little buggers to beat me! Help, please.

Relax, you're doing exactly the right thing. The only ingredient you need to complete this behaviour soufflé is perseverance. I was going to say 'and time' but that would have been two ingredients. Good luck.

Supply teacher going under

Dear Tom

I'm a Year 6 supply teacher; the regular teacher has been off for months with stress. In my second week now, I'm beginning to see why she's off. Some of the kids behave like animals: late to class and refusing to enter, running around the room and corridors, leaving the room when you tell them off, swearing, watching rude videos on YouTube when I'm trying to teach, ignoring me, ignoring punishments – they can do whatever they want!

The school has NO sanction system – any offenders simply get sent to the head, and then returned after about fifteen minutes. Oh yes; they have a positive sticker system too. I must say that lots of our kids have very unsettled (sometimes abusive) homes, but surely we can't use this as justification for bad behaviour? My contract runs out with them in a few weeks.

You know, normally I would write the same kind of advice I always try to give something encouraging, specific and practical based on my experience of people and children. But for once I am scratching my head, possibly at the idea that a school would choose not to have sanctions. How absolutely, barn-stormingly bananas is that?

For once being in a supply position plays to your advantage – you can run for the hills, and don't look back in case you turn into a pillar of salt or something. Stickers for classes? God give me strength. From what you describe I'm not surprised that the pupils are fairly feral. Seriously; I regard that kind of weak-willed communitarian exper- iment as a sickly cousin to abuse, or at least neglect. Children need rules, so that later on they can learn the pleasures of breaking them … but they need rules first, so that they can know what to break. Don't tell me – are the kids allowed to 'design' their own school rules? Seriously – don't tell me, I'm about to burst a blood vessel.

Grit your teeth and count sheep until the bitter end. If you were staying I would grit mine too and write you a battle plan that could keep clipping their wings all by yourself. But I should simply weather the storm until D-Day.

Getting them to Go Straight after some Porridge: I'm dreading some kids coming back to my class

Dear Tom

Just before Easter I had three really troublesome lads taken out of my class for a spell in the naughty house up the road. Since they've been gone my class has run like a dream. They return next week. Now I'm dreading having them back. What do I do when they get dumped back on me again?

Your apprehension about their return will communicate itself to the pupils subliminally through your reception of them, unless you take control of the situation. *You* have the power in the classroom; *they* are naughty children who are learning to be human beings. *They* should be apprehensive about returning to *your* class.

Reintroduction meetings are a must, and individually, not en masse. Possibly have a senior teacher present to show them it's serious.

Reiterate the class rules. Personally I explain why I have them first, but I don't invite their opinion on the matter, mostly because I don't care what they think of my rules, only that they follow them.

You must get a verbal (even a written) contract established that they understand your rules and agree to abide by them. Then you can be sure they know when they are misbehaving. You need to show them that things will be different for them, from now on.

Obviously seat them away from each other. Introduce them one at a time, and try to praise them for anything *legitimately* praise-worthy that they do. Show them that positive behaviour = good, misbehaviour = bad. Of course, the discipline stick still needs to hang above their heads, but if you can convince them there's advantage in being on the side of the angels, then you won't need it.

As each member returns talk up how well some people were doing in the previous lesson. Name a few names and try to include the most recently re-integrated inmate, just in passing. Any good intentions they might have can be destroyed if you go nuclear on them too soon; try to give a stern warning first before you come down on them.

Vet feels like a rookie: when you've been doing it for years and can't get the magic back

Dear Tom

I've been teaching for 11 years; now I've gone from a tough school to an even tougher one. Most of my classes are bottom sets, but all the wheels have fallen off my behaviour control. My kids all play the system (if they get two detentions in a day then they only serve one detention) and I'm starting to bore the parents with the same call home every day. I feel, to be honest, pretty low about the continual misbehaviour. It's like I'm being worn away. SLT only show their faces if OFSTED are around, or to give people hassle when things aren't done. I'm looking for my mojo, but I reckon it's knackered.

Your situation is probably useful for any NQT to be aware of; so many of them can't understand what they're doing wrong when they seem to be doing things by the book. Yet as you can testify, even experienced, respected teachers catch hell when they move schools. Long gone are the days when students would defer automatically to rank and seniority, and now we live in an age where, for many teachers, deference must be 'earned'. It is, of course, tragic and ridiculous that we face this dilemma, but there we have it.

Issue One: it sounds as if your school behavioural system is rotten with the silverfish of ropy management. How can 2 × 1 Detention = 1 Detention? If a child incurs a detention twice in a day then they get two, without question. Sure, kids can earn some time off for exceptional behaviour, but it should be a privilege, not a right nor an expectation. Can you bypass this cowardly nonsense and simply impose your own behaviour strategies? Who knows? Sounds like the system hasn't been looked after very well.

SLT not pulling their weight? Maybe you can make them by bugging them as much as possible and making them realize that if they don't support you, you'll make things miserable for them! Sounds odd, but sometimes managing upwards is your only option. Are all SLT craven, or are some sympathetic to the cause? Enlist them if possible.

I would do some market research on the behaviour of the kids with various teachers. Why do they behave for them? Do they have any strategies or tips you can use? Or can you borrow authority from them in any way (possibly via your HOD/HOL etc.)

You've been round the block, so I hardly need remind you about consistency, following up, fairness and doing what you say, always. Remember that it takes time for relationships to build up, and until you do, you have to fall back on your charisma, tenacity and stubbornness. For my hardest kids I act like tough Dad – I tell them I care deeply about them (tough, serious face) and that means that I'm going to make them succeed even if they don't want to (points finger, etc). Sweeney jacket optional.

I don't think you've run out of strategies; I think you're probably doing the right thing and suffering while you wait for the results to trickle in. You'll get there in the end because you're a professional, a grown-up, and better still, a real teacher.

Quite contrary: a boy who does the opposite of what you want

Dear Tom

I work in a special needs school for boys, mostly a mix of autistic and behavioural conditions. One boy who has Oppositional Defiant Disorder (basically he refuses to do anything you tell him to) is challenging me beyond belief. He produces no work in literacy and numeracy sessions, and he takes up most of my time by being disruptive. Even detentions don't work with him, and it's exhausting me. Reward systems don't work, even though my line managers have told me to keep plugging away. I can't go on like this much longer.

ODD must be extremely hard to contend with, and I commend the patience and professionalism that powers you to work with these children. I spend most of my day advising people how to deal with 'fringe' behavioural issues; for you, it's the 'mainstream'.

Everything I've studied about ODD suggests that no single strategy has been proven infallible, and that you will have to try different approaches. It sounds as if your curriculum head might know what he or she is talking about, and given their background in the institution, their approach might well be the correct one, no matter how debilitating it is for you. It seems to be the approach of 'keep plugging away and you'll get there in the end', which works for the majority of people, ODD or not. It may seem tiresome in the extreme right now, but possibly it will pay off.

What do you do in the detentions? If it's making him do the class work then you put yourselves (both of you) back in the classroom context, and his behaviour emerges. Could you instead put on a film / movie related to one of his topics/subjects and just play it with no comment? Trick him into getting interested in something. Then ask him what he thought of the movie at the end, perhaps see if you can get him into a conversation about the themes, or what he thought. Listen to what he has to say. Given that one of his prime delights is getting a rise out of adults, you'll have to go softly softly. But as he's in the room, it's really hard to avoid watching or at least listening to TV.

A wise man once made the point that if you try to pull a cow into the cowshed at night, it'll pull against you. But if you get smart and try to pull it away from the shed, it'll run straight in. I don't suppose you need to get this boy into a cowshed at any point, do you?

Can I get naughty kids to bake cakes?

Dear Tom

I am not from the UK, but I notice schools here seem to rely on detentions a lot. I cannot see the point of them. I have some suggestions for things they could do instead: get them to cook or bake something for the class, do more homework, or call the parents in. Can I do any of these?

A detention needs to be simultaneously unpleasant enough to act as a deterrent and useful in some way. I always make my pupils do work, preferably class work they should have done or work they have missed. Better yet, give them something that extends their knowledge or skills beyond the lesson. If they fail to do this work then they are deemed not to have 'done' their detention, and are set another. They soon get the message. Detentions are useless if they just have to sit quietly – most students can phase out quite happily and listen to the voices in their heads – and they often have a threshold of boredom approaching Olympic standard.

I would love to set pupils useful pastoral activities, like removing chewing gum from tables, picking up litter, or painting a fence, but alas I have discovered that our child labour laws have rather set their shoulders against such ideas. (Ah, we threw the baby out with the bathwater on that one …) In an ideal world pupils that misbehaved would be set something profound and slightly ironic to do (I still can't get the cake-baking out of my head) but in the tougher schools this just isn't possible. It would, I imagine, prompt them to phone their lawyers and invoke the UN Declaration of Human Rights. If they could spell it. Or indeed, use a phone.

No baking I'm afraid. Or painting picket fences. Or chimney scouring. Better stick to the detentions.

The domino effect: the boy who can't take criticism

Dear Tom

I need help with a Year 3 boy from a severely dysfunctional family. Even the most delicate criticism has him downing tools and refusing to work. If I take golden time off him, he's not bothered; he says he doesn't care – about anything. When I send him to the Head, she chews his head off, he comes back crying and even more determined not to work.

Now the other boys are beginning to act like him because he seems to be getting away with kicking off. It really is awful and I can't deal with it.

Sounds a very complex young man, and it must be hard dealing with him. I've seen a lot of kids who are both very able and also exhibit behavioural difficulties. These kids aren't often on the G&T list, for example, because their behaviour inhibits classroom achievement. Many of them have serious issues with failure and achievement, and have a complex relationship between their own self-image and their external successes and failures. If they are criticized at home, or their parents are demanding perfectionists, or if their family sneers at success, or if Mum and Dad are really good at something, if, if ... the list goes on. There are so many ways for children to learn that they mustn't fail, or worse, mustn't try.

Confrontation clearly doesn't work with this young man – it only encourages him to repeat patterns of defiance that are learned at home. So give him something that we are ideally placed to give: inspiration. Praise him consistently, but only ever for genuinely praise-worthy activities. Have one-to-one chats with him where you tell him that you know he's able (ham it up a bit at this stage for impact) and that you want him to be as great as you think he can be. Then try to get him to self-criticize in ways that sound entirely positive ('I love what you wrote there- how can you make it even better?') and get him to critique himself; it's far safer than being judged by others, and it will develop his thinking skills.

Above all, try to show him that he is valued for things other than his academic achievement; if he doesn't get a lot of esteem from home, he might cling to his classwork as a way of feeling good about himself, so naturally he won't let it be mocked or criticized. Give him compliments for pastoral activities, or being helpful. Give him a star (or whatever) for being funny, or kind. Never shout at him, and tell him that you'll work hard with him for as long as you're his teacher. It sounds like he's crying out to be valued as a person, so the next time he acts up, simply have him calmly removed to a quiet space and when you do get round to 'the chat', say something non-confrontational like, 'How are you feeling?' as an ice breaker. If you give him anger he'll give it back, so give him something that he can't use as a weapon.

Good luck.

When Smiley Faces aren't enough: the class isn't responding to positivity

Dear Tom

My first class ever has 27 pupils (reception year). Most of them are lovely but of course there are six or so who are causing lots of trouble by chasing each other, breaking stuff and hurting class mates. Now I use the Smiley Face on Board system (and sad faces too) to give warnings, I use time outs and sticker charts; but they all mean nothing to these pupils.

I used to feel so happy going into my job but now my love of teaching is crumbling. They don't want to play, they only want to hurt others and break things. Even when we had a class discussion on rules they didn't care! Help!

First of all it's essential that you keep perspective. Twenty-seven *is* a large class, and fortunate indeed is the teacher who doesn't experience trouble with a new class. Things will improve massively over time.

Twenty or so of them are great. Looking at it like that, you've started extremely well! Don't be too hard on yourself and expect perfection from the get-go. Teaching, as you have no doubt found, is quite unlike the adverts. Or indeed any other depiction of schools in the media.

I advocate the stick before the carrot; at that age they are still learning how to be human beings, and it's our job to lead them there. They need to be aware of what's wrong before they know what's right. They are innately selfish, and need you to draw boundaries. So focus on class rules and punishments for transgressions before you focus on rewards. That comes later, once they understand that you're not to be messed with.

Persevere. It could take an entire year of sanctions with some pupils to get the message across, particularly if discipline is weak at home. You *will* get there in the end.

The road to redemption: getting small groups of small people to make small steps to improvement

Dear Tom

I team teach a Year 2 class with another teacher. There are about half a dozen children who behave badly in a variety of ways, all supporting each other's misdemeanours. These include rudeness, chatting, answering back, throwing things. Strategies tried include consequence codes, the language of choice, chats, talking to parents, positive praise, missing golden time, everything, but they keep on disrupting lessons, although one seems to be responding a bit.

This kind of situation is incredibly wearing, and can make you feel that you're doing something wrong as a teacher. If there's a group of pupils acting up there are a few points I can suggest:

These kids are seeking self-esteem from their peers, looking for the boost to their egos that only mates can bring, so supply it yourself, and praise them for any achievement, particularly anything pastoral, evidencing kindness, thoughtfulness or helpfulness.

Sit them as far apart as possible, with neutral pupils in between. Really sandwich them in an ocean of nice kids!

Keep applying the sanctions ... every time, every time. If they keep it up then escalate the sanctions. Your chief asset is the ability to grind them down over time, and all but the toughest kids will break before this. You say you've made some progress with one. Great – this is the beginning.

Don't stop what you're doing; it might simply be a case of keeping up the pressure until they give up. We run marathons, not sprints, and almost every kid will wave the white flag if they see they'll be under siege forever.

I would pump up the pressure a bit. Don't give them choices, and once you've discussed their behaviour with them calmly, once, then they don't need it again. They need to start learning more about negative consequences.

It sounds like you've started already – keep it up.

You are SO unfair: getting kids to understand why some people get special treatment

Dear Tom

My Year 6 class have a variety of hard backgrounds, and many of them have had a tough time at school. One boy in particular has really violent and extreme episodes and outbursts; even with help to manage his behaviour he finds it difficult. We've worked out coping strategies with him, and he has a learning mentor.

But now the other kids think that he gets special treatment, and openly say it's unfair that he can leave class to calm down when he's hyper or aggressive, or spend time out of lessons with his mentor. I've told them he doesn't go out for treats, but does so to help them learn and for him to calm down. Most accept this, but some still think he gets favoured. It's causing friction in my whole class.

Ah, the delights of *inclusion-at-all-costs*. I sympathize. In my opinion our school system is badly letting down a generation of pupils of all needs due to this insane social experiment. Cheers, David Blunkett.

But that's no help to you. I would say that after four years of being together it's unlikely they'll spontaneously form a barbershop chorus anytime soon. Every class has a different dynamic, and some classes have dynamics that really, really suck, simple as that. They will never settle easily together, in the same way that some people will never get along particularly well.

And that's no help either, but I think it's an important thing to realize before you are too hard on yourself. As with so many other problems involving behaviour, we don't have the luxury of unpicking years of difficult upbringing. Sometimes all we can do is deal with the behaviour, and that means clear guidelines and clear sanctions. Apply them whenever they are broken and the pupils will understand. They may always wriggle, and this may just be their destiny.

As to the allegations of unfairness, I agree that there needs to be a class conversation about it, and then an *instruction* from you (not a suggestion) that there has been a line drawn under the situation. I would tell them that we all need different help to get to the same level. I wouldn't expect a pupil on crutches to climb stairs, and I wouldn't expect a pupil with anger management issues to be able always to resolve them successfully without time outs, etc. Some people wear glasses, some people need scribes, and some people need to leave the room when they get angry.

If they still bitch about it after this then it's too bad for them – you've been reasonable and explained matters. Get the detention stick out.

Music to motivate

Dear Tom

Do you have any suggestions for fast music for children to tidy up the class to?

I usually use *It's Chico Time*. Or *Flight of the Bumblebee*. For some of my classes I feel like I should be using *Tubular Bells parts 1 and 2*, given their general torpor.

I yelled; she bailed. I failed? Feeling guilty about shouting.

Dear Tom

One of my 'delicate' Year 10 girls was late to one of my lessons (with the usual excuse of 'her mate had her pen' and so on) and she refused to answer me when I asked her about it. After ignoring me for a minute I'm afraid to say I shouted at her in front of the class, and then she swanned out to see her Head of Year. How could I have acted so that it didn't get that far? Such a simple situation ...

Don't be hard on yourself. Oh, that we all had a rewind button to go back and change things. Until they invent such a thing, we're only human. And teachers have to make snap decisions constantly with multiple participants, so it's only to be expected that we don't make the perfect move every time.

Yes, in retrospect you could have left it and dealt with it later – kept her behind after lesson to explain why lateness is wrong and giving her a detention for it so that she doesn't lose face in front of her mates. Many kids have no problem being shouted at; they're used to it at home, and you shouting at them holds no fear for them. All it does is put them in 'home' behaviour patterns, where they just shout back, rebel or in this case, withdraw. Shouting at a pupil in front of a class almost always ends in bad blood. We've all done it. If the pupils are even remotely hard, it just winds them up, and gives them an excuse to shout back. Surprise them with calmness and reason. It's what most of them don't get at home.

Good luck with her in the future.

Veni, Vidi, Vicky: when kids are nice by themselves and not when they're together

Dear Tom

I thought I'd crossed the Rubicon with my class; I was wrong. I've had them since I started, and individually they're fine, but en masse they are murder. Simple problem is this: they keep talking and I can't teach. Seriously, almost every single one of them will talk at one time. The sheer numbers of the equation defeats me; I can't get all the names, and when I put one fire out, another one jumps up. I've tried fresh starts, seating plans, rewards and so on, but it still comes back to me simply writing the work on the board for the nicer ones because I can't be heard above the chatter.

It's strange how universal this behaviour is with some classes. It's clearly something hard-wired into the teenage mentality, a sort of pack instinct.

What I think is happening here is that the class know you well, and know exactly where your boundaries are. And in classic teenage style, they're rushing right up to them and poking you. I suggest reestablishing where the boundaries are; it also sounds like they are taking advantage of your good nature, which is one of the most frustrating things a class can do to a teacher. When we present them with positivity and generosity of spirit, it's heartbreaking to see that treated lightly and meanly. Here are my suggestions.

Stop smiling. Seriously. They need to learn that you're all about business. In the animal kingdom, particularly among primates, a smile is a 'fear' reaction, designed to placate more aggressive animals. So automatically it signals to them that you want them to be nice. Smiling at people of equal status is a different matter but they aren't equal to you. So look stern, but not angry. Try to look dignified, unconcerned, and calm.

Take a lesson to reiterate your classroom rules, focusing on the 'don't bloody dare speak over me,' ones. Give them copies to stick in their books. This can take all lesson if needs be. I talk *at* them for about 45 minutes, just to watch them get crushed with boredom.

Don't get involved in *any* discussions about 'Why me?' or 'It's not fair!' or any of that rubbish. These are diversionary tactics that they have learned work with you. The classroom isn't the venue for discussions about behaviour. That should be done after lessons, always. Just be calm, take names and then *always* follow up. Issue detentions, keep your paperwork tight, and if anyone doesn't attend then *always* escalate, with the assistance of a more senior teacher. Half an hour becomes an hour. An hour becomes exclusion, whatever the procedure is in your class. They have learned that they can argue with you. Don't argue with them any more. Just tell them what's forbidden behaviour, note it when it happens, and then punish them for it. They don't need substantial warnings, perhaps once or twice, said calmly. Children are far more impressed by what you do than what you say.

You can have *any* behaviour in your lesson that you desire; the question is if the teacher really wants it or not. If you want them to work in complete silence, then draw the line in the sand that says, 'Anyone who talks gets a detention', and then stick to it. That means being tough with yourself, not just them. If they see you back pedalling, or if they see you waver or hesitate, then you're back to square one. But if they see that they will *never* get away with it, then they'll adjust their behaviour in almost every case. Push for exclusions if need be, but get the paperwork done so that you can press the case.

At first they'll think you're having a laugh: you've allowed them to do X for a while, so why would they expect any different? Show them they're wrong.

Et tu, Brian? One child wants to ruin our drama day

Dear Tom

We've been working hard for months on an RSC visit to our little village school which takes place next week. The children have been so excited abut this happening, but now one boy (a notorious bully) doesn't want to get involved anymore, so he's planned his birthday party for the same day. Now he's intimidating as many people as possible to come to his event and not the RSC event.

His parents totally support him in everything (probably why he's such a big bully), and know that there's a clash, but they don't care.

Your frustration is understandable. But any attempt on your part to thwart this boy's birthday party would be meddling with factors over which you have no authority, which will make you unpopular. It would also be unprofessional.

Your best weapon is to work with the things you can control, namely, the event itself. Talk it up in lessons, even more than before. Enlist other teachers to mention it, and how fantastic it's going to be. Perhaps you could sweeten the pot and guarantee attendees some kind of wonderful treat on the day itself. Talk it up until you're hoarse, and make everyone see how unmissable it will be.

How do you know that he's bullying people into attending? It sounds as if someone has told you, which in itself constitutes evidence (this isn't CSI after all – we don't need to convince a jury) which could then be used to support disciplinary action against this boy, or at least support a stern talking-to.

Have you tried talking to the boy himself? Tell him you'd love it if he could be there, and that it would be a shame if some of his peers couldn't make it because of the clash, so why not shift the party date/time instead? You never know, he could be won over if he's spoken to like a potential ally rather than a nemesis.

Do you think he's engineering this deliberately? If so, why do you think he has a bee in his bonnet about it? If you get to the root of that mystery, you might be able to negotiate a solution to his antagonism.

Finally, if all else fails, just forget about it. After all, how many friends (bullied or otherwise) could he have? Surely he won't be so magnetic that he attracts the entire cohort of your school. Or perhaps he is, in which case maybe the RSC would be interested in taking him on as an understudy.

The show will go on. Somehow.

There's going to be a murder: are role-plays a good tool for naughty kids?

Dear Tom

I need help getting a rough class in a rough school in a rough area of Glasgow to focus; to get their attention when I want to change tasks, or just to talk to them in general. I'm a supply teacher. I can usually hold their focus for a few minutes, and then a few drift off, then more, then more. Whole class discussions start easily – but not ones started by me!

I'm thinking of doing some circle time activities to help them bond as a group and with me. Besides, it might help for me to talk about some social and moral topics with them, maybe include a few role-plays too. Another thing I wanted to try was 'hot seating' students, and getting them to play at being teacher, trying to control the noisy class.

Danger, Family Robinson! I wouldn't advise the role-play activity you suggest; such strategies can be useful, but only when the majority of the class are on task and on side. If you introduce it to a difficult class, they will turn it into a wrestling match, defeating the object of the exercise. I think that activities that rely on the children empathising with others (including you) are best used when the children have some empathy with you already, and you're building on that. Right now I think this might just be giving them another stick to beat you with.

At this point in your relationship they need consistency and firmness from you, not understanding. I suggest some back-to-basic behaviour management.

Of course, fun, interesting lessons will help; but initially, it's not the content that dictates the behaviour, but the format of the lesson. If they have short attention spans, create lots of short activities that engage their tiny concentrations and work with their mental patterns. Keep the pace up.

It will take them some time to get used to your rules, but once they see that you have teeth then they'll fall into line.

Problems with the naughty list

Dear Tom

My last school was well behaved, and this one isn't, frankly. I use Names On The Board to keep a list of warnings and detentions, but it's really getting me down how difficult it is. Problem is that so many of the pupils get their names up that it takes up a lot of time. Also when I turn around to do it, somebody throws a pen, or shouts out, etc. because they know I can't see them.

And when I do put the name up, half the time I get into a big argument about why their name is there in the first place. It's exhausting, and my classes are so noisy too that even with this strategy I can barely get half the lesson taught.

Names On The Board only really works in a class where decent behaviour is the over riding norm. It takes too much of your time otherwise and as you've indicated, it causes situations where they can moan en masse about the severity of your discipline. By all means take names if you want, but in your planner or notepad, so you don't have to turn away from the class. I tend not to do this with challenging classes, instead just making a list of the ones who misbehaved and keeping them at the end/telling them to see me later. Once they're there, then I tell them how long they've got, and why. They don't have the right to know during the class – my time – and besides, 99 percent of the time they know fine! If they want to argue/discuss it, they can do so in their time, not when I'm supposed to be teaching.

If you find it difficult to take so many names, try dismissing only the kids who behaved immaculately instead. That will leave you with the rump; you can tell them that they are there for general chatting during lessons, and dismiss them in reverse order of obedience. Any acting up in detention is legitimate cause for escalation. That'll learn 'em.

In general there will be a core gang of trouble makers in every class, the ringleaders. One approach is to target them first of all, even if it means ignoring low level disruption from lesser fry that makes you grind your teeth. In that case, you would only nail the ones who *really* break the rules, but you go in *hard* – long detentions, phone calls home *the same day* (best before they get home – devastatingly effective) and press for exclusions in the case of recidivists. And make sure you nail every single one of them hard – never slacken off, keep up the pressure. Then you move down to the medium offenders, and finally the misdemeanours.

Persevere with your great intent, just don't be afraid to change your technique. Whatever tool tightens the nut is the right one.

Wait for it: how long *should* I wait for silence?

Dear Tom

I was reading in a behaviour management book that if the class was talking, I should stop the lesson and wait for silence, no matter how long it took. With my Year 9s yesterday I realised that I would be there until I grew a beard. How long should I wait?

The 'wait for complete silence' trick is far from foolproof (as you have seen). Some classes, particularly the more spiteful ones, will see this as a stick to beat you with: 'If she's not going to start until we stop, then let's keep going and she'll have to be quiet all day!'. To avoid this, I definitely suggest using your *impressive teacher voice* a little and repeating your instructions in a slightly different tone, and try to personalize it as much as possible by addressing pupils by name: they find it much harder to ignore a direct address.

Waiting in silence until they stop is something that requires a little innate respect from the pupils or a certain level of relationship between teacher and class. In tougher, inner city comps, for example, it just becomes a game for the class to bait you with, so get the other tools out of your strategy kit. Complex classes need hard work, lots of grit, determination and tough skin.

The Coursework Whisperer: getting it in at short notice

Dear Tom

Just moved to a new school and I have to get coursework from over 100 students in the next few months. They have done no coursework so far, and refuse to do any. I feel like flying a white flag right now.

Are all 100 refusing to produce any coursework? That's amazing. If so, then set them an essay, or project, in lesson time itself, and then submit *that* as course work. Sneaky. If it is a few, and only a few, then you may be looking at giving up some of your after-school time to round them up and make them stay in order to do it, possibly over a series of sessions. You can start off with the carrot approach, and explain to them that the coursework is a compulsory component, and that with it they can improve their grades. But start to use the stick too, and make the sessions compulsory, punishable by further detentions etc.

Have you any support in this matter? It sounds like you are a new HOD, in which case your line manager needs to be part of this process, even at the communication stages (to parents, pupils, etc), as this is a big ask for a new member of staff. If you are not HOD, then the HOD needs to be intimately associated with the solution to this.

Tie me to the mast: the same kids get detention all the time

Dear Tom

This is my fourth school in six years. I really enjoy teaching, and most of the kids are great, but I'm starting to get tired of asking the same people to come back after school. I know the school policies, and I follow them, but it's just beginning to get to me, how long it takes to build up good behaviour in your classes.

How do I stay focused and do what I need to do, when I feel that I could so easily fall off the wagon and take it easy?

Four schools in six years. Tenacious. If you've changed schools before then you know the stark truth: it takes time for them to warm to you, and for your behaviour policies to start sticking. There will always be this initial period of disheartening levels of poor behaviour, and there is nothing you can do to make it go quickly. Not even Valium. I suspect that you already know that eventually, in almost all situations, your endurance will be rewarded with better discipline, so keep at it. I can offer these ideas for staying focused:

Keep your eyes on the prize. Nothing worthwhile was ever easy, especially with manic kids, but the effort you invest with your behaviour management now will pay dividends. Gradually they will come round to seeing your way of thinking, and that, as you know, is one of the chief satisfactions of teaching – watching them flourish around your style of teaching.

Remember you are playing a long game – the behaviour tends to improve incrementally, like acid erosion. We wear them down until they comply. It's rare to see a miraculous improvement that is visible in a week, so remember that when you think they're not coming round. They probably are, it's just hard to get a perspective on matters because you're so close to it. Think about how they were when you first met them, and take a mental picture of it. Compare that to now. I bet there's been an improvement.

It's your job and your duty. This sounds hard, but I mean it kindly. Every job has its downside, and for us, this is it. Whenever I think that my job's hard, I think of coalminers or people cleaning toilets and I think, 'I can put up with this.' In some ways the depth of the downside magnifies the height of the reward. Be proud of all the effort you put in, because you deserve it.

Remember the negative side of the equation – what will happen if you *don't* keep on at them? The consequences of woolly behaviour management are long term problems that never get resolved and a world of pain for you and them. Plus they won't learn as well. So aim for what you want and be aware that the alternative sucks.

Remember the good kids. It seems that we are biologically primed to remember, or look out for, bad things: it's a survival mechanism courtesy of our ancestors. But it means we dwell too much on the negative. I bet that, in your classes, the majority of the pupils are on task for the majority of the time. That sounds like success to me. It's only a handful that needs your special attention, so remember all the good things that are happening.

Make a list of all the good kids for a change. I bet it's longer than your naughty list. I also suggest sending home some positive comment slips (or whatever system you have) for every negative referral you make or detention you give out. *Make* yourself get a balance. Don't make paperwork all about the bad side of teaching. Why not just send a letter or a postcard home to the good kids, thanking and praising them to their parents? I find the free postcards in cinemas are great for this.

Don't give up! You are a trained professional and an adult. They are children, misguided and often very lost, but still kids. *You* aren't trapped in a room with *them*. *They* are trapped in the room with *you*. *They* should be mindful of *you*, and suffer the consequences when they fall out of step.

Remember your work/life balance. Don't take your problems home with you. They're not sitting at home worrying about your feelings, or how you're taking everything, so don't do the same. Go for a pint. Watch Ugly Betty. Get it out of your system. We work in a job that can suck us dry, emotionally, so cut off the supply when you leave the school and recharge your batteries. We work to live, not the reverse.

My Spitting Image is too close to the bone: one of the kids is mocking me

Dear Tom

I've just marked a set of creative essays; one of them has a nasty caricature of me written in it, disguised just thinly enough that it doesn't directly point the finger at me. But it's fooling no one. Actually it's upset me a bit, so what should I do?

Treat this seriously. Although it's true that you don't want to give him the satisfaction of seeing that it's upset you, it also needs to be dealt with. So show him that it hasn't upset you, just disappointed you. This is the kind of situation where the best punishment for the child is to arrange a meeting with parents present. It is usually painfully uncomfortable for a pupil to have their nasty comments read out publicly in front of authority figures. And even if you feel a little uncomfortable yourself about the comments made (especially if they're personal or something that touches a nerve), don't show it. Just keep up the 'disappointed' tone and awaken any latent qualities of shame that they possess.

Sometimes you have to dig deep, but every human being has the capacity to feel ashamed, as long as it is clear that their community disapproves of their actions. So make a community of supportive adults in a quiet space, and make the pupil associate disgrace with their nastiness.

The devolution of the species: my class has gone backwards

Dear Tom

I've come back after Christmas and my KS2 primary class have gone backwards somehow. It's top heavy with boys, and although we'd started making some good progress before we broke up, I feel as if they have no recollection of who I am. I've tried House Points and rewards; I am loth to shout at them, and anyway I'm no good at it. I am so friendly and nice to them I can't understand why they'd be so ungrateful.

The one thing you haven't mentioned is sanctions, and although it makes us uncomfortable to confront it, it seems to be a part of human psychology that we fear the rod far more than we crave the carrot. If pupils misbehave it is because they know that they can get away with it. If you are very friendly and nice to them, they will exploit it in the way that only small children can. They haven't yet learned the habits of gratitude and generosity of spirit as well as most adults have. Right now they are at quite a selfish stage in their development, and although many of them will be capable of largesse and self-restraint, many will not. So you have to put up mental fences in their heads, rules that they can't break. You have probably already told them the rules. Next you need to make the fences electric – make it hurt for them not to obey (not physically, obviously). Just make the pain of the punishment greater than the pleasure of the misbehaviour.

This means detentions, withdrawal of privileges, severity and consistency. Make them see that bad behaviour *always* means a punishment, and make the punishment mean something. And when you have them alone in detention, take the time to explain to them exactly why they are in detention, and what they can do to avoid it next time. Let them see that they get themselves in trouble, nobody else.

It's going to take a lot of effort on your part, but I practically guarantee it's the best investment you ever make. It will be hard for a while, but afterwards you reap the dividends of your effort, and life gets easier, and the pupils will enjoy the calm environment you provide. Most of us don't like to get tough with kids (good thing too) but we as teachers need to. The kids need it. Your marbles need it.

Rocking a tiny boat: disruption in very small classes

Dear Tom

I teach a class of nine Year 8s. Two of the boys are really big trouble together so I seat them apart, but in such a small class it doesn't make much difference.

One's slightly better, but they're both rather foul – they make dirty jokes, swear, and speak to classmates like they're dirt. One of them got a bit better when he was summoned for a chat with the Head (we'd all discussed it was necessary), but the improvement lasted about a heartbeat. He still looks at me as though I have no right even to speak to him; he's so arrogant, and still a child.

I think he's quite bright, and I do provide G&T work, but they have to finish the normal work first, which he never does.

For God sake, get the detentions out! And when they do them, make them do work; catching up with work unfinished is a tried and tested favourite (of mine, not theirs). There is no reason on earth not to do detentions, because without sanctions, pupils will treat you as if you are weak or careless – it is as brutal as that. You need to get tough with them to show them that you care about their education, so I would keep the sweets in your bag until you've shown them some teeth. Apply sanctions consistently and never give up! If they don't show up, pursue it and escalate. The greatest weapon we have in our artillery is resilience – we will wear them down before they wear us out. It's not a sexy solution, but it's absolutely the way forward.

One thing that sticks out here is the pupil's ability; if he is more able or gifted in any way (or underachieving G&T possibly – their test scores might be average but check out their SATs or CATs) then simply adding extension work on to regular work won't do. This is because able pupils often look contemptuously at work they consider easy. So you need to get creative about how you set work. Make it more challenging from the beginning of the lesson; don't make him plough through simple (to him) work until he gets to the good stuff. Many G&T pupils simply see this as a punishment for finishing quickly. Speak to your G&T adviser if you have one. Give him tasks that cover the lesson content, but in a unique and challenging way that makes him feel that he is being tested. I have found many aggressive, difficult pupils can be turned around because they are secretly very bright indeed, and once you treat them as if they are, they flourish. Couldn't hurt.

Top-set chatter: the clever kids want to talk about what they want to talk about

Dear Tom

This might not seem much like a problem, but it is for me. I have a top-set Year nine class who really struggle not to talk over each other all the time. The positive thing is that they talk about the work, but they can't seem to get into a pattern of letting each other speak. I've tried to go with the flow and let them speak in this way, but they still haven't learned how not to let it get personal, and arguments break out all the time.

If you feel that their discussion is of good quality then have clear times when they are allowed to sit and discuss, sharing opinions, and then mark the points clearly when they are not allowed to talk over one another. Use a bell, a whistle, a raised hand, a visual cue, whatever, to indicate the demarcation.

This could take the form of getting them to prepare a speech, role play, whatever, on a particular topic, and then once they have done this, move into listening time when it is imperative that they have to pay attention to one another. Be ruthless with your sanctions when pupils transgress the rules of both periods, so that you reinforce the importance of good discussion, good listening, and appreciating the difference between the two periods. It also teaches them respect and good discipline, as well as allowing them to express themselves in a safe environment.

And even if their conversations are relevant and worthwhile, they are unacceptable if it's not the right time for them; after all, we often have interesting relevant things to say, but aren't allowed to blurt them out whenever we feel like it – funerals, interviews, churches, etc. It's a skill they need to learn too. Get Victorian!

Supply and be damned: getting respect when you're not the regular teacher

Dear Tom

Due to being perpetually skint I have had to accept some supply work in a school that I don't really like. The pupils have next to zilch respect for people like me, and they just see the lesson as a chance to catch up with their texting and heavy petting.

How can I get them to see otherwise? I'd love them just to listen quietly to what they have to do, and then at least make a start with the work, or at least let the ones that want to work, do so. I think that supply teachers are treated appallingly in many schools and I don't just mean by the students either.

I have boundless sympathy for supply teachers; the abuse they sometimes endure staggers me, and the tenacity required to stay sane is humbling. They routinely experience the 'new teacher' syndrome that most of us suffer only a few times in our careers. I do believe there are things that can be done to make the role harder/easier though. Firstly, preparation. Most supplies are smart enough to do as much of this as possible, but you can see the ones who don't, and it shows in the reaction they get from the kids. Get to school early. Get a map of the school, and for God's sake get to the room before they do. That way you can start to prepare the ground so that the room becomes your space: make sure it's tidy – clear up and straighten chairs if you have to. Wipe the board and put tables in rows. It sounds trivial, but if the room looks chaotic when they come in then they subconsciously find it easier to assume that no one's in charge.

If you can, get the lesson instructions on the board before they get there, so that there's no question of what they have to do, and they can't complain that there's no work. Textbooks on every table – again, before they get there. Have a small pile of spare paper and a handful of pens ready for the whiners who claim that they've lost them (although there is a danger in this too, that they may take advantage of your generosity). Basically do everything you can before they descend on you so that you can ...

Be on the door when they arrive. This is important. Stand firm; don't move or shuffle about, cross your arms and look mean but not angry. Look vaguely annoyed, if you can imagine it, as if you've just noticed it's raining outside. When they turn up to your class, be polite, say good morning and deliberately eyeball everyone that comes in, saying 'Good morning' to them. Don't let them enter until you feel they are ready. This is the time to say, "Jackets off/sit down/the work's on the board," to them. Give them space to get in but stand firm so that they have to walk just a little bit around you. Don't give an inch. Don't even move your feet! This sounds odd, but your standing firm sets a standard: this is *my* room, and you have to accommodate *me* in it. Children size you up in about half a second (this is true – all research points to this snap judgement as being hugely influential on attitudes), so the way they see you at first must be rock hard.

Think yourself into being the boss. This means accepting that you are in charge of the room. You're not 'just a supply teacher' – you're the *teacher*, and that means something. If it means something to you, it will show, and mean something to them. If it doesn't mean something to you, then they will smell it from the end of the corridor and treat you with the contempt that children reserve for adults they can push around.

You really have to believe yourself to be in charge. Imagine someone you know that exudes authority, and constantly say 'I have the same authority' and 'What would they do in this circumstance?' Speak slowly and softly, and carry a big stick, as a bouncer friend of mine once said. Don't rush into rash sanctions, and only raise your voice if you have to, which should be next to never. If you start screaming, go back to square one. One nil to the kids.

Get some ammo. Find out the name of a teacher that they fear – not always the regular teacher! – and get a prior agreement with them that if they mess about you are at liberty to take names so that someone can kick their backsides later on. Sometimes these names can act as a talisman to naughty kids. And always follow up. Chase teachers if you have to, but show the kids you mean business. Summon SLT by all means – just get a good kid to get them. You deserve the full support of the management team, just like any other teacher.

The family that fights together, … when bad behaviour is tolerated by the parents

Dear Tom

I teach a pair of Y8 twins who get into fights like I get into the shower. They will fight with anyone, and it doesn't help that they're really tall for their age, and frequently find themselves in scraps with Y10 and Y11 boys. Their older brother (who's just left school) was the same, and had a real reputation as a scrapper. How can I stop these boys turning out like him?

This is an octopoid challenge; family reputations are hard to shake, particularly in a community where they precede you. The perceptions that others have of these pupils will be extremely resistant to any intervention you can make. The boys themselves may not be entirely angelic in their way of dealing with the situations; perhaps even they have something of the fighter in them and it's their own reputations that are at stake, not their brother's. And of course, once aggression is out in the open, violence begets violence, and revenge is often sought in a spiral of tit-for-tat fighting. The attitude at home might be an obstacle or a boon.

The things that we as teachers can tackle are usually external: keeping the boys apart from aggressors through careful playground monitoring; harsh punishments for any aggression observed so that aggression becomes too unpleasant. Sometimes sitting all the parties together in a safe room can help resolve differences, although I suspect they are based more on dominance and 'face' than anything rational. Anger management can have some effect, as might moving forms so they avoid patterns of encounter.

Finally, if there is an adult they respect, ask them to mentor the boys and keep, keep, keep reinforcing the message that they are better than what they are doing. Young men often turn to violence to feed their self-esteem, so if they can find it in other areas then they may be less willing to get their fists out. Find out what they are good at and try to focus your time and praise into developing them in these areas. If they can find face in something less violent, you may be able to convince them that fighting isn't worth it.

No prize for being first: pupils who can't bear failure

Dear Tom

I have a lovely, very bright girl in my Y9 class. She works hard and gets great grades, but whenever she makes a mistake, she really takes it to heart. She holds it in, but I can see it's upset her. How do I get her to relax about not being perfect?

More able students often present a whole raft of unusual challenges to any teacher that wants the best for them. I find that many gifted students base a huge amount of their self-esteem on their academic competence. Some of them feel that the only reason they are worth something is because they get all the questions right; at least then they have a tangible yardstick by which they can judge themselves, something numeric and solid that says, 'I am worth a lot'.

This often masks a host of anxieties they have about themselves, and to me indicates that the girl suffers from low self-esteem (which doesn't always manifest itself as shyness or any typical sign of low confidence) and has a poor or uncertain perspective towards herself.

One way to help her might be to make sure that she feels valued and rewarded for herself, and not just for the work she produces. This could simply be praise for other areas of her life, something pastoral, or even just for being kind, thoughtful or punctual. Best of all it could be a simple affirmation of care towards her that even teachers can provide, e.g. 'I will always try to help you in what you want to do, ' or 'I always care about how you are feeling and I want the best for you,'; that sort of thing.

And of course she needs to receive this at home too, where unconditional love at some level is always essential. I have seen very bright students from large families suffer from this condition, or where Mum and Dad have split up and the child feels a lack of love, real or imagined.

Finally, and as an addition to this approach, she needs to shake the idea that perfection is the only goal. Do this by teaching her that perfection isn't really possible in the world (not in a meaningful, permanent way) and that there are *levels* of success that are all important.

Ransom demands: a sudden influx of new pupils in my class

Dear Tom

My reception class has just taken in another ten students, five of whom
are incredibly needy, with everything that entails – whiny, desperate, loud,
arrogant and demanding of my time. If I give them what they want then I
literally have no time for the rest of the class. Where do I find a balance?

Right here, Boss. Aargh, needy children! Demanding people (and
small ones) need to be trained by the people around them. They
have become demanding because they've learned that as a strategy it
works great for attracting attention, as it's so difficult to ignore them.
In a way though, this is exactly what we need to do with them, at
least as much as possible. Of course this won't always be practical
as their misbehaviour needs to be tackled, so the best thing to do is
to move them to the part of your room/school where it's quiet and
there's no audience. Without the attention they are craving they will
soon be hungry to return; when you readmit them, make sure your
integration discussion involves a warning along the lines of, 'Any
more monkey tricks and you're back in quarantine,' sort of thing.

Then, once they're back, give them praise and attention whenever
they do something good; even say publicly, 'Well done Bill, you're
behaving really well.' Repeat this throughout the day, and if (when?)
the attention-seeking behaviour re-emerges then remove the pupil
quickly and quietly with as little fuss as possible. They will learn that
bad behaviour results in loss of attention, and good behaviour gains
it, although it may take a few days or even weeks.

5 | School issues

There's a lot more to teaching than turning up, looking glamorous and being showered in glory (if you substitute the word 'teaching' with 'accepting an Oscar'). Managing behaviour involves a lot more than just terrorizing your charges with incident slips and detaining them; eventually every teacher starts to come across the theme of pupil control in other areas of his or her life or job. Should I tell kids off on buses/in supermarkets/other countries? What should I say at an interview about behaviour? What's a good policy for a school to have on exclusions? How should a school deal with swearing? When should a pupil be referred to a department head, and when should they be marched to the head's office?

Of course, this is when behaviour management enters the theoretical realm. As I said in the introduction to this book, I view fashionable theories about human behaviour (and the policies derived thereof) with a scorn I normally reserve for astrology. Too many children have been sacrificed on the altar of educational experimentation for me to have patience with Utopian fixes and Magic Bullet remedies to improve behaviour and learning (*Brain Gym*? I'm talking to you. Yes, *you*. And *Personalised Learning*, don't think I can't see you). But every action is preceded by a thought, and I have tried to present the practice of teaching as springing from a set of simple and clear axioms that can be used to generate a complex range of responses.

For example: I proceed on the assumption that our role is to help them develop from children into adults. Taking this as a given, I find it much easier to know how to behave around my students, because I am guided by the aim of improving their thinking and behaviour; so on a school trip I don't get drunk, in the playground I don't light a roll-up, and in the classroom I treat them politely and firmly. Another premise I have is that I have a responsibility to them that is more sacred than what they think of me, so I really don't are if they like me or not, as long as they are doing well (besides which they probably will like you a bit if they respect you for your role). So simple rules can guide and govern complex situations.

If you are clear about why you are teaching, and the attitudes that you have towards yourself, the students, the school and the profession, then you'll find it a lot easier to answer more general questions you might have about behaviour in school. I believe it's what they refer to as being a 'reflective practitioner', but I prefer to call it 'being a professional'. We've been trying to professionalize teaching for decades now; well, if we want it to be on any kind of footing with the other professions, then we'll have to go a long way to understand what our teaching is about.

So ask yourself, *Why am I a teacher?* I'm hoping that the answer isn't *Because I couldn't think of anything else to do*. You face a long struggle (although it isn't hopeless at all). Establish what it is you think education is for, and what the purpose of the school system is. Is it to produce a workforce (cynical, but partially realistic)? Is it to create rounded human beings who explore their souls and consciousness (beautiful, but who's going to clean the toilets?)? Of course, I'm being deliberately provocative. But establish your viewpoint you must, because without some kind of understanding of why you do what you, it will be difficult for you to have a strong idea of what to do when you need to do it. You won't be flexible enough to deal with situations that arise. Even if you teach because that's just what you do, you do it for a reason. Find out what those reasons are. Then ask yourself, do I still agree with those reasons? You might even find that you've changed your mind. It might even make you change how you teach. You'll certainly feel a lot more passionate about teaching, and probably enjoy what you do even more.

Yes, even more than you do right now. Can you believe it?

Does permanent exclusion actually work?

Evening Tom

My school is designated 'challenging', and I've just been appointed as the member of staff in charge of behaviour. This school hasn't permanently excluded a pupil in four years, and I've been asked to write a report on the effectiveness of permanent exclusions as a method of controlling behaviour in school.

What's your view? Is it used too much or too often? Does permanently excluding a pupil actually work?

Works for me!

OK, proper answer. Permanent Exclusions (PEs) are an essential part of the school's disciplinary toolkit. Imagine a society that had laws, police, judges, lawyers and courts ... but no prisons, no ultimate sanctions. People would understandably treat every other part of the legal process as ridiculous if there were no punitive measures available to back them up.

PEs are the big guns of behaviour management, the last resort for many. But they are necessary for the well being of the school. If a pupil persistently disrupts lessons, ruins the education of others, harms, threatens or endangers the physical and mental safety of pupils or staff, then unfortunately their rights have to take a back seat to the rights of the majority, in a victory for utilitarianism. Everyone else in the classroom has rights too – the right to a safe education, and the right to a safe workplace.

Some pupils – the minority, I'm sure, but a significant minority – have needs that cannot be met in the conventional classroom. They need one-to-one learning environments, whether because of social, emotional or behavioural difficulties. Our education system lets them down by enforcing universal inclusion at all costs, but in the meantime we have to play with the cards we are dealt. We can only do so much with some pupils, and their problems are often beyond the limited power of the classroom teacher to address. So in some circumstances, sadly, exclusions are by far the best thing to do.

Incidentally, it drives me potty that schools and heads are applauded for low exclusion rates; it encourages school leaders to shy away from the ultimate sanction and push the problems back into the classroom. You can't expect the majority of teachers to have the skills/patience and time to deal with the minority of real troublemakers. SEBD teaching is a profession requiring specialist skills, and until every teacher possesses these kills, PEs will be necessary.

Where does duty lie? Can I act like a teacher when we're not in school?

Dear Tom

Recently I was on a bus and there were some schoolkids (not from my school) standing on seats, shouting, and intimidating passengers. Should I have intervened, or did I do the right thing by keeping my head down? It made my blood boil that no one was doing anything to chastise these animals.

As this isn't a school issue as such, I can't really offer any teacherly advice, but I can attempt to answer this from a *citizen's* point of view.

I repeat: this is *not* a school issue, therefore we can't expect to enjoy the benefit of professional authority, or pupil deference. I sympathize with this situation – this is something that we all face from time to time, teachers or not, and it's hard to know what to do. In fact, this is real behaviour management 'in the raw' – how do we influence the behaviour of others to coincide with the wishes of society?

First of all, they may be amenable to a polite request – after all, remember how you or I were, when we were fourteen? Much as I hate to admit it, maybe there were times when we were a bit noisy or inconsiderate. Many young people genuinely can't understand why most people over 25 prefer a bit of peace and quiet to constant noise.

Even if they're not, every citizen has the right to say something, or to make such a request. The best way to do this is to speak in a flat, neutral way, in an even register and a deep tone. Don't in any way betray fear or anger – both will mark you as an aggressor or a weakling. Make it sound as natural as possible, and say something non-accusatory like, 'Excuse me guys, that's a bit loud. Any chance you could turn it down a bit?'

If they're jumping around, or being in any way deliberately intimidating to passengers, then it's obviously not just high jinks and larks. In that situation I always speak to the driver and complain that there are some passengers making trouble. Often they will stop the bus and make an announcement that they won't carry on until things calm down.

Young kids in groups are massively concerned with face, and prestige, so try at all costs to avoid embarrassing one of them in front of their friends. Give them a chance to withdraw without losing honour. That's why it's important not to show anger or fear. But if it does get to that situation, then enlist other passengers, speaking directly to them if necessary. We are terrible at standing up for ourselves.

I have to confess that I am a serial busybody in these situations. I always speak to kids (or adults) who are drunk, rude, noisy etc and ask them to cut it out. Then, if they start to get dangerously aggressive, I withdraw, move away, whatever. It's not worth a smack in the kisser just because life is noisy. But at least I feel that I have stood up for myself and said what I thought was right, even in a small way. I am neither big nor hard (quite the contrary – I look, and am, soft as a toffee in Simon Cowell's pocket), but I have never been assaulted for doing this, and in many cases I have persuaded kids to cool it; on several occasions other passengers have joined in.

Just remember that we have the right to safe passage and a quiet life; and we all have duties to each other. Stand up for yourself and see what happens.

Who can tell me what the capital of f*****g Chile is? Can kids swear in lessons?

Dear Tom

Recently I read in the Daily Mail that a teacher at a church school had been fired for encouraging her students to write down all the swear words they knew as part of a lesson on cooperation. Is this the kind of behaviour you would encourage in school pupils, and do you think it was right she got the sack?

I researched this article and I couldn't find any reference to the named teacher being dismissed in this or any other version of the story – merely 'disciplined', which of course could mean anything from solitary confinement to a 'tut tut'.

I think that a) her union and b) an industrial tribunal would eat up any dismissal for breakfast as I can't see how it breaches her contract, unless it is the last misdemeanour of a thousand warnings.

Amazingly enough this story got carried over the wires to news agencies in New York, Singapore, Sydney etc. How utterly bizarre that a lesson which I imagine many teachers have at least skirted round, if not carried out in practice, should become so controversial. Classrooms are supposed to be safe environments where pupils can discuss ideas in a calm and rational manner. Analysing and critiquing aspects of language is a legitimate area of learning and discussion, even offensive words.

To be fair, this is a really tricky lesson to make work – it can quickly degenerate into a competition, where pupils (usually boys, depressingly enough) try to say the most outrageous thing they can, and in effect the classroom is in danger of becoming another playground, where some pupils are swearing in order to offend or upset other pupils. In this situation, some pupils will withdraw from the class completely, at least mentally.

We need to remember that although of course every child knows and hears most of these words (didn't we all?) there are many kids for whom hearing them is still offensive and/or upsetting. It's hard for us to imagine that as adults, when we've heard (and used) them all so many times, but for many pupils (and other people) these words have a potency. Of course they do – that's what some of them are designed to do! There will also be many terms, particularly neologisms and portmanteaus referring to niche sexual acts that many or most of the pupils will not have heard before, so there will be an element of bragging among (yes, you guessed) – the boys about who knows the muckiest sex act.

In essence, I think that this lesson can work really well in a room where the teacher has a good relationship with the class, and exerts good control in order to prevent it becoming a classroom of profane malice. Personally I would only do it with older classes, as I would worry that not enough primary pupils would really get the aim of the lesson, but I'm sure that some groups could cope with it.

Poor teacher, though. Bet she never thought that her lesson plan would get her in the *New York Times*. I imagine she'll think twice before planning any more lessons on, for instance, rolling her own smokes, or burning the Union Jack.

Managing behaviour on the biscuit aisle: should uniform codes apply as far as the supermarket?

Dear Tom

My school has an (extremely) strict view that the students should wear their uniforms properly, even when not in school itself, as they represent the secondary school wherever they go. When I go into the supermarket in town, I often see a few of them, obviously not having ties done up properly, shirts out, skirts rolled up, etc. Also, I sometimes see them in the shops making a nuisance of themselves, being rude to assistants and shopkeepers. I feel that I should say something, but I don't want to look like a nag or an idiot.

I wouldn't make a big deal about it at the time, although you might want to have a gentle word with them as a warning. Gentle, though – outside school they will feel a lot braver about answering you back, and you're not *in loco parentis* in the real world.

What you can do that is more foolproof is to make an issue of it *in* school. Give them a detention after lessons for misbehaviour outside school. But you need to make it watertight. First of all make sure that you have the tacit support of SLT, in order that they will back you if parents complain/kids refuse to cooperate. And really it shouldn't be you, but an SLT that conducts the detention, unless that be ye.

Secondly, it really has to be for something serious, like swearing at people or severe public disturbance; there will be few written school policies governing acceptable behaviour in supermarkets! There will probably be something in a policy about not bringing the good name of the school into disrepute, so check that this exists.

Or you could speak to local shopkeepers/supermarket bosses etc., and ask them if there is a problem, and that the school would like to support the community in some way. Offer to look at CCTV footage and see if you can identify culprits. Then, most satisfyingly of all, grass them up to the law. It will feel like Christmas if you get a result.

But to reiterate, this all really needs to be passed on to a senior school leader. And if they don't support and follow up, then I advise you to do likewise. Of course, you can still tackle them as a citizen – just don't expect the magic of your position to work miracles!

What happens when the dust settles? Worried about the result of a bullying incident.

Dear Tom

There's a nice boy in my Year 11 class who recently apparently beat up another boy in school because he was a notorious bully. He's been temporarily excluded, which made him miss an important GCSE oral exam. Now the other boy's parents want to take it to the police. What will happen to him next? I'm worried about him.

Very difficult to say without further information. I can only speculate. Without significant previous form, most students progress to an exclusion for fighting in school. However if the fight involved a weapon, or resulted in significant damage/injury, he could be looking at a permanent exclusion.

Schools are very reluctant to press charges. Parents are very happy to talk about it. It could be hot air. But even bullies deserve due process, despite the temptation to celebrate when one gets a smack in the kisser. This isn't *Grange Hill*. Most kids don't realise that assault is assault, and that if the parents get the police involved, what seemed like a classroom ruck will be treated as GBH by the magistrates.

If it's his word versus the alleged bully, he's normally safe from prosecution. But if anyone gives witness evidence (and the police are a lot better at getting it than the Head of Biology) then it's anyone's move.

Hot for teacher: the pupils all fancy me

Dear Tom

I'm 28, a woman, and in every post I've had, I've had a group of young lads who obviously have a little 'thing' for Miss. I've never been sure how to deal with it, but I hope I've got the balance right. Without wishing to sound too vain, I'm quite attractive, or so I've been told, and I like to take care of my appearance. The boys always say things like, 'Have you got a boyfriend, Miss?' and, 'Can I get your number?' That sort of banter.

The problem? I don't always see that sort of a thing as a problem, if I'm honest. I don't see it as weird if a healthy teenage boy tries to sneak a peak at my backside when I'm bending down, or has a quick look down my top. I mean, when I was their age, my girlfriends and I checked out the good-looking male teachers. It's really rare that any boy has taken it too far and touched me inappropriately. Even the traditionally 'creepy' boys never do anything you could report. At worst, they just give off a weird vibe, but I'm not concerned by it.

But how are you supposed to deal with pupils that fancy you, especially given the media concern these days, and how sexualized teenagers are. Is it OK when I say something like, "Yeah and I'm old enough to be your mum," or, "You'll never pull with that kind of chat-up line!"

It's not an issue really for me, but I get a bit embarrassed when students make it obvious they like me in front of other teachers – some of them fall over themselves to help me, and some make themselves look like pillocks by trying to impress me. I'd be interested to know where you think I should draw the line, because I often wonder if I'm getting the balance right with the boys.

This is one of those subjects that rarely gets talked about, yet must affect many teachers in a number of ways. I'm sure the majority of us can remember getting a bit peculiar when a good-looking young teacher walked in the room, and for the vast majority of students that will be the extent of their reaction – getting a bit shy, tongue-tied, or for the braver pupils, showing off a bit so that Miss will notice you. I think all of that is both harmless and perfectly natural.

I think where the problems start is when covert attraction starts to spill out into overt attraction; pupils explicitly saying that they find you attractive, or making suggestive comments that are more single entendres than double. This spells trouble because it damages and subverts one of the basic necessities of the classroom – the proper relationship between pupil and teacher, which although it can take many forms, from light-hearted to solemn, must always maintain a professional distance between the two parties. We cannot advise, guide and sometimes discipline students if they feel too close to us, and if they feel that we are their pals instead of a paid professional who is there to do an important job, then we are at risk of losing a great deal of ability to run the class as we want it.

Crushes are fine; if students want to carry your books or behave well because they fancy you, then who's to stop them? Sexual comments need to be squashed however. Make no mistake; when a young student makes a sexual comment, there's a lot of bragging rights in it to his mates ('Look what I said to Miss') and it's very creepy – this child is suggesting that there could, or should be a sexual bond between himself and the teacher. It is an attempt to bring you down to his level, so to speak, and reduces you to an object of lust. Obviously, there will be many different ways of handling this, and you can go in hard or attempt to be more conciliatory in your rebuke, but you must stamp on it.

Some teachers, not wanting to damage the relationship they have with the student, don't wish to spoil all that lovely good behaviour that seems to come with the comments, but in actual fact the relationship that shows is one of being submissive to a student, and showing them that they can dominate by using sexuality. If a student realises that sexual language will get a certain reaction that makes him look like a big man, he'll repeat it.

Furthermore, if students learn that it's *ever* acceptable to make sexual comments, then this will only encourage them to do so in other contexts with more vigour. If one female teacher allows it, then the student might replicate the behaviour to another female teacher who is less able to cope with it. There is no doubt that students who end up groping or seriously sexually threatening staff/pupils start off initially by making inappropriate sexual comments, which then lead to further acts of increased unpleasantness once they start to get their courage up.

My advice would be to get serious when they do make comments; it doesn't have to be a screaming match in the corridor, but it does need to be firm. If they say anything, just stare them down and tell them it's not appropriate; if they carry on then discipline them as you would for any bad behaviour – and treat it seriously. Without the lines drawn between teachers and pupils we have no authority. And a teacher being treated like a sexual object is never a laughing matter – even if initially it seems harmless.

Do we need a behaviour policy?

Dear Tom

I've been made chair of a behaviour working party, with a remit to design a clear policy for behaviour for the whole school. What systems do other schools use?

A solid set of behaviour procedures is essential for the running of a tight ship at school. In my experience the only places where they are not essential are schools where there is already a culture of good behaviour and/or it's a small school and the majority of teachers are great with behaviour. Additionally the Head and his support team must be visible and most importantly, visibly in control. Pupils respect strength (and they actually want it too), and it's a mistake to imagine that their primary desire from a school staff is understanding and cuddles. They would far rather feel secure that there is order in their school community than chaos.

This sounds contradictory given that many pupils are so wild and undisciplined, but in fact this behaviour is, at least formally, totally predictable behaviour from young people growing up and defining who they are, usually by first of all rejecting authority. Of course, there are far too many students who take this rejection too far; the reasons for this are beyond the classroom, and are out of our remit to address directly.

Therefore in the vast majority of schools a behaviour system is necessary. It provides the students with the knowledge of what will happen to them if they do certain prescribed behaviours, and because it provides a safety net for teachers who are often swamped by minor (and major) disruptions; they can refer to its guidelines and issue consequences to students, safe in the knowledge that they are clear in their use of sanctions.

The best behaviour policies are the simplest ones. There is absolutely no need to go crazy for scores of different types of forbidden/ permitted behaviour, and they should be vague and broad enough that the students can't use them as a stick with which to beat the teacher.

But the only policies that work are the ones that are used by the majority of teachers consistently, and that are consistently backed up by the SLT. The students need to know that there will be outcomes for more persistent behaviour, and that at the end of the path there is some kind of ultimate sanction that can and does happen. If they think that they can beat the teachers by being more stubborn than we are, then they will.

A correspondent added:

I agree in general, but are you sure it should be vague and broad? Surely if it's too vague then nobody knows what they can do and what they can't? Kids need to see solid examples of what they aren't allowed to do.

Perhaps I have myself been too vague so let me clarify. I mean that policies can often become *too* specific, to the point that students then start looking for loopholes to claim a foul when they are chastised.

I'll give you an example: I once saw a school policy that listed in great detail the activities that were forbidden to students in case they hurt themselves or others (fighting with peers; throwing scissors; slamming doors). Unfortunately such lists are never exhaustive, and students started to kick off if they were pulled up for something that wasn't on the list but was clearly in the spirit, if not the letter of the prohibition. They worked on the basis that 'everything not forbidden is permitted'. Far better to make a broader rule which simply prohibits 'dangerous behaviour'; give some examples if you wish, but indicate that they are simply examples.

Also, if you introduce something like a consequence system, as many school successfully do, with escalating indicators of offence (C1, C2, C3 etc) then they need to be aware that in normal circumstances teachers will proceed up the list one step at a time; but that in extreme circumstances they will automatically receive a higher sanction. (This avoids the situation where you immediately proceed to a detention or whatever and the child howls because they haven't received a C1 first. If a child slapped you in the face you wouldn't be worrying about whether it was a C1 or a C2!).

That's all I mean by keeping it vague enough to be helpful. I fully agree that it is behaviour suicide to be wishy-washy about what's allowed and what isn't. We need to be as hard as rocks sometimes; not because it feeds our egos, but because children learn better in an environment where they feel safe, secure and where they know where the boundaries are, and those boundaries mean something. And it also creates a better place for us to work. I think many well-meaning teachers are unsure about asserting what they think is right and wrong in a classroom, and that is precisely one of our duties to the pupils and to our profession.

Job application at an SEBD school

Dear Tom

I'm just about to apply for a job as Deputy Head of a SEBD school. One of the interview questions will be 'How will you improve behaviour?' Any ideas?

Obviously any whole school approach to raising standards in behaviour needs to be structured, consistent, and as simple as possible (but no simpler, as the man said). Some types of things which apply to all schools could be:

A clear behaviour policy for all pupils and staff – what is and isn't acceptable. This should also include behaviours that are encouraged.

Clear sanctions that will be applied whenever this policy is challenged. These should escalate depending on severity or repetition of the incident.

Clear communication of this policy to all parties so that everyone is clear about expectations and consequences.

Dedicated time set aside for staff to make these procedures happen, particularly at a senior level. This means that heads of year, curriculum, SLT, or whoever carries out the phone calls, detentions, meetings etc need to have allocated time in their timetable to enact the procedures.

Internal observations of staff who have good behaviour management, by members of staff who need support. This could be voluntary or timetabled, but it needs to happen. Teaching is an active verb, and no amount of behaviour INSETS can replace watching good behaviour management modelled before your eyes. At best, INSETS can be an opportunity to reflect upon learning, but this doesn't need to be external to the school. I would suggest that after an observation, the observer is required to write their reflections on what they have seen, and think of ways that they will emulate the best practice. Then after a suitable period of putting it into practice, they should have a second debrief with line managers and reflect upon what went well, etc.

Get tough. By that I don't mean boot camp, just say what you mean and then do it. Every time. If students realise that sanctions have teeth, then they will avoid the behaviour that attracts the bite. If they think for one minute that they might get away with it, then they will punish you for your moment of weakness by continued bad behaviour.

Finally, and as a nod to your application, I would suggest having a period of observation yourself in the school, walking around corridors, visiting classes to say 'hI' to teachers, standing in the playground, being invisible for a bit, until you get a feel for the behaviours. You can make this a period of data collection, and back it up by looking through any hard data that the school might already have (records of exclusions, etc. Who is getting in trouble? With what teacher? When? Are there any patterns?)

When will the nightmare end? How long does it take to control a class?

Dear Tom

A general question: how long do you have to be teaching before you lose the fear, and start to feel confident controlling classes? When is the point you stop worrying that SLT will put you through a mincing machine for being rubbish?

Most teachers claim they go over a bit of a threshold with behaviour in their second year; of course this is only to say that they experience a gear change in their confidence in dealing with students rather than a watershed where everything is fine and dandy afterwards. And the third year usually sees a steeper improvement, as lesson planning and subject knowledge stop being quite so insistent on our time.

Most of us, if we're honest, would say that things get incrementally better as time goes on as long as we never stop trying to improve. And some levels of misbehaviour are incredibly hard to get used to dealing with; it is a pertinent question to ask whether it is legitimate for teachers ever to be expected to deal routinely with levels of disorder that, if they were repeated on the street, would result in criminal charges. We are neither social workers nor constables, and are ill-fitted to be either.

The dangers of Nick O'Teen: they're smoking at the gates

Dear Tom

Every day I walk into school and pass pupils smoking away – worse still, some of them are in uniform (they're Year 11s, so legally they can smoke)! Just ignoring them seems like cowardice on my part, but at the same time I feel uncomfortable with telling them off for doing something both outside of school and legal. What should I do?

While in uniform, students represent the school and the school has a legitimate right to govern how they choose to do that. Also, although the school's powers over a pupil outside of school premises starts to become a rather philosophical question, it could be described as inversely proportional to their distance from the school gates. I have no hesitation telling kids to pick up litter they've dropped just outside the school, or asking gangs of pupils to disperse from the street at 4pm, so I would apply that to smoking, particularly immediately outside the school.

As to their legal rights in this matter? In school we establish the precedent of reducing pupils' rights in order to look after and teach them – after all, it is impossible to be responsible *in loco parentis* without having some say in their behaviour, so I would also apply this to kids outside the gates with a Dorchester Black stuffed in their gob. I have, however, been blessed to see a teacher admonish a pupil for smoking, while they themselves had a proud B&H hanging out of their mouth. Balls of steel, certainly.

Is there more to behaviour than a policy? What other principles should we use in school?

Hi Tom,

In an interview I was asked how I would deal with misbehaviour, and I said I would use the behaviour policy of the school. Then they asked what ELSE I would do – I came a cropper on that one! Is there anything else I can do?

There are plenty of ways to manage behaviour that don't fall under the umbrella of a school's behaviour policy, no matter how broad or particular a beast it is. For example: consistency and routine in your relationships with the students at all times; do what you say, and mean it every time; professionalism: be on time; be available when you are supposed to be; be mannerly and gracious.

Get to know the students' backgrounds by talking to them, or consulting pastoral representatives in school. Discuss schoolwork or other issues with them when things are going well, or indifferently, rather than only dealing with them when they are off task/building pipe bombs, etc.

All of these areas are good for discussion re: this topic. The school policy should be the skeleton of your techniques, but your person-ality and professionalism are the flesh. Body language, tone of voice, posture, idiom, charisma, relationships, etc. are all big guns in managing other people. They must be; so much of our (non-school) lives revolve around managing others' reactions and actions, and I see precious few behaviour policies helping us there.

Danger: trip hazard. Worried about safety on a day out

Dear Tom

My SENCO wants one of our Teaching Assistants to take some statemented kids out on external visits to football stadia etc. She is terrified about doing this, as she thinks that some of these kids pose a real threat to their own health and safety. Surely you need at least two adults for this kind of trip? After all, what if the child is rude to her, or a member of the public? Surely she needs witnesses to protect her?

Any school trip should have at least one teacher extra beyond the ratio, as a redundancy measure. What happens if the sole teacher has an accident, or falls ill, or gets forced off the train, etc. (fill in your own unlikely but possible drama)? Yes, it's expensive to run, but if a trip can't be run safely, then it shouldn't go ahead. You're not being paranoid. Given the responsibilities we have in this profession, we must ensure that we are planning for success on trips, not failure. She isn't required to do this trip, by contract or otherwise, so she should simply refuse, and give her reasons for doing so.

Kids today, they don't know they're born: getting kids to realise how lucky they are

Dear Tom

For a while I was fortunate enough to teach maths to pupils in Uganda, and I was amazed by the difference between how much they value their education compared to the kids in my school. They're so poor, and they know that getting ahead at school is one of their only realistic ways out of poverty.

Some of the teachers from the village visited my school and were horrified at the behaviour here and how little we dealt with it (they still have the cane and sackcloth there!). How can we make British students realise how valuable education is?

A salient question. One of the reasons children muck about in schools (one of the many, many, many reasons) is an underlying failure to appreciate the value of what they have. I think we live in one of the most fortunate societies in the world, a country where, compared to our historical context, we have almost banished want for the basics of survival. So much of what we have on tap has become an expectation. Our grandfathers and grandmothers fought and prayed for much of what we call normal: free health care, universal suffrage, a welfare state, education as an entitlement.

But to quote a chap with a beard, 'It is the doom of men that they forget.' In other words, it's almost second nature for us to fail to appreciate the good things that we have until, to quote a lady with less of a beard, 'They're gone.' And if we as adults forget how lucky we are, then children are doubly doomed, having been raised in a world where privation means being denied access to online tournaments of *Zombie Grandmother Liquidiser*. Or something.

The only way to make them appreciate it (apart from hopping into a TARDIS and taking them into 2021 – in Scrooge style – to see their futures after 12 years of larking about) is to remind them by education and by example. Talk to them about other people, who aren't so fortunate. Tell them stories of struggle, and loss, and inspirational men and women who stood up and risked everything they had so that their children would live in a gentler world. Don't let the past be forgotten by them; if we forget the mistakes and triumphs of our forefathers then we'll never learn from them, and our culture stagnates. Unlike science, the social advances of the past can be forgotten in a generation.

Shall we agree to differ? Do behaviour agreements solve behaviour problems?

Dear Tom

I'm just about to go into my GTP year after working in corporate training for years. I can see that behaviour management is important; most guides stress the importance of establishing rules, and agreeing with students from the beginning how the class should be run. This is similar to the business world, where rules of engagement have to be established and agreed with new team members, senior management or people you'll be working with. But most teachers rarely mention behaviour agreement or shared values or referring back to rules made on day one.

Rules, as Thomas Hobbes would say, are the basis of the state. It is impossible to conceive of a community that does not have an agreed set of laws, tacit or explicit. Apart from anarchists, no group has ever attempted to claim that societies should not be based on them to some extent (and no anarchist group can point to an example of such communities either existing, or existing beyond a certain point of implosion). This 'social contract' that permeates our behaviour doesn't have to formal or signed, it just needs to be subscribed to, for the society to exist. In the UK we never formally sign citizenship papers (at least residents don't) but it is assumed that we agree to abide by the rules because we choose to remain. There are holes in this theory you could drive a combine harvester through, but that's pretty much the way it stands.

One of our primary roles as adults is to guide children into adulthood, by setting an example to emulate, and by communicating the values, skills and knowledge necessary for the pupils to flourish. What I don't believe we should be doing is breaking sweat explaining, convincing or discussing the rules we impose with them, and certainly not at the lower end of the Key Stages. When a child is a babe, we don't discuss why they shouldn't touch a hot iron: no, we simply tell them 'you mustn't'. There's no discussion. We might explain why afterwards, but it's because we know better about such things than they, who have never experienced the matter.

As they get older, we introduce them to the complexities of ethics and morality and we can start to discuss why people do such things, and is it ever right to bend the rules etc. But it's wrong to say children should only buy into rules that they agree with, simply because it's not up to them. We live and abide in communities where we have input into the rules by means of elected representatives etc., but we have no right simply to disobey the ones we don't fancy. Or to take it even further, disobey if you like, but don't be surprised if the community bites you on the ass.

Of course, I'm not advocating that we should obey unjust laws, but my point is that as adults we have presumably the intelligence and maturity to question, challenge and interpret the laws as moral entities, as agents of choice. Children are still getting to that stage, and although many of us quail at the prospect of being authoritarian, it's what the students need. They don't need us letting them get away with murder; they want, need (and partially despise) guidelines and rules, if only to know when they can break them. Requiring that they agree to them is an inversion of the natural process of teaching. Of course we can learn from them; of course they can stimulate us.

But I've yet to find an opinion from a Year seven pupil about how I should run my classroom that was an improvement on what I do.

Teachers teach, and students learn. Until that changes, I'll be setting the rules in my room, for the benefit of their futures. With or without their agreement. Make agreements with them by all means – as long as what they agree to agrees with the things you agree with.

Kneel before Zod! Bringing corporal punishment back to the classroom

Hi,

I'm a NQT and I have good behaviour control. Is it actually illegal for me to make a Year 6 kneel down in the corner of my room? I would like to introduce this as a deterrent and punishment with my Year sevens instead of ineffective rounds of detentions. What is the law of this country on this?

Don't get any kids to kneel in the corner. Other things to avoid include waterboarding, dunces' caps, caning, belting, long term solitary confinement, Chinese water torture, iron maidens, crucifixion and stabbing. (Sorry, I've just been informed that apparently one of them is a doddle. And stabbing takes a second.)

I'm not sure how anyone can call detentions ineffective, but kneeling in the corner productive.

Er ... good luck.

Does anyone here speak OfSTED? Translating what they mean

Dear Tom

How do OfSTED inspectors characterise unsatisfactory behaviour? When they say something like, 'Behaviour is often inappropriate and badly managed'? Is it when a pupil kicks a door and the teacher doesn't do anything? Or does it refer to when pupils create low-level disruption and the teacher sets the odd detention? I'd like some guidance, because I don't understand them sometimes!

Trying to define bad behaviour from the OfSTED observation criteria is like herding cats on a boat in a storm. Cats made of bees. The definitions they have are maddeningly nebulous, despite the excruciating detail it appears to describe. It means whatever it is needed to mean.

For instance, one teacher I knew was delighted that during a lesson observation his normally fractious class was immaculately behaved. No one spoke out of turn, everyone was on task for the entire lesson, everyone completed their differentiated tasks and pupils regularly volunteered to contribute. His chin fell off a cliff when he received a *satisfactory* behaviour grading from one of the observers – not even *good*. The reason? the observer wasn't able to see if the pupils were capable of independently good behaviour, and whether they were only behaving well because it was an observation (i.e. 'it's because I'm in the room' – give me strength). When asked in exactly what context the observer *would* be able to witness this sort of behaviour, the answer was, 'Well, if you'd left the room for a second to get something.' Believe.

Any value judgement will be observer-dependent – this is inescapable. Turning a value judgement into an objective number involves a process which I like to call 'magic'. Behaviour is complex – as we all know, a chatty class can often learn *more* than a quiet one (within reasonable limits of course), and sometimes noisy kids are calling out because they're engaged with your lesson. The OfSTED criteria, IMO, looks for intensely polite pupils who are prepared to get enthusiastic at the drop of a hat, but then return to passive obedience at the teacher's whistle. This can happen, of course; I remember when I was a spotty Herbert I would have behaved for any teacher, no matter how rubbish they were. But other kids come to school intent on mayhem in all but the toughest teachers' classrooms.

From my experience, if the class listens when you speak, jumps when you say 'go', smiles when you crack a funny, stick their hands up like their lives depend on it, and can contribute to your 'evidence of progress' plenary then you get an *outstanding*. If there's any mucking about, but you deal with it effectively, then you can get a *good*, with all the above elements. If there's some mucking about, and not much enthusiasm/progress, then you can squeeze a *satisfactory*. If they taunt you mercilessly about your deodorant, then prepare for an *unsatisfactory*.

They've never had it so good? The difference between rich children and poor

Dear Tom

I've noticed that there is a huge difference in attitude between British schoolchildren and those in other countries. In poorer countries, many students see education as a huge privilege, and try their best to get as much of it as possible; they'll even walk miles in the morning and evening to get to school. Why doesn't this value system exist over here? Maybe some pupils see school as an imposition on their rights, because it is involuntary, and they have no say in attending or not. Do you think they don't value school because they have no choice about going or not?

Economics (seen by some as a science, rather than the combination of witchcraft, devil worship and entrail divination it is) has long recognized that the more available a commodity is, the less valued, and therefore valuable, it becomes.

Galbraith (one of the few American economists writing after the war I can stomach when reading) talked about the post-WW2 'culture of contentment'. By this he meant the idea that, although life in the western European democracies is far, far from Utopian, it at least promises and delivers a reasonable level of social welfare and comfort relatively unknown throughout history, for a broad demographic of people. People's memories are short, especially newer generations, which explains the relative disdain our existing school generation has for democracy, education, universal suffrage, welfare, etc. – they simply haven't experienced a world without these commodities, and assume that they are universal rights enjoyed in perpetuity at no cost, oblivious to the sacrifices made by their grandfathers and mothers to obtain such basic human wants.

I see this truism expressed every time a school pupil moans about having to be in school and moaning that they aren't allowed to play their MP3s during lessons or chat to their friends. They have grown up in lives of such relative ease that they simply cannot imagine how a bigger problem than what to watch on TV or what Happy Meal to have next could exist. Arguments about having to do homework or having to remove their jackets remind me of the sort of tantrums four-year-olds throw when frustrated, because their parents refuse to buy them the latest toy or treat. Children in countries that deny them the treasure of suffrage and schools would look on our chubby, indolent whiners with confusion and envy.

Many pupils leave school with eagerness, expecting ... what? What do they expect? A Shangri-La of ease and luxury, free from the privations of evil, pedantic pedagogues? A Brigadoon of cool contemplation and philosophical freedom? An exuberant riot of hedonism and sensual pleasure? A few thrive, of course – there are always exceptions. But I have lost count of the number of ex-pupils – *and* their parents – who have said to me, years after their departure,

'I wish I'd got my head down a bit more in lessons', or 'I was a bit of a pain, wasn't I?' To which I always say, 'yes, you should have,' and 'yes, you were.' Not out of malice, but simply glad to see that, despite the negativity that a substantial minority display towards education, most people *do* still value it, when they are mature enough.

Amen.

The Teacher's Bill of Rights

Dear Tom

I'm a Further Education teacher retraining as a secondary teacher. What sort of rights do we have in the classroom? Reason I ask is that I have a Year 10 girl who is extremely conniving and accuses me of unfairness all the time. Eventually I'd had enough of her whiny voice talking over me, and I told her to shut up.

Of course she then wouldn't let it go for the rest of the entire lesson, and said I had 'no right' to say that to her. So – what are my rights? I need something to say back to her.

Here's my Classroom Charter, my Bill of Rights that I rely on:

1. Anything they do which disrupts their education (as defined by me) is forbidden.
2. You know fine well what that means.
3. Anyone who objects to this charter has the right to put their objections to me in writing, whereupon it will be recycled as toilet paper.
4. I reserve the right to make up new rules as I progress: pay attention.

You can laminate that if you want.

Seriously, the amount some kids bang on about their *rights* is comical – they have no idea what they mean, they simply have a vague conception that it's something they're entitled to, like telly, E numbers, or dole money. Unfortunately 'responsibility' is a much bigger word to learn, so they fail to grasp it, until they have it shoehorned into them during Citizenship lessons, at which point they associate it with castor oil and cold showers.

Unfortunately there is no genuine charter of teacher rights that I can refer you to, so I suggest that you invent your own (and I invite you to adopt the one above). I tell my kids I'll bust my ass making sure they get a good education, and as a result they will have to acknowledge that they don't get to decide how that happens.

Perhaps they can bring it up at the next Student Voice meeting. I will be constipated with excitement to hear the result.

'I am a valuable, confident winner. Today will be a good day!' The link between self-esteem and behaviour

Dear Tom

In my opinion there is a clear link between self-esteem and behaviour. The more a pupil has low self-esteem, the worse their behaviour. This seems clear. Would you agree with me, and how can we promote self-esteem, in order to improve the students' behaviour overall?

Thank you

Despite attempts to nail bad behaviour and low self-esteem (LSE) together in some necessary causal way, the two issues remain slipperily independent. This, I venture, is because self-esteem is certainly linked to many aspects of bad behaviour, but that link is both contingent and partial, i.e. LSE *can* cause behaviour problems, just as high self-esteem can *also* cause behaviour problems. But neither of these links *have* to occur. LSE can clearly be one factor contributing to bad behaviour, but there are many, many others, and they all have a subtle interaction with each other before producing something as complex as behaviour.

Also, linking all bad behaviour to self-esteem issues is problematic because it medicalizes (and if that's not a word it bloody well should be – if it's good enough for Shakespeare it'll do for me) and therefore legitimizes poor behaviour. 'Ah, he can't help being rude/bullying etc. – he's got low self-esteem,' as if behaviour was as predetermined as the cogs in a clock. This removes responsibility from the student and thereby reduces us all to fatalism, what will be, will be and we can't help it. This is the opposite of the libertarian moral system upon which our entire social structure is based. Start down that path and before long, anything is possible.

If we want to entertain notions of right and wrong, we need to be able to sustain them with the oxygen of responsibility. Certainly, use phrases like 'low self-esteem' as diagnostic tools to aid the creation of strategies to deal with behaviour (praising the shy child, the bully etc.) but let us retain the sense that saying someone has LSE is a description of their behaviour rather than a prescription of psychological inevitability.

And finally, saying that LSE causes bad behaviour runs into problems of definition; after all, what is bad behaviour? A simple definition might be 'any form of behaviour not desired by the observer', which could run to an infinite series. The law defines smoking pot as bad behaviour but Bob Dylan might not. My neighbours banging out Hard House at four in the morning comes under the bad behaviour banner for me, but they appear to have no trouble with it. In neither instance is low nor high self-esteem the significant factor. Contributory, perhaps, but not causal.

I suspect that if we want to embark on a project to raise a student's self-esteem, we should tread carefully that we're not doing so because we equate SE with 'good', and we should be careful what aspect of their SE we're feeding. Telling a vain, arrogant, self-indulgent, narcissistic, egocentric, self-obsessed, over-indulgent and spoilt child that they're the cream in your coffee will have as much effect as telling Jenson Button he drives quite fast.

I dedicate this mini-rant to all the shy, unconfident kids working their backsides off for their exams right now, not making a peep, disturbing lessons, or telling teachers to stick their three-part lessons up their backsides.

The X Factors of bad behaviour: what are the triggers that cause mucking about?

Dear Tom

I think more attention should be paid to the kinds of factors that affect pupils' behaviour in lessons. Before school it can be so many things, from the quality of parenting, to the number of kids sleeping together in one room, to when Dad comes home from work, or the fact that their Gran is in hospital.

In classes, they can be affected by the teacher's style, the preparation of the lesson, where they are in the room ... so many different things to consider. How, then, can we truly blame children for misbehaving, when so many things influence their behaviour that they cannot control?

If we assume that every child, man and woman is simply a product of innumerable pre-existing factors that dictate their behaviour then we slip rapidly down the slope of psychological determinism, i.e. we are helpless automatons with no free will. Does this appeal to anyone out there?

I'll take free will as a given. This means that I can believe in personal responsibility, and the ability to change. So, given that I am neither a trained social worker, nor a neurosurgeon with god-like omniscience, I will instead get naughty children into trouble and reward those who behave well. May God have mercy on my soul.

Bad behaviour is because of your bad teaching: how do I respond to SLT saying that?

Dear Tom

My SLT say that bad teaching = bad behaviour. Now I agree that lessons should be well planned, differentiated, etc, but I feel very uncomfortable with the theory that not having an all-singing/all dancing/personalized lesson for everyone equals bad teaching; it basically means it's our fault for the behaviour of a class.

This is a common call, usually made by people who have no idea how classrooms work. Good behaviour is completely prior to fun, exciting differentiated lessons. Until you have control in a room, all the bells and whistles won't help. And it will ruin your self-esteem to watch all your hard work dashed against the cliffs of their indifference. I read a good line on a poster about decisions made by committees of managers. It read, 'Meetings – because all of us are dumber than one of us.'

That sums it up for me. Meetings generate this kind of well-meaning rubbish. Once they're under control then you can focus on the T&L. It can be done simultaneously, but T&L is never prior to good behaviour. Never.

Tell them that from me. Indeed, I suggest that you advise them to put it in their pipes and smoke it. Or say, 'How d'ya like *them* apples.'

Naughty parents need love too: do we have a policy for parents' behaviour?

Dear Tom

I think it's shocking that my school doesn't have a complaints policy for parents who are badly behaved to us. Is there no such policy?

In an ideal world we could give 'em all detentions. Unfortunately a minority of parents act in a way that would be legally actionable were it in a 'non-school' context. A Parental Policy is difficult to enact simply because parents aren't part of our sphere of influence, so they couldn't be expected to comply with it. At best such a policy would have to govern the school's reaction to parental 'misbehaviour'. This would be a good step towards ensuring consistency of expectations between SLT and teaching staff in the event of a crisis.

Unfortunately this is further complicated by the fact that many leadership groups might consider such a policy less than politically expedient. If you have a policy like that, it will inevitably be explicit about acceptable and unacceptable behaviour from parents, which might be considered confrontational by parents (in a world where schools compete for pupils and parents compete for schools). A good SLT should have the chops to stand up for what they know is right, including facing down aggressive parents (after conciliation has failed).

However I *have* seen isolated incidents of parental contracts being signed between schools, parents and pupils, where parents promise to provide uniform, ensure attendance, etc. These policies still seem to be very weighted towards the school's responsibility to the pupils, and say little about acceptable parental behaviour. I would be interested to see examples of schools that actually have such a policy.

Giving time outs

Dear Tom

What's the best way to give time outs to pupils in a primary environment? After years with Reception classes this is my first time in 'little-big' school.

I think time outs work best when there's some kind of re-integration meeting – it may be only a few minutes, or a more formal meeting after school. But the essential aspect is that the emotion is removed from the situation. We make many poor decisions when a red mist clouds our judgement (or theirs); harsh words, once spoken, are hard to take back. Emotions cloud the issues, and prevent us from seeing the real objectives to our actions.

So pupils only return from time outs once you've had a chance to ask for an apology, or a tacit acceptance of their wrong doing. It mustn't be a big stand off, fuelled by ego and aggression. Instead the miscreant needs to accept your authority calmly and quietly.

Otherwise they need to spend a bit more time thinking. If they re-enter in anger, they'll simply repeat the patterns of behaviour they exhibited before.

Talking to kids after school about incidents that generate time outs at the start of the day is really good practice. By that point the initial trigger of the time out is usually so far away that even to the kid it seems a bit pointless and silly to feel angry about it. In that way, we encourage them to have perspective on triggers that normally set them off. And hopefully they learn to anticipate and deal with them as they occur.

6 | Extreme teaching

If this were a Jackie Collins novel (it's not. Were you fooled by the suggestive title and the embossed cover?) from a public library (Google it – I believe they're called *Idea Stores* or *Knowledge Shops*, or something now. Presumably you go there to download celebrity autopsies onto your Zune, or your Kindle or something. I don't know) then this is the chapter the book would fall open at. This is the good stuff. This is the kind of behaviour that really grabs the headlines, and everyone's attention: *bad* behaviour. Actually I believe we don't refer to it as bad behaviour any more – that would imply some kind of moral judgement over the behaviour of the students (or 'Learning Stakeholders'), and imply that we had any right to tell them what do. *Behaviour at the upper end of the acceptability spectrum* will undoubtedly be the new title we have to embrace. I just call it 'Extreme Teaching and Learning'.

This is what terrifies the beginning teacher. Actually it terrifies the rest of the profession too, but until it is experienced it grows large in our imaginations, and there are few things more unnerving than a thing unseen. As soon as the monster steps out of the shadows, it might still be scary, but at least it has a shape, a definite form. Extreme behaviour is awful to endure, but a lot of it isn't actually as bad as it sounds – more perplexing than shocking or revolting. Of course, there are many behaviours that are genuinely upsetting. This chapter discusses the entire range, from unexpected mentalists to intimidating and dangerous behaviour. Every job has its risks. Every school is different. Some schools and careers will see a life unblemished by controversy. Some schools are breeding grounds for aggression and danger. My experience is that the latter are rare, because extreme behaviour is rare – that's what makes it extreme and unusual.

One thing that any new teacher needs to be reassured of is that this kind of thing is still exceptional – the incidents of genuine assault and intimidation are still infrequent enough to get reported in teacher journals. Another thing to say is that a lot of it is dealt with in the same way you would any other misbehaviour, i.e. you record the behaviour, pass it on to your line manager, and punish accordingly. If a child point blank refuses to follow any of your instructions, and just sits there, defying your orders to leave the room, then take a tip: don't go mad and start raving at them. Just note it down, and make sure you bring down the whole weight of the school disciplinary system on it later. Seriously, just knowing that you will get your way ... eventually ... can have a huge calming influence on you at the time.

But it doesn't do any good to brush this part of the teaching experience under the rug either: many of the questions I have received concerned pupils who behaved so inappropriately that teachers felt dazed, unable to know what to do next. Not just pupils either, but members of staff or parents. Another common experience for such people was that often school senior leader sometimes don't know how to handle it either. After all they're only human, just like you. Part of the problem also seems to lie with a minority of spineless line managers who refuse to face up to their responsibilities towards a serious situation – unless it happens to them. Another part of the problem in this equation is that the newer teacher is often so confounded by the experience of being told to f*** off (or whatever) that they fail to escalate the response to the situation appropriately. I've seen teachers giving a kid 15 minutes detention for grabbing something out of the teacher's hand, or calling them a m****** ******. That'll teach them!

Clearly some ways of handling such incidents are better than others. For a start, the witnessing teacher needs to make the response to the extreme behaviour a DEFCON 1 priority. Clear the decks and get it written up and reported forcefully to line managers and responsible senior management. The next step is for these people then to take the same attitude to the behaviour and deal with it as promptly as possible. Pupils need to be pulled out of lessons (preferably in front of their peers) to demonstrate that crime doesn't pay. External services need to be consulted as soon as possible. The teacher affected by the behaviour (and possibly other pupils in the class) needs to be supported in an appropriate way. If line managers and senior staff don't take violence, threats, swearing, sexual intimidation and assaults and racism seriously, then God only knows what would get their magisterial backsides in gear. Note to SLT everywhere: for Heaven's sake, reschedule the meeting with the borough SEAL coordinator if something like this comes up. It's called leadership.

Governors can play their part too: incidents where insipid governing bodies overturn sensible exclusions are thankfully rare, but not rare enough. Note to Governors everywhere: have some guts. Ask if you'd like your son or daughter to be taught in classrooms where there was a tangible risk of violence. In reality, it's the responsibility of *everyone* to keep a lid on this kind of extreme behaviour. Pupils famously model their behaviour on their peers, and if somebody pushes the envelope of acceptability by evading punishment, then others will realize that the goalposts have moved in favour of chaos and madness.

Take heart, if you have experienced anything extreme; there are many bodies (from your union, to the staff association, to a responsible senior teacher) that will back you up and make sure your wellbeing is looked after. You'll have to do some of the looking after yourself, but life was never designed to be easy. Console yourself with the knowledge that it almost certainly wasn't your fault in the first place. And you're never alone.

Running the gauntlet: coping with an assault

Dear Tom

I work in an EBD school and I was involved in an incident on Friday during which both myself and my TA were assaulted by a pupil. I was punched repeatedly in the back and my TA was punched once in the chest. The child was arrested but has been bailed pending further investigations. I have just been informed by my TA that the child has not been excluded for this incident and furthermore I am expected to teach this child on Monday when he returns to school, with the same TA who was also assaulted.

Apparently SMT want the child to return to school so that he can be present in the class when interviews take place for a new member of SMT later in the week. They want to see if the applicants are capable of dealing with this child along with the rest of the class.

Good God, what an awful position to find yourself in. If this is really what SLT have said then they should be ashamed of themselves. This assault isn't a hurdle on an interview; it's a crime, and a threat to your safety. Refuse to teach this child. Given the urgency of the issue, take action now and get the union to back you retrospectively. Legally we have no specific right to refuse to teach a child, but at the same time the school and the LEA have a duty of care to you as an employee, which is clearly being threatened here. No teacher should have to teach a child that has assaulted them. I would dearly like to see the Head teach his/her attacker if the positions were reversed.

Freedom to hate? The fine line between free speech and race hate

Dear Tom

What do I do if I have children in my class expressing extreme views? The child is happy saying that all white people and non-Muslims will go to Hell and he wants to grow up and go to Pakistan and get a gun to come back here and kill all white people. I was distressed by these comments and wish to protect other children from this view; I was also personally affronted by these comments being white myself; I felt I had been racially attacked.

Unpleasant in the extreme. We as teachers have a duty to uphold a shared sense of community values, and these can be as general and liberal as 'we all have the right of freedom from attack, verbal or otherwise.' The students have a statutory right to their SMSC education. However everyone also has a right to express their own opinions, even unpleasant ones. How do we reconcile the two rights?

The solution in any society of liberal sentiment is generally to tolerate beliefs and draw guidelines of acceptable conduct as to how and when those views are expressed. It is perfectly legitimate for a teacher to tell a student that certain views will not be tolerated in open expression. Liberal societies do not permit every behaviour; rather they support the private sphere, but disallow any actions that harm others in the public sphere.

As to religious beliefs, it is usually enough to add the appendix 'some people believe' when you express a view that is controversial. I am an agnostic (handy for a Religious Studies teacher) and append almost all my statements with this, e.g. 'some Christians believe in Salvation,' or 'some Druids believe in the Great Horned One'. I am happy for atheists to make claims about the membrane universes theory, or for Pentecostals to express claims about the blood of Jesus. As long as these claims are:

a) recognised as truth claims i.e. statements that can be challenged or accepted, and

b) expressed politely and respectfully. An atheist can deny Hell, but it's hurtful and rude for him to tell a peer that someone will 'never see their mum again', etc. And vice versa.

Incidentally, I don't think it would be wrong to report this to the authorities. If a pupil made regular claims that he wanted to kill (for instance) prostitutes or somebody famous and the views were shared by the parents, then there are grounds for a police investigation. It's not too alarmist to imagine that it is a possibility. Personally I think that this issue touches on your responsibility to the community and to the future.

Cuddle or smack? Do we appease or condemn aggressive behaviour in a parent?

Dear Tom

I was recently in a school (as a governor) and witnessed a member of a pupil's family throwing an extremely violent tantrum. He was ranting at staff and waving a baseball bat about as if he would hit someone with it! His wife (who is a teacher) kept shouting at us to 'Back off and give him space to calm down,' which of course we did! Then there was an hour-long meeting which was conducted like an argument in a pub. Awful.

My question is this; is it now standard practice for teachers to give people 'space' who are displaying behaviour like this? I seriously considered phoning the police as we were all threatened. Surely the best reaction to this behaviour isn't immediately to placate it?

Emotional states can be exacerbated or ameliorated by how we allow them to unfold. As Bertrand Russell once said, "We can act as we please, but we cannot please as we please." Essentially, although our emotional states often seize us without warning, how we handle those states is our responsibility. If an inconsiderate driver cuts me up and flips me the finger, I would be furious; but rather than following my instinct to follow him home and decapitate him, I hold it in and say, 'Bother!' under my breath. (That'll teach him.) We're not robots – we have choices in the matter.

If, however, I felt like expressing the anger, I would get myself into a state of heightened anger. Expressing this heightened anger would inspire others to act angrily towards me, and my anger would be multiplied again. The notion that we have to 'get it off our chests' in all circumstances is, I reckon, pretty ridiculous. What are emotions, poison? They're not objects, to be 'let out', to disperse in the wind. They're states of mind, attitudes. The parent acted like an idiot.

I once worked with a wise bouncer who never struck anyone first, ever. His motto was, 'If someone lifts a fist to me, *then* they get a sore face.' So if you wave a bat around, you can expect a ton of consequences. Obviously I wouldn't recommend chinning him, but it could certainly be a police matter, as I think you have already noted.

Better out than in? Only if it's a bad egg. Grown-ups shouldn't throw tantrums; that's what babies do.

Is this a dagger? Pupils who bring knives to school

Dear Tom

A pupil was recently caught in school with a knife, but three days of exclusion later, he's back in school! Surely he should be out permanently? Plus next week he's back in my lesson. Should I refuse to teach him?

Bringing a dangerous weapon into school sounds so obviously like a permanent exclusion issue that I can barely bring myself to type it. However there may be extenuating circumstances. Some stupid boys bring in things to impress others. I can easily imagine a lonely, unpopular boy bringing in a knife to look tough, just to show his friends. In that case the boy should be given a temporary exclusion, especially if of previous good character; you wouldn't want to spoil his educational career for one mistake. But if the offence was repeated then permanent exclusion should follow. And if he used or displayed it in a dangerous or threatening manner then it's time to get the Yellow Pages out and open at 'Schools'.

How much is too much to deal with? Discovering the limits of acceptability in your room

Hi Tom

Is this acceptable in a Foundation classroom? I have two children who repeatedly kick off and hurt other pupils and/or trash the classroom and play areas. They throw everything about, and the class had to leave once because I was fearful for their safety. They scream as loudly as they can in lessons, and move all the learning equipment This happens every day, and I feel awful for the other kids in the class. These children won't do any work,or join in with the others, and I feel like a total failure. Is this acceptable?

No, this isn't acceptable. If it were then God help us, because these kids sound like they've been reared by dingoes. If you are applying sanctions consistently and regularly, and you are positive that you are using the strategies that you have described, then it's clear that the current strategies aren't working.

Of course, it's possible that they simply haven't worked *yet* – how long have they been in the class, and how long have you been using the strategies? Frankly, if the answer to both is 'more than a few months' and you haven't seen a significant change in their clowning, then something else needs to be tried, and I suggest something more drastic.

Definitely enlist your SENCO; there may be something identifiable or certifiable behind their behaviour, in which case they can get special provision.

They need to be removed from the classroom situation as much as possible. Social exclusion is required for two reasons: a) for the good of the class; the needs of the many must outweigh the needs of the few. Think how the education of so many of this class is being ruined by the disruptive behaviour of a couple of poorly behaved children. The others deserve, and are entitled to, a safe and calm educational environment. b) the two miscreants, if they are merely misbehaving due to poor self restraint/ill manners/choppy parenting will get the message that their behaviour is bad when they find themselves removed from their peer group. Children, and people are social animals (don't blame me, I'm quoting Aristotle) and dislike isolation more than most sanctions. They need an audience, and perhaps by depriving them of one they might reassess what they are doing. *Every* time they misbehave, take them away from the rest of the group. Let them feel the full force of the disapproval of the community.

What mustn't happen is some wishy-washy attempt at keeping them in class if their behaviour isn't appropriate for being in a group. Children learn to be socialized by realizing what is and isn't permitted. If we let them stay in the group when they misbehave *without* punishment, then we teach them that they can be unpleasant and nothing will happen – the last lesson we need to teach them. More awfully, socialization works both ways, and the rest of the class will learn to imitate their capering.

Look into options for removal – TAs, mentors, learning support, other teachers – and look into procedures at school that lead to removal. Apply normal sanctions for misbehaviour, and don't make special provision for their misbehaviour. If we want to teach them to be part of society, then they're going to have to live by society's rules.

So if they continue to misbehave then escalate the sanctions and start proceedings for them to take some time off from school. Perhaps then, with time, they can learn that crime doesn't pay.

Urinating in the classroom: is it acceptable?

Dear Tom

I had an unusual experience in school the other day. Unfortunately a fight broke out between some boys and I tried to intervene. At this point I was knocked to the floor and one of the more 'naughty' boys urinated on my face. I was so shocked but had to continue the lesson at the end of the day I feel upset and do not wish the incident to be repeated. Do you have any teaching strategies that could help me?

Have you tried peer observations?

(My spider-sense tells me that this one might not have been 100% genuine. Yes, I'm a cynic.)

The state of nature: scared to teach my new class

Dear Tom

Hi there; I'm due to start teaching in September 2009, and therefore completely green. One particular class is beginning to worry me, a Year 10 English class, where every lesson observed so far seems to degenerate into a riot. The teacher is told to go f*** herself, things are chucked, pupils graffiti the tables, the kids walk in and out of the class at will, and they show each other porn on their phones. There is zero respect in the room for the poor teacher; at one point one of the kids hugged her, and she looked petrified. I'm terrified too and utterly mortified for her. Please tell me this isn't normal …

God, that sounds awful. No, that isn't in any way normal, and it's not what you have to expect. Of course, the teaching adverts nowadays bear more resemblance to *The Prime of Miss Jean Brodie* than to the *Apocalypse Now*-style *Heart of Darkness* that some people seem to experience. In my experience, the vast majority of school pupils are on task, polite and behaved, almost all the time. There are pupils, classes and even schools that are nightmarish, soul-destroying even, but it is not the case that we could in any way describe this as the norm. I often hear comments from teachers denying this, claiming that all children are feral, and we should all retreat to the Channel Islands before kids start eating people.

But in reality, there have always been bad schools, bad teachers, bad kids. Society has always suffered from terrible extremes of privation and privilege. I wonder when the alleged Golden Age of youth behaviour was supposed to have existed. When were children rosy-cheeked models of virtue? When were we? I certainly agree, also, that as a society we have badly let down many sections of our young communities by pandering to their whims, by forgetting what we are responsible for as adults (the list would be wearying) and that we are damaging their prospects because we sometimes forget that they need guidance more than indulgence. But a brief examination of history teaches that few eras have enjoyed the mythical good and positive behaviours that we would like them to have had. Kids up chimneys, anyone?

This class sounds revolting. The teacher needs some serious help and support; every single incident you have described should have been recorded, reported, and punished. If the teacher didn't do this because she's too scared or depressed to do so, then her SLT needs to know (and I'm not suggesting that's your job either, although perhaps as a human being you might want to have a chat with her and ask what she's doing, maybe even suggest she speaks to a colleague to get some encouragement and support, before she goes boogaloo).

These types of classes aren't normal. Too common, yes. But you'll find all sorts. A lot depends what you do with them. *Very* good luck to you.

Facebook libel

Dear Tom

A girl I thought was smart has set up a Facebook page that is dripping with venom about the school. She's called the Deputy Head a chubby f*** who stuffs herself in the canteen, and also called the Science head a 'daft mongo'. In all there are about twenty-five staff slagged off. When we found out she got a couple of days in the internal exclusion room. How should the school have dealt with this? I'm not sure it was handled properly.

Ah, brave new world that hath such people in it! Each new wave of technology brings a new spin on old problems – and that's what it is, just another example of the same problems, served up in HTML (or something. Don't quote me, I teach RS).

A Facebook page can be private, open or limited. If the page is open for all to see (as this witless child apparently has permitted) then it's a gross and public insult to the named (or undeniably identified) colleagues. In which case, it should be dealt with in the same way as you would if she shouted out 'The Head's a retard!' or something to a whole class. An exclusion sounds pretty right – whether it should be internal or external depends on the quality of punishment or rehabilitation that you think it should produce.

Certainly it's not slander, which is verbal; it might be libel – the law permits fair comment, i.e. opinion, unless it could be proven to be factually inaccurate in some way *or* if it can be proven to damage the reputation of the victim. But I suspect Plod wouldn't drop his doughnut to deal with this one.

If the page was limited access only (i.e. only she and her Facebook friends – as opposed to her real ones – can view the page) then it is, to some extent, a private conversation, and surely therefore no one's concern, no matter how unpleasant. We are all entitled to have opinions, even if they are unpalatable to others, as long as they don't cause harm to anyone else's private sphere.

If she's stupid enough to imagine that teachers won't access this then she's not as bright as she thinks, and deserves a bit of a roasting for her poor manners and lack of foresight. She should also be made to apologize personally to every teacher and member of staff that she insulted, with the insult read out in front of her, the member of staff, and a senior teacher (plus, preferably, a parent).

That'll teach her!

Squeezed gentials

(NB All emphases, spellings, the correspondent's own. Seriously)

Dear Tom

The Head of Year told us today that there is a group of boys in Year 7 squeezing other boy's gentials [sic]. A mother has phoned our school to say that one of the boys has been peeing blood. One of the Assistant Heads has said we will have to have an assembly about this for all Year 7 boys.

There is a twofold question here: what do other schools do? And – much more importantly – this is happening more regularly and more often as well. What can the staff do in order to resolve soft management as regards to boundries [sic] and punishment by *some* of the Leadership team? As an experienced teacher and I don't wish to be self-identified as an agitator; I

will not stand by and allow things to continue. My fellow teachers believe that the senior team are **not** dealing with this and that it will **continue**. Your comments please?

Ah, the old 'squeezing the genitals until they bleed' problem. We've all faced it. Have you been taking *all* of your pills?

Where is the justice? I've been pushed and no one cares

Dear Tom

A Year 10 pupil pushed me in the corridor; I nearly fell over completely. Why did he push me? I told him off for play-fighting in a classroom while I was teaching. The outcome is that the Head wants 'restorative' justice (which is?), so I have to endure a meeting with the pupil – who has accused me of being a liar, anyway – where he will deny he did anything wrong, or sob crocodile tears that he knows will let him wriggle out of it. The stress of this has affected my eating, sleeping, and I now feel like I'm the one on trial. Why is he being treated as if his word was as valid as mine?

Once I was pushed by a pupil who thought it was funny – the pupil never returned to school again, because my management took it seriously and moved on it immediately, and because I pressed for the highest sanctions.

But sadly, if SLT don't treat it as serious, then the whole situation deteriorates – as a classroom teacher there is only so much you can do before the only option left is to withdraw your services. I genuinely wonder when the balance between the rights of the practitioner and the imagined rights of the pupils will be redressed. Still; sometimes all we can do is fix our feet squarely in the ground beneath us, look ahead, and fix the problems in front of us.

Good luck to you, and I'm sorry you were another victim. And I'm sorry you were let down by the people who were responsible for looking after your wellbeing. There are better schools, and better SLT, I promise you. Talk to your union if your SLT fail to grow a backbone over this, because the school has a duty of care to you as an employee, and it could be argued that you are being exposed to possible harm if they don't ensure that this doesn't happen again. If this pupil was, say, a bare, live electrical cable hanging from the ceiling, you can bet your interactive pen they'd be on it in a flash. Insist on sanctions. Or go to the police if you have witnesses. Good luck.

The second blow was harder: when the school won't support you against a pupil

Dear Tom

A few days ago, a nine-year-old girl hit me when she was angry. She did it because I wouldn't let her work with a friend. I waited, and she marched up to me and slapped my arm hard. So I sent her to the Head (who was teaching) who sent her back in five minutes with a message: 'Why have you sent her to me? I am teaching.'

When we spoke about it later, the Head said she needed some witnesses to the assault before she would do anything. Hang on, I thought I was an adult and a teacher? The girl refused to apologize, and came into my lesson the next day as if nothing had happened! She had been told not to apologize to me. What? Then the Head spent about an hour with the girl devising 'strategies' to help her enjoy lessons more. I feel like I'm to blame here, or they think I am ...

Farcical were it not so tragic. There's a girl that should have been on a fast track to serious trouble; exclusion at the very least. This attitude that *understanding* a child's inner needs is somehow more important than your assault is moronic. Of course her needs are important, but right now she *needs* to learn that hitting people is very serious, she *needs* to understand how to deal with adults with respect and she *needs* to apologize. Incidentally it sounds like your Head *needs* a few things, too: a backbone; sense knocked into her. There are many things that we need but we don't particularly want – like restrictions on our whims – there are many restraints on our freedom that develop and encourage us to be better, healthier people in other ways. And children need to learn restraint so that they can flourish as adults.

Union's in the phone book. And talk tough with the Head. This isn't good enough. Let her know that you were assaulted, the girl needs some quality time in an exclusion unit to cool off, and that you won't put up with her in your class unless you have some more support. Good luck.

A thug in my classroom

Dear Tom

I love teaching in a FE college. But ... There's one boy (18) who is really bright, speaks cleverly, and a total nightmare. He recently had a fight with a new student (he's Romanian Roma gypsy, as is my pupil – I hate to mention it though, in case I'm accused of victimisation). In a meeting, I got him to sign a behaviour agreement, but it's meaningless. He just accused us of racism while he did it.

For the last six months he has spoiled every lesson he's been in with his texting, shouting, strolling in and out of the room... Of course, I'm a '***', '***' and numerous pejorative curses. He's loathsomely sexist, and sometimes I feel like throwing that in his face when he says we're racist.

My line manager is like a marshmallow – totally ineffective with them. She's no help at all because she just wants to duck responsibility – and she's hardly ever there.

This is clearly a desperate dislocation in managerial responsibility. This boy should have been out on his ear a long time ago. In any school I've observed, he would have been excluded for persistent and wilful misbehaviour – the damage he is doing/has done to the others in the class is shocking. They have rights too: the right to an education unblemished by disruption and chaos.

And what about you? You are entitled to a safe working environment, free from unnecessary stress as much as is practical. Any manager that throws unruly kids back in the classroom without an effective sanction procedure is being negligent in their responsibility towards you. It would appear that senior members of your department are never there – this might mean that you need to ...

... manage upwards. Find the member of staff who *is* there, the one above the one who should be there, and complain that you aren't being supported. Or, if you don't feel comfortable complaining, say that you need support and that you're not getting it. You've tried your line manager and they are too busy, etc. Whatever it takes. *Somebody* must be in charge, and they are ultimately responsible for this situation's resolution. You have been, it seems, shockingly abandoned by the people who are supposed to be there for you.

Incidentally try to avoid playing the sexism card. What he's doing is wrong, and an insult to the victims of genuine racism, but I believe my mother taught me that two wrongs don't make a right. Also, sexism isn't illegal by itself, the Sex Discrimination Act makes discrimination against someone in terms of wages, employment etc illegal, not simply being unpleasant to women. That's why Bernard Manning avoided prison.

My word against hers

Dear Tom

I can't believe this is happening to me: one of my Year 9 girls told me to 'F*** off' in a lesson today, and when I told the SLT he asked if there were any witnesses. I said no, so he said he'd have a chat with her. At the end of the day he said he'd spoken to her but she denied it, so there was nothing he could do. I'm choked with anger. How can he not take my word as being stronger than hers?

Infuriating to hear a member of SLT being so spineless. Unfortunately there have been instances of teachers being nasty and then covering up so I suppose from his point of view he was just being safe, but it's a pretty poor show to take the word of a student over a trained professional in the first instance.

Also, this isn't *CSI, LA Law* or indeed, *Diagnosis: murder*. This isn't a court of law; we don't need proof beyond reasonable doubt or even probable cause, reasonable grounds etc. This is a school environment, and as such we don't have to provide the level of evidence that would secure, say, a conviction on a charge of manslaughter. Were it a criminal charge then we would, but in cases of he said/she said, then the school should keep it simple and back up its staff, otherwise it might find itself without any.

Educational managers: grow a backbone! And stop watching too much telly, even if the kids do.

Pupils mock my sexuality

Dear Tom

My dilemma might seem trivial, but it feels so bad I felt compelled to ask for some advice. I'm an NQT in a reasonable school but as I walk past some pupils in the corridors they shout 'gay boy' and similar comments. Thing is, I am gay (but definitely not 'out' at school). Basically I don't like the tone or content of what they're saying; after all, it's none of their business to talk about my sexuality (although what they do behind my back I couldn't care less about).

Problem is, if I raise this with my HOD then I'm basically coming out to my colleagues, and I'm not ready for that. This really bothers me, and it's affecting how I look at my job. I'm in a Catch 22 position because if this was racial harassment then I wouldn't hesitate to bring it up with SLT etc.

Now I try physically to avoid certain groups of boys, humiliating as that might sound.

A far from trivial issue and the worst thing you could do would be to ignore it because you think it's not important. You really have to tackle this head on – if you ignore it then they have absolutely won and how could you expect to teach these pupils anything if they can say things like that to you? Of course tackling them isn't going to be a piece of cake (when was standing up for ourselves ever easy?) but it isn't the worst thing in the world either. Remember, you are an adult, a professional, a teacher, a tax-payer and a man. The people making you feel uncomfortable are children – spotty, charmless and lacking in hygiene.

You could tackle them head on. Next comment you hear, stop, slowly turn around and call the offender over to you. If you had 'form' in the school you could walk right into the middle of them, but that will encourage them to act up for their mates. You need to divide and conquer. Just say to him, 'What did you just call me?' Serious face. No nerves, no fear, no aggression, just all business, like you're speaking to someone in a call centre. Unlikely he'll say, 'you, gay boy,' so on the basis that his answer will be something like, 'What?' or, 'It wasn't you I was talking about,' or whatever, then your reply should be along the lines of, 'Good. Because I thought for a second you were being incredibly rude to a teacher. But seeing as how you're not, then we don't have a problem. For a second there I thought someone was going to be excluded. Good thing they're not.' That sort of thing.

Then explain to them that they need to be more careful in future; if you hear it again in earshot you'll assume they're making comments about you and you'll proceed down the sanction avenue (see below). Then walk away. If you hear it again (then, or later) do the following.

Tackle it obliquely. Have them brought to your classroom, or get them yourself after school (or better yet, in the office of their HOY, SLT etc, as back-up for you). Explain to them that you heard some extremely offensive language from them earlier on in the day, you felt it was directed to you, and did they have anything to say about it? Explain that the sanction for offensive comments to a teacher is exclusion. They then either have to admit it (unlikely, but you never know, they might grass up one of their mates. Jackpot!) or deny it, in which case you get them to admit how it could be interpreted by someone that they were being rude ('yes sir') and that it could be seen as a very offensive slur ('yes sir'). By then they've effectively had to back down in front of another teacher, and paid at least lip service respect to you. Whatever; it's a mild humiliation for them. Of course, the next time you hear it, it becomes a serious matter for sanction, because you've made it clear you're not even to hear the words. Proceed with the normal whole school sanctions.

Do this for every one of them if you like. You'll need a sympathetic SLT etc. to back you up, but for God's sake man, that's what they're there for! It doesn't sound like you're 'coming out' if you simply object to name calling – after all, students aren't allowed to say that to any staff member, gay or straight – it's rude because it's personal, and designed to be offensive, even if *gay* isn't an insult. There will be (or should be) a member of senior staff happy to help with this. It's not an 'outing' – you only think that because you see your innermost thoughts as transparent to others. They're not. You're as in as you want to be. Boys make gay jokes about most other boys, without any implication that any genuine Ugandan discussions take place. It's just a common slur among the weak-minded and the insecure, so don't take it personally.

"You're rubbish, Miss." Dealing with direct criticism of my teaching

Dear Tom

A girl in my mixed ability art class told me I was rubbish today. I tried to tell her I was trying my best. Unfortunately some of them aren't taking art as an option, so they're turning off a bit. Even when I do a seating plan they just creep back and let me know that they couldn't care less about me. What do you do when students openly criticize you as blatantly as this? I'm not sure how I should have responded. What should I have done?

Exactly what you would have done if they had chucked a pen at someone, or sworn at you. Give a detention. Ignore the comment apart from a simple, 'see me later, Morgan,' She's been rude both in content and intent. She is trying to embarrass and pull you down in front of her peers in order to look hard/funny/clever. Teach her the price of her costly manoeuvre by calling her on it.

And don't tell her you're trying your best – you are, I'm sure. But she has no right to judge you publicly or criticize you about a skill that she is incapable of evaluating. She should count herself lucky that she has you as a teacher and shut the hell up. I think we get so used to observations by peers that we develop paranoia about our own abilities. Maybe you could critique her on her abilities as a student?

Words are sometimes not enough: getting physical when punches fly

Dear Tom

Today I had to stand physically between two boys who were fighting in my classroom. I shouted at them to stop, but they kept going. I haven't been trained in this kind of thing, and I have no idea if I was right or not. My line management have been great, but I'm still wondering what I should have done. What do you think? Thanks.

Context is everything in this one. The law allows us to use *reasonable force* to restrain a pupil in order to prevent further harm. And that word *reasonable* is as vague as it sounds, which is helpful when you're looking for clear instructions. Mind you, life isn't simple either, and fights never are.

Teachers are in no way *required* to intervene in a fight – we're expected to be so many other things, from social worker to psychologist, but one thing we bloody well are not is police. There is nothing to compel us to intervene physically in any situation that could put us in harm's way.

That said, there is possibly a greater responsibility on us as citizens, and as adults. I have intervened in dozens of fights, usually on the basis that they are kicking hell out of each other, and I'm a grown-up, and I can't stand by and watch it happen. I am prepared to take a punch or two (and have done) in the course of my choices, but this is entirely my call, and no-one has the right to make it for me. I know that if I had a kid and somebody was beating him like a piñata, I would take a dim view of any teacher who stood by and said, 'Oh I just watched. Looked a bit scary.' I certainly wouldn't expect anyone to intervene in a situation where the kids seriously outweighed the teacher. Sounds terribly old guard, but I also wouldn't expect a small woman to intervene in a fight between two big Year 11s, either. (Sorry, Andrea Dworkin. The Hell of Unreconstructed Men awaits me.)

Like I say, it's all about context. I find that standing in between them works best, because you prevent them from getting at each other. Of course, it might also get you a sore face. But from my experience of pub fights, 90 per cent of brawls are about face, and at the first chance to back down gracefully, they'll take it.

Sexual assault in the classroom

Dear Tom

A Year 6 girl from my form came to me and told me that two boys held her arms, stroked her chest, backside and worse. She looked like she was stunned by it, and I immediately went to the SLT; but they told me they were busy, and I should wait for the Child Protection Officer (CPO) to finish her lunch. During this time I allowed the girl to phone her mum to come and get her. Then two Child Protection Officers came and took her statement, plus that of witnesses. She spent all day at home today, but the boys are still in the school, and this afternoon they were interviewed by the CPO.

Now, I don't know what really happened, but hasn't this all happened a bit fast? All that has happened now is that the boys have admitted inappropriate behaviour, but denied anything sexual. They have written apologies. That's it. Is this just a cover up?

I completely understand the way that the seriousness of this situation has left you feeling, and I commend your actions in dealing with the situation. For this young girl you behaved in exactly the way children should expect us to: swift, decisive and protective.

Bear in mind that a lot *has* been done in respect to this incident. The CPOs were called in swiftly – extremely so, given that you received the report at lunchtime and the CPOs were in action by the afternoon and interviews took place almost immediately after the event. In this situation I would call that exemplary, an absolute model of best practice. Although the speed with which it has been resolved might suggest carelessness, I think it speaks of swift resolution and professional care from all concerned. After all, if the case had dragged on for weeks, it could equally be open to accusations of being low priority, etc. Also the trail would have gone cold.

It seems that protocols worked quickly in this case. I suspect that you feel the boys are guilty and that the wrong punishment has been handed out; but if the CPOs are minded to accept their stories then I don't really see there's any way (or indeed any reason) to contradict that, given that they are used to dealing with these situations and we are simply not. After all, these boys may be at least partially the victims of false accusations, despite appearances. It does happen.

If the girl's testimony was detailed and emotional it could indicate that she's telling the truth, that she's expressing some other form of abuse in her life, or that she's a liar with a grudge and a cold heart.

Obviously it's impossible for me to comment, but without further information about her background and the incident in question, it would be wrong to speculate.

You should be very proud of yourself for getting so involved in child safety.

I'm scared of looked-after children

Dear Tom

Started a new job with looked after children – a week later some of them were jumping in my car (smoking!), spitting around me, chasing me while holding a lighter. It's not a school, it's a social service institution, and I'm alone a lot with them. The teaching assistant has been off ill for a while. To be frank I feel a bit scared, but if I leave now, will it ruin my chances for another job? I'm stuck.

I think you're very brave indeed to persevere with this situation. I'd also like to remind you that some of the incidents you have described are clearly assault (remember that assault doesn't have to involve actual physical harm, merely the threat to do so) or intimidation. All of these are actionable by law, and I wonder if you shouldn't take the matter further. It's a common theme, but we as a profession appear to be expected to endure aggression and behaviour that would justify the involvement of Plod in any other arena. Sometimes I think we are complicit with this expectation by allowing it.

Either way, you have the protection of the law should you choose to pursue this. I can't imagine any circumstance in which such behaviour would be seen as 'mucking about', and perhaps these kids need to be reminded that in the real world, actions have consequences.

Make sure you are never alone (or at the very least, next door to a colleague) whenever you have the kids; if your employer cannot guarantee this then they don't deserve to have you. At least in mainstream education we usually have lots of witnesses, other kids and legions of colleagues nearby.

Make sure you are safe – that's absolutely paramount and absolutely your right. No job is worth getting hurt for. Please don't let them fob you off with half measures – you deserve better.

I was called a c**t

Dear Tom

Today I was called a c**t by a Year 11 boy. As nobody else was there to hear it seems he won't get any punishment. Would this happen everywhere? Is a student's word equal to that of a teacher's?

He called you a Celt? How odd.

A teacher's claim alone should be able to justify a substantial detention, and IMO a short exclusion (actually in an ideal world it would be grounds for a very long exclusion, but let's walk before we can run). Much depends on your SLT's style; some will back you to the grave, some will wet themselves at the thought of standing up to a draught. Have you actually reported this yet? When you say 'it seems' does this mean that you've asked for it and been refused? If not then do so ASAP, otherwise the crime becomes cold and punishment becomes less relevant.

A pupil's word certainly shouldn't count as much as a teacher's given that we are a) adults, b) professionals, and c) not given to calling people c**ts on a regular basis. Unfortunately there are a few teachers who would abuse this system by maliciously inventing claims, but I still don't think that this would justify devaluing the word of every teacher. The weakening of our status has, I fear, been matched by the rise of the 'student voice' in education. Which begs the question: are we teaching them, or are they teaching us? Will they get paid? Can I bunk lessons? Unanswered questions, all.

Make a fuss, and show the kid and the school that you're not to be crossed.

Twisted fire starter: dealing with arson

Dear Tom

Here's the drama: girl in Year 10 goes to the cloakroom crying, and another girl goes in to see why she's upset. The first girl (who has a bit of a track record of instability) takes out a lighter and singes her scarf. The second girl gets a bit frightened and takes the girl to a mentor in the school. Apparently the scarf was left in the cloakroom smouldering. So they talk to the mentor and she says she'll get to them in a minute. Ten minutes later the fire alarm goes off and we all have to be evacuated. Both pupils excluded, permanently: the first girl for the fire, and the second for not telling a staff member about a fire risk. The parents are launching an appeal. What should have happened?

There's never a moral philosopher around when you need one.

Sounds complex, and a little perverse. *If* the second girl thought there was no fire (i.e. she was sure the scarf was out) then she can't be held responsible for failing to report it, as she didn't believe there was anything to report. Responsibility usually entails a) awareness, b) intention, and c) freedom to act otherwise. Sounds like she had (c) but neither (a) nor (b). If I thought there *wasn't* a fire then I *wouldn't* call the fire department. Presumably the school believes that the scarf was alight when the girls left it? It sounds like only the very stupid would ignore that, and the fact that she brought the girl's distress to the teacher's attention indicates some degree of altruism and compassion, as well as a hearty amount of conscientiousness. Ladies and gentlemen of the jury, I ask you: does this sound like the sort of girl who would be willingly complicit in a wilful act of arson?

Of course, this is only based on the evidence presented, and we need to be careful not to make a judgement based on partial evidence. It could be true that the scarf was only smouldering, because as any camper will know, smouldering fires can re-ignite. Or maybe it was fully ablaze and the girl thought it was groovy, but wanted to talk to a teacher about ... no, it doesn't strike me as likely either.

Unless there's a lot you're not telling us then it could be that this girl's permanent exclusion is on thin ice. Can you be PE'd for failing to report something? Possibly, but the prosecution would have to prove that there was forethought and malicious intent.

Naturally, the Year 10 girl should be out on her ear. I mean, who sets fire to their scarf because they're upset? What is she, mental? I notice she didn't smash her mobile phone or something – I mean, that would be inconvenient ...

The class biter: do I get a muzzle?

Dear Tom

My Year 2 class has a boy who regularly runs out, and when he gets angry he bites, kicks and scratches. He's had exclusions, and I've asked everyone else in school for advice on how to handle him, to no avail. I only have a TA sometimes, so often I'm alone with him. Apparently he's been like this since he started school. As an NQT I'm getting annoyed and frustrated that he takes me away from the rest of my class so much. Any advice?

This level of behaviour at such an early stage is a harbinger of much, much worse to come. The kindest thing that can be done for a pupil in this position is to escalate it into the hands of people best suited to deal with his issues and support him as much as possible in a process of socialization. Make no mistake: this is not a classroom fix. This pupil exhibits serious symptoms of antisocial problems.

It's a tragedy that it hasn't been addressed earlier on, but the problem is in your lap now, and for his sake, your sake and for the sake of the class, you need to facilitate his engagement with an educational psychologist, social workers, etc. Take this to SLT and demand that something be done. If they drop it back in your lap then they are guilty of neglect. If one pupil is making it impossible to teach then that pupil needs to be isolated and dealt with. Get your union involved if school won't face up to their responsibilities.

How far should I take it? Allegations of teacher assault

Dear Tom

I chose to be a primary supply teacher because I love the challenge, but now I've hit the rocks with one class. I don't care that they moan about how strict I am, but I was disgusted when the Head told me that two of the girls had phoned and texted home to tell their Mums that I had pushed them both over in the lesson.

Fortunately the Head knew them well enough not to believe their stories; plus other children corroborated my version of the story. And one of the girls retracted her story and admitted she made it up; the other didn't. Thank God the Head supported me and told the parents that the girls were not being entirely correct.

Now the girls are back in my lessons and nothing has happened to them. But they made serious charges against me, and if I'd been under suspicion my career could have been over. Surely they should have to pay for what they have done?

How awful for you. Great to hear how supportive the HT was though. Now let's see how supportive your HT really is ...

Because this girl needs a sanction against her; what she did was dreadful, and could have had serious professional and financial implications for your future career. It was (excuse the analogy) like a false rape allegation where the fantasist gets away scot free. Not a chance. She needs to feel a ton of bricks fall on her. What she did wasn't a little thing – it was one of the worst things a child can do to a teacher, and far more serious than bad behaviour or chatting.

If the HT knows the girl is lying, then she needs at least to be temporarily excluded for her actions (and I wouldn't put it past being serious enough to warrant a permanent move). You could have been sacked for this! This girl doesn't need a cuddle, she needs Alcatraz. She needs to learn that actions have consequences, and serious actions have serious consequences.

If the head won't support this, why not? If they accept that the pupil's point of view isn't the way things happened, then they need to take the next logical step which is to support the rights of teachers to a safe workplace, free from fear and bullying. If they won't do that then they're looking for the quiet option, the easy option, rather than doing their duty, which sometimes means getting your sleeves rolled up and standing up for the rights of their staff.

Get a TA in there. These pupils are time bombs, waiting to detonate under a teacher's career. If they get away with it this time, all they will learn is that their strategy didn't cause them any harm.

The whole class is being rude, boy

Dear Tom

My whole class has zero respect for me; I've been teaching for years and never had one like this – even when I give the whole class minutes on the board they don't stop talking. I've done seating plans to no effect, called home, written letters, detentions; it's as if they didn't exist.

They really seem to be spiteful towards me and clearly enjoy winding me up. When they make stupid noises they smile at me as I'm telling them off! SLT are being very helpful, but the class turn into monsters the second they leave. I am totally out of firepower. I nearly swore at them today, which is totally out of character for me. But I feel like I'm losing my grip. Help, please.

This is a long fix, I suspect. Sometimes classes 'take' to teachers and sometimes they resent them, for a number of reasons. They can often act as a pack and 'decide' that you are liked or not. It takes a while to turn around, although there are things that you can implement immediately in order to start turning the ship around. And essentially, it is about that: like a cruise liner, it takes a while. Use all the normal sanctions and disciplinary/behaviour methods you have already described, but most importantly, *don't stop*. This is exactly the time when, dispirited by the perceived failure of your measures, it can seem worthless carrying on. Remember that we play a long game, and we wear them down by degrees, not in quarters. Keep at it and you *will* win.

Also remember that, despite how awful they all seem, the class is composed of individuals, not a hive. Some will be working and some will not. Some will want to work and some will just want to look hard. It will only be a hard core that are actively working against you, so try to keep your punishments individual and try not to punish the whole class, otherwise you risk losing the nicer ones (they are there, honest!).

Take their books in and assess their work positively. Marking homework and classwork is an excellent opportunity to start having a 'clandestine' conversation with your pupils, if they don't like to receive praise in front of their peers.

Essentially it will take time. Not a particularly exciting answer, but if you persevere you will reap the benefits of your investment. Remember, they're children, no matter how horrible or hard they act. You are the adult, and you will win if you believe in yourself. I'm sure you'll get them in the end.

Losing the fight against racism

Dear Tom

After being at the same school for over a year I've concluded that the pupils treat me disrespectfully because I come from a different ethnic background from the majority of them, and I have an obviously non-Anglo accent. The pupils openly mock me whatever the quality of my lesson.

They've called me things like terrorist (or more usually, a f***ing terrorist), and I hear an imitation of my accent around the school. This is constantly wearing, although I love teaching. I can also feel disdain from the parents when I call home about it, which makes me feel totally humiliated. Being at school used to be great – now I feel like everyone is laughing at me, and I am incredibly stressed and depressed about it all.

I have been told by my line managers that I need to improve my classroom control, but when I do what they say, I get accused by the kids of being too strict. I have no idea how to solve this problem, and worse, I'm starting to feel like I don't want to any more.

If you are the victim of racial abuse, then log it, report it and demand action to be taken. If nothing is done then your school becomes an accomplice to racial abuse, and leaves itself exposed to litigation – and rightly so. Your union rep needs to be your closest ally on this, although there must be other members of your school who a) sympathize and b) will press for action in these instances. You absolutely deserve the right to a safe and non-racist working environment, and in my opinion, pupils that make these kinds of rude, hurtful, personal comments need to be spending some time out of school, in order to emphasize the seriousness of the situation.

The school needs to be on side. You say that you are accused of being too strict when you apply the policies. By whom? The students? Their opinion is irrelevant in this context. They're not supposed to like you; they're supposed to respect you and get an education. If they like you it's incidental – nice, but a secondary consideration. Is it the parents? Ditto. If it's the school, then I am confused about the mixed messages you are receiving, and no doubt you would be too. Ask for clarification about their expectations.

As I say, speak to your union rep. Ask for classroom observations from teachers you respect, and get their feedback about your behaviour management. We all fall into patterns where we use the same techniques with the kids, and it's always useful to get another perspective. Observations in this context aren't a burden, they're a real support to your practice.

You aren't the laughing stock at all – you're a victim of cruelty.

An acceptable level of violence: does an IFP justify agression?

Dear Tom

Is 'The child has an Individual Education Plan' enough to justify allowing any child to hit people and throw things when things don't go their way? One child in my Year 5 class is so difficult that the whole class is constantly disrupted by his screaming and outbursts. And I can't send him out because he has minimal support. He makes me want to scream sometimes too. How much violence should a teacher or TA suffer before the child is excluded?

As little as possible. This is a topic that starts my blood fizzing with frustration. When did we allow the expectation that teachers were supposed to put up with being assaulted? OK, so an eight-year-old isn't going to knock anyone into a coma, but these behaviour patterns are prophecies of the future, unless interventions are made with the child before he becomes a man and thinks with his fists.

The child may lack support, but you shouldn't. Any time a child lays a finger in anger on a teacher, it should at the very least warrant exclusion for that pupil. He needs to learn that this behaviour will not be tolerated, or in any way 'understood.' He is the one that needs to learn and understand the rules by which we conduct ourselves, not you. Of course, there are undoubtedly many reasons why he acts the way he does – biochemical, social, genetic, societal, etc. – but none of these gives him an excuse, even given his age. Most of his peers don't think that hitting adults is OK, so he needs to catch up with them, and realise that he's the oddity.

What sanctions have been applied so far? Depending on their severity, he may have learned that he can do it and, relatively speaking, get away with it. The next time he does it, he should get the impression that he's just robbed a bank – seriously. March him off to someone more senior, demand that the child be out of your lesson all day, demand a meeting with the parents etc., and finally demand that he be punished severely. If the school won't support you in this matter then unfortunately you'll have to get serious with them. Get your union involved, mobilize other teachers' support, and make the SLT aware that this boy is not going to be mollycoddled or placated.

He doesn't need a hug; he needs a wake-up call, as does the school if such a boy is allowed to interfere with lessons. After all, the needs of the other pupils in the class are every bit as important as his, and they outnumber him. The damage he does to their education, and to your right to a safe workplace, is considerable. Time for damage limitation. If you do it right, you might just save this boy from himself, teach him something about self-restraint, and save somebody in the future from being clobbered. Violent behaviour patterns in children repeat themselves as they grow up, unless something (or somebody) intervenes.

Teaching NEETS to participate

Dear Tom

After working in the private sector for a few years, I've been offered a job in a FE college teaching NEETs and similar in 'Life Skills'. The college was very open about how disadvantaged, challenging and cynical these students were. I remember in my PGCE year I was totally rubbish with hard classes, so have you got any tips for me, apart from, obviously, buying an anti-stab vest?

To be honest you need to be ready for this mentally, and be prepared for a devastating level of disconnection. That doesn't mean you should accept it, but that you need to have your shields up before it crushes you. These kids have grown up thinking that not only is the world *not* their oyster, but that it isn't even their world. They feel as if they are useless, and there's no point in trying not to be. These kids have spent a lifetime being told they're good for nothing – and let's face it, many of them don't make it easy to challenge that stereotype – so now you can amaze them with the following.

◆ Total sincerity.
◆ They have bull s*** detectors that could spot Bruce Forsyth from the Moon. Always tell them the truth, and always do what you say you will.
◆ Total enthusiasm – if you can't see this as a vocation (and sometimes even a bit like missionary work) then it's going to grind you down. You have to love the subject, the kids and the project. Be evangelical. Tell them you'll never give up trying so they shouldn't either. Tell them you believe in their potential (but be careful; see above).
◆ Finally, total positivity. Many of them are trapped in cages in their own minds, built by themselves out of every 'No, you can't,' they've ever heard. Tell them that they can. And mean it.

Nothing goes right with this class: are they unteachable?

Dear Tom

I've just started in an inner city boys' comprehensive, and one of my Year 9 classes is unteachable. They won't be quiet at all, they throw paper at me and each other as soon as my back is turned, and they have no respect for me. None of them seems to want to learn. Hardly any have a school bag, and every lesson I have to give almost all of them a pen. They take their phones out whenever they want!

This isn't teaching – this is handing out worksheets and hoping. It's wearing away my will to teach, and although my HOD has helped to punish the very worst offenders, the class remains my worst nightmare. I don't want to go in anymore, and I'm thinking about giving up teaching as a career.

Large scale disobedience is, I think, one of the most depressing experiences any teacher will face. Sanctions are all very well, but when it's most of the class, where do you start? It makes most people want to call it a day, so you're not alone. I spent all week dreading my classes in my first year, and wondered if teaching was the right choice. Remember, every teacher goes through this, at least any teacher in a reasonably challenging school. Realize that you are not alone, and that it's almost to be expected (although never accepted).

You set detentions – that's a great start. Where do you go from there? It sounds like they don't turn up much, so what do you do then? If they can dodge detentions by not showing up then they'll never learn to do what you say. So make sure that *not* attending detentions results in the offence becoming more serious, and make sure that the more senior teacher responsible for the sanctions does their job. They are just as human as anyone else, and sometimes need pressure put on them to follow up their sanctions too (although many will do this automatically).

If they no-show for you, then make sure you communicate this to your HOD as soon as possible, and every time – names, dates, punishments.

Kids throwing paper at each other makes me want to give them detentions. I can't help it; it's a twitch or something. Take their names, every time. Set a detention. Do the paperwork. Then when they don't show up, escalate.

There are kids in there that want to learn, so good for you for going down the worksheet route as a behavioural tactic, not as a last resort. If the class is behaving as badly as you say, there's no point designing OfSTED lessons until you've tamed them a bit, so get the work out to the ones that will do it, and then work on your ever growing detention list.

The key here is support. You need to enlist it, and it sounds like you do already, so keep it up. A teacher's main asset is working as a team; we play the long game. You *will* get them, but if you're not consistent always, they will keep on testing you forever. It's when you become predictable and severe that they start to obey you. They can smell uncertainty a mile off.

Total defiance, then he melted down

Dear Tom

What would you have done with this? One of my Year 3 pupils was blocking a door to a classroom, so that the others couldn't get in. So the teacher uses the language of choice to try to get him to move. He refused (of course). The teacher asked again. Again, no go. The corridor is now dangerously full because the class can't get in, so the teacher takes his arm and marches him to the thinking area, and then escorts the others in. The boy runs back in, shouting, and the whole class erupts, so the teacher takes him by the arm again and puts him back.

A minute later there's a smash; he's thrown a glass timer against the wall, and shards go everywhere. Eventually SLT take the boy away and he's sent home. I feel terrible.

It's difficult to say without knowing more about the boy and the situation, but on the face of it, it sounds like you did everything by the book, followed procedures, and focused on the wellbeing of the majority until you had time to deal with the boy. I understand from your question that you're wondering if there's anything you could have done differently. My short answer is: maybe not. Sometimes we do everything that should be done, and we still find that we can't solve or fix anything. As people who care about the wellbeing of our charges, that can be incredibly frustrating, but there it is.

In the kind of time frame you're suggesting, it's not so easy to make complex empathic decisions that create the best possible outcomes for everyone involved; we just have to call it the way we see it on the spot. Hindsight is legendarily a wonderful thing. It sounds to me like the boy is either very upset about something, or is being (unusually?) needy and attention-seeking. Everything you described suggests that he wants your attention for something. Did something happen, prior to the situation you explained, that upset him? Is something happening at home? Has he just been bullied? Has he had an accident and been embarrassed, and now wants to take it out on everyone?

Lots of variables, and of course, you just have to make a decision on the spot – you don't have time to get Freudian or terribly empathic. Possibly he could have been reached by a quick attempt at reaching him – 'Are you OK?' That kind of question might make him feel he is being paid attention to, and he might calm down. Or, 'I can see you're upset. Why don't we talk about it in five minutes, and you just help me by letting everyone in so I can speak to you more quickly.' This could appeal to his need for attention without charging up to him head on.

But at the end of the day, he also needs to know that selfish, obstructive behaviour will result in consequences, so I think you acted very professionally.

So violent, so young

Dear Tom

In my reception class there is a boy who is more violent than any pupil I have ever taught. He started with lots of anger issues, which we've worked on with him, but now it's developing into something a lot more sinister. He will deliberately walk over to another student and hit them hard in the face, the groin and so on. He is very aware of exactly what he's doing. Just as bad, he acts incredibly inappropriately to the girls, climbing on top of them and touching them in an unpleasant way.

Horrible – and tragic. Unfortunately this sounds like one of those behavioural issues that might be beyond the abilities of mainstream education. If this boy isn't responding to the normal classroom discipline, then he needs extra support and care beyond the capacity of a teacher's time and ability to provide. Star charts etc. only work if the child prefers the praise to the crime, which he might not. Possibly he is repeating patterns of behaviour that he witnesses/has witnessed in his private life, so there might be a child protection issue here. Schools have a designated member of staff for such matters (the Child Protection Officer), so you should bring this to their attention.

There is a greater issue of duty of care here, too: towards the other pupils. If I was a parent of one of the other students I would be furious if another child regularly assaulted my child, especially in a sexual way. This child needs to be removed from the theatre of his crimes, in order that the other children can be safeguarded from his actions.

It could be that he seeks attention by misbehaviour and gets it, in which case there is a slight hope that removing him from his peers every time he misbehaves into an environment where he works by himself/with a mentor might convince him that his misbehaviour is harming his ability to mix with his peers. But I suggest that you speak to your school/cluster school SENCO or equivalent to discuss withdrawal, support and a visit to the Education Psychologist. If this is not available then you need to enlist senior management. This might not be a fix that you can do by yourself. And the other pupils deserve a safe learning environment.

No one person is more important in the classroom than another, and in this case, the majority's needs must take precedence.

Sexual threats are never a joke

Dear Tom

I confiscated a note from two Year 9 girls. In it, they were talking about torturing some boys using a technique they called 'gas pedalling' – I'd never heard of it, but the note described it in detail. So much detail, in fact that I presume it took them over a lesson to write it in the first place.

It was a really foul, filthy thing they were planning to do – but of course they didn't, and if I challenge them about it they'll say it was a joke. But I find it disturbing they would even find it funny.

In all honesty I bet that most pupils involved in this kind of writing don't really mean to carry it out, and are simply enjoying the thrill of fantasy.

But even if they're not, there's still a whole heap of trouble to get them in. Writing notes in class. Passing them in class. Passing on notes of a violent or threatening nature. Remember that even the threat of violence can be a criminal offence and anything as detailed and as cruel as you describe is unacceptable. Can you imagine if two boys had been passing notes planning a rape? The door would come off the hinges of the Head's office.

Is there an in-school police officer at your school? They can be really useful for showing pupils that this kind of stunt is incredibly serious, and they're useful for giving them some perspective on the real world that can really put the fear of God into them. If not, then it definitely needs to escalate.

I suggest getting them in detention for the note writing, and inform them solemnly that it's going further, then pull the HOY into it and get them to consider their options. They need to be dragged over the coals for this. Don't worry about not having enough evidence. Sometimes I think the kids watch too much CSI; we don't need to have proof beyond reasonable doubt, nor do we need a room of witnesses, handwriting experts or sniffer dogs. We just need a reasonable suspicion that we believe in our hearts, and we can pull them in for most things.

Book 'em, Danno.

Back to haunt me after he assaulted me

Dear Tom

I was recently assaulted by a pupil studying A2; the school has said that, after a few days exclusion, he can come back into school and into lessons.

This just doesn't seem stiff enough, especially for a boy as old as he is. The union rep seems to believe that SLT are right to let him back in, but in any job he would have been sacked for what he did. I mean, it's not like school is compulsory for him anymore.

What was the level of the assault? I know it sounds a stupid question, but there are different degrees of offence, and they can be treated differently. A teacher getting hit by a paper aeroplane can expect a proportionate response; a teacher getting smacked in the nose can expect a different retribution and resolution.

Still, if it's as bad as you suggest, I hope this isn't another example of senior management being too weak-willed or lazy (or indeed incompetent) to deal with a serious issue because it affects someone else and not them directly. I saw this a lot working in the catering industry – waiting staff were expected by management to take a mountain of grief because the managers were scared to stand up to unpleasant customers, who were instead treated with servility.

If SLT won't make a case of this, then *you* should. Refuse to teach the boy, on the grounds that you're being treated incredibly unfairly. Threaten to take criminal action against the boy unless something else is done to your satisfaction.

It's a lot of effort, but this is one of those things that is too serious to ignore. And the price of ignoring it can be exorbitant: will other pupils think that it is now acceptable to assault a teacher? Where does it end?

I worked in a school a while ago where a female teacher was touched in a sexual manner by a pupil. The school excluded him for two days and then he was readmitted. Enraged, she took him to court (with union support) and the boy was successfully prosecuted and convicted. As a result he was permanently excluded. SLT should have died of shame.

She'd argue with her shadow

Dear Tom

In my Year 2 class I have a girl who could pick a fight in a coffin. She's SEN and although she's the oldest girl in the class, far behind the others academically.

She's become, to put it politely, the class bully, and stomps her feet and waves her little fists when life doesn't go her way. She's becoming absolutely intolerable in lessons, and I mean that as specifically as possible. I try to praise her and encourage her to be kind and nice, but it always falls apart and she usually tries to hook someone, or tell them off to me for some imagined slight or offence.

The parents are struggling with her too; what hope do I have?

This may be a case where the needs of the child exceed the capacity of the classroom to meet them, and I truly sympathise with you. I am sure that you are in regular contact with your SENCO or similar, and perhaps there are some extreme measures that need to be taken – constant one-to-one support, removal to a quiet space at times, etc.

But assuming that there is anything to be done with the pupil in class I would suggest that you keep going with the praise, and also start to focus on the critical behaviour. Pupils that criticize others are sometimes looking for praise from the teacher, to reinforce their own worries that they are unloved. However you say that you already do this, so the problems may go deeper. Why do we criticize others? Sometimes it's because we fear being like them, so if she picks other people up for failings, it may be that she is herself terrified of appearing stupid, clumsy, etc.

How to handle this? It might require a degree of isolation from the class, either extreme (separate room) or simply a remote desk. Give her individual work sometimes when others are in pairs or groups, and explain that you have a special task for her. The less contact with her peers, the less she will compare herself to them, perhaps. At the same time she needs a more rigorous assessment by a qualified specialist to ascertain what needs she has, and what support she will require to resolve it.

As for the stamping, etc; do what you would for any pupil – sanctions, rigorously and consistently applied. Don't treat her behaviour as special, and she'll learn that rules apply to her as much as anyone.

This school's tearing itself apart

Dear Tom

I've just started in a school which is in special measures with serious behaviour issues. Some of the SLT believe that behaviour will improve if lessons get better; others believe that the behaviour should come first. A lot of the teaching is unsatisfactory; the children expect to mess around and don't really listen, no matter what lessons are like. Pupils assault each other frequently – hospitalized in one case recently – and sometimes staff if they get in their way. Swearing is commonplace, and you couldn't discipline a kid for it.

How on earth can I make a difference? The simplest request gets ignored, or a fight breaks out. Children sent out just run off. Detentions don't happen because they don't come back. Senior staff don't follow up on anything either, so nothing happens as a result. It's totally depressing, and the kids deserve better. We all do. Is it hopeless?

I really do sympathize as you seem to be in a very difficult situation, and I think any teacher would find it extremely challenging. I also applaud your integrity in wanting to find solutions for the situation, in order to improve the students' education.

The most serious issue here is the lack of whole school unity in its behaviour policy: in order for behaviour to improve there needs to be consistency of attitude and a hierarchy of unbendable sanctions that is supported by the management structure. There are, after all, many more students than teachers, so they will naturally control any environment (classroom, corridors) where it is a simple battle of you versus them. The student body is, at heart, a disorganized group, and the key strength that the teaching staff have is working as a team. If neither side is organized then the teachers will struggle to achieve any kind of dominance. But if the teachers work together then they are unstoppable.

Unfortunately from your mail this seems absent in your school's behaviour stance, so let's look at what you can do to improve the situation. You say that the HODs and SMT are unhelpful. Are there any senior staff at all that seem to pursue discipline effectively? Or are there any other members of staff who seem to have good behaviour in their lessons? If so, enrol their aid and ask for their help in these matters. It might be useful to ask them if you can observe their lessons, with a focus on what they do, and how the students react. See if you can pick up tips, and if there's anything you can take back to your classroom.

Additionally, they may be willing to pursue behaviour follow ups with and for you, perhaps phoning home on your behalf if detentions are not attended. Perhaps they have a relationship with your most troublesome students that you can use to your advantage.

Think about what goes on in the classroom itself. Teenagers are humans, no matter how remotely connected they seem to that species, and they respond to some very primitive signals, namely the need to be reassured by authority and the need to be valued. This means that you need to make two things perfectly clear in the classroom: you care a great deal about their education and you won't be satisfied until they have got the very best opportunities out of your classes, but also that you will do everything it takes to make sure that it happens. Remind them at all times that they are all important, but no one is more important than any other, so you will be enforcing your rules with sanctions.

In the classroom you can adopt strategies that are immune to bad behaviour: for instance, have material and work ready for them that is on the board or delivered to the table via worksheets etc. That way, there is work for all the pupils to do and the well-behaved pupils will get on with it, glad for the chance to do something. And that way you have more time to focus on the badly behaved pupils

What about the parents? To help you enforce sanctions, approach other members of staff (see above) and phone as many parents as you can – while some are very unhelpful, most are extremely good allies. The best way to get them on your side is diplomatically to praise their son/daughter, and then mention the bad behaviour:

'Hi there Mr/Mrs X. Listen, Robert is normally pretty good in my lessons, and when he wants to he can do some really great work; unfortunately today he let himself down a bit. Have you got a minute to discuss ways we can get the best for him?' That sort of approach. This really works; avoid making the parents think it's their fault or that you blame them, and you will avoid defensiveness on their part.

Interesting lessons vs. behaviour management: great, well planned lessons are one tool that can be used to improve behaviour, but it is foolish to think that they are the same thing, or that interesting lessons are a magic solution for unruly classes. A disruptive class will tear through your well planned masterpiece like a Japanese wall, so I really do think that senior staff might be passing the buck somewhat here. It's a bit too easy to say that 'it's not our responsibility, it's yours' when in fact it's *everyone's* responsibility.

There are other approaches. This is going to take a lot of courage and self-reliance on your part. I don't know from your message if you are new to teaching, and if you are then the best advice I can give you is to be consistent and dogged with your rules; apply them at all times and never give up, even when it seems hopeless. You will wear them down, but don't let them do that to you. They are children, possibly rude and offensive at times, but you are the adult.

If you're *not* new to teaching then take courage for the task ahead of you. Don't work alone, and get as many teachers of all levels on your side. Perhaps you could ask to be part of/form a behaviour committee that addresses these issues and creates a behaviour policy. Talk to your union rep and see where they stand on violence towards staff. Take your concerns higher, right to the head if you can.

If you try your best and things still do not work out, then you can look around for alternative positions with honour, knowing that you've done what you can. No one can be expected to change a school by themselves. If the SMT won't support you in trying to make things better then they don't deserve you.

7 | Dealing with other grown-ups

Kids: the only thing wrong with teaching. Take them out of the equation and our lessons would be delivered in worshipful silence, proceeding at the pace we dictated. The lesson bells would ring and their echoes would hang in the corridors until they dropped away into a velvet silence. Life is full of regrets.

Assuming that we will be teaching students instead of robots, we're all going to face behaviour issues throughout our careers, and that's been the focus of this book so far. Lick the problems with the kids, and all will be well, right? Alas, no. There is more to the job than the student/teacher relationship (I mean the regular type, not the Chris Woodhead variety). You will have noticed all the other grown-ups that keep sticking their noses into your day; some invited, some not. We have to learn to deal with them too; not as problems, but as potential allies, mentors and sources of soul food. Or you might be one of these groups, a non-teacher (which is a little condescending, in the same way that using the adjective 'coloured' is), wondering how to deal with the kids, the teachers, and everyone else. Students learn from everyone around them, which I suppose makes teachers of us all.

Parents terrify some teachers: a lot of them feel that this group is somehow the 'them' to their 'us', and that as a group they have to be managed rather than consulted. To be fair to teachers, a lot of parents don't exactly make it easy for teachers, and imagine that we are somehow out to get them. If you've ever had a parent threatening to come round the school and 'fix' you then you'll know what I mean. To be fair to parents, a lot of teachers don't exactly make it easy to be reasonable; these are the teachers who phone up and start conversations like, 'your son is disgusting, how on earth have you raised him?'

The key is to identify some common ground between you and the parent, and proceed from there, talking to them as if they weren't an antagonist, but a partner. And what common ground do you always share with a parent? The pupil's welfare: their flourishing, their progress and education. That's what you both want. And frankly, no matter how much you care about your students, rare is the parent who won't care a hell of a lot more than you. Some teachers talk to the parents as if they have no idea what's good for their children. OK, there may be some car crash families out there who seem to base their dynamic on the *Jeremy Kyle Show*, but if we're honest with ourselves, most of the times we tut-tut about other people's parenting, we're simply expressing a cultural dislike or a personal preference compared with how we would do the job.

Whenever we talk to a parent, we should always do so in the belief that this person is the primary carer in the student's life. If you can convince them that what you want is what they should also want for the student, then you've formed a team that will multiply each other's powers. So we need to make sure all of our conversations run along the lines of, 'Sammy is letting himself down, and I know he can do a lot more; if he keeps this up then he's at risk of exclusion, and I know that none of us wants that ...' If we can keep that attitude in mind then all but the most unbalanced of parents will jump on the back of your bus. And of course, there's always the chance that the parent will be able to tell you a thing or two to make you think about how you handle the kid. Just a possibility ...

And of course schools aren't just run by teachers (thank God – they'd always be skint); there is an ark of administrators, bureaucrats, supply, support and auxiliary staff to make sure that light bulbs work, fire exits remain unpadlocked and bills get paid. Many of them will intersect with the students and teaching staff alike in a number of ways. Some of them have asked me how they are supposed to conduct themselves with children and with other professionals. In a school it is vital that everyone is clear about their responsibilities and defined areas of interest, in order to know what we should be doing (which is why it's so heartening to see so many schools unable to issue written contracts to new staff – that'll teach them). If teachers themselves feel at sea with behaviour management, then you can only imagine how challenging it must seem to a cover supply, a TA, or a caretaker.

It seems painfully obvious to state that all members of staff should conduct themselves with dignity and decorum, and treat everyone else they encounter with basic manners, whether they get on with them or not. I get very uncomfortable with demands from teachers for respect from their charges, as if respect were something that could be summoned at will. I can think of maybe half a dozen people I deeply respect in my whole life. But manners ... now, that's something we can all expect. And the beautiful thing about expecting manners is that everyone knows roughly what you mean by it. It means treating people, not as you wish yourself to be treated, but as if you were a person of some value. Because you are; you're a human being.

We all are.

I'm dashing myself against the rocks: cover supervisor being ignored by students

Dear Tom

I've been working as a supply Cover Supervisor for the last year, and I have one problem that has me stumped for ideas: what do you do when students ignore you and refuse to do what is asked of them, such as waiting outside before entering the room, standing outside when they've been misbehaving, not throwing paper aeroplanes etc? I have been leaving notes for the absent teacher, reporting it to behavioural management and, if it is persistent, reporting the students to the Head of Year - but the students keep reoffending. What should I do?

Trying to get someone else to punish them sounds as if it might be the problem here; I know that as a CS you may feel uncertain about your rights to set detentions etc., but until you do, they will treat you like any teacher who doesn't follow up personally on misbehaviour – poorly. Unfortunately many teachers don't give support staff the support *they* need to cover their lessons properly, and fail to follow up on any misbehaviour that occurs when they're not there. Actually I understand this to some extent, without condoning it: most teachers have enough to do in their own professional lives, without taking responsibility for what happens when they're not there. But I always recommend that the regular teacher and the cover teacher collaborate to work out ways to discipline the children together. If the teachers aren't following up, then you need to change your strategy or you'll keep getting the same results.

Phone home to parents. Set detentions yourself. Follow up on failure to attend. Use the school behaviour codes. Refer to personnel in charge of form groups/year groups. Speak to department heads and ask WHY nothing has been done, and explain the need for sanctions in these lessons. After all, teachers should regard cover lessons as valuable in some way. When they don't, that's when problems start, because the kids realise that the lesson is low-value.

If the previous strategies aren't possible because the school has a policy against CS setting detentions etc. (and God help them if they do) then insist that action is taken. It is your right to expect reasonable support from the people you work with. Otherwise you're just being thrown to the dogs.

Why can't my daughter do pottery instead of detentions?

Dear Tom

My daughter has recently moved in with me after living with her mother all her life. She's always been extremely bright and a model student in every way but recently the school has been extremely unfair on her. She has been getting into trouble by truanting from lessons, but I work a long distance away and can't just drop it all to come into school on a regular basis. Now they are telling me that she should try to find another school if she doesn't want to be at this one!

Surely the school should be doing more to find out what's really up with her rather than just washing their hands of her? I feel that the school simply can't be bothered to help my daughter, and are being grossly unfair – she was perfect every year before this. What's wrong with education today? Apparently when she gets detentions they make her do pointless things like lines and copying. Surely the point of education is to educate, and she should be doing any one of a million interesting things like pottery, or writing an essay on politics?

There is, as they say, an elephant in the room in this situation – her reintegration with you in a family unit. This is always a challenging period for anyone, but especially for a teenager who is coming to terms with all the difficulties of adolescence, developing a sense of identity, or coming to terms with moving from one parent to the other. Even with the best of intentions and support, teenagers in this situation can feel alienated, abandoned and unsure. The fact that she was previously exhibiting compliant behaviour and high achievement suggests that something new has come into the equation, and that something may very well be her moving in with you. That's a big change for you, so imagine how it appears to her: is she still loved? Who's the boss now? What are the ground rules now? The security of her life has been overturned and now she feels slightly adrift.

Teenage rebellion is natural and desirable; it's how they find out who they are. Add the uncertainty above, and she sounds as if she is desperate for someone to tell her what the new rules are.

Children crave boundaries. She needs to know what is acceptable and what isn't. If no one does this then she'll decide what they are for herself, often to the detriment of others. Teachers often experience sudden character changes in students when family life has been upset.

Bad behaviour in previously well behaved children is often a cry for attention from the primary adults in their lives. If they feel neglected at home then they can turn to adults who *are* there and present behaviour that demands attention; unfortunately that tends to be *mis*behaviour.

I can't comment on how teachers have performed in individual circumstances, as it's important not to judge events at which we weren't present. I bet the teachers mostly have her best interests at heart. Detentions etc., may sound pointless to some people, but the range of strategies open to teachers isn't limitless. In general, the broadest tactic is to punish bad behaviour and reward good behaviour. Punishment usually involves detaining them. In order for it to be a deterrent, it has to be undesirable. That doesn't mean that it has to be pointless (I make mine do work applicable to their subjects) but it has to be testing in some way, to remind them that being rude to teachers and students (for example) has consequences they won't like. It's a universal principle of deterrent and reward that is as old as the hills.

If a pupil persistently truants, then the school will have done some investigation into why it is happening. But they don't have the resources to be welfare officers or psychologists – schools are, after all, institutions for education, and the school's priority will have to be dealing with the symptoms more than fixing the underlying reasons; that is, to be fair, more the responsibility of the parents, who know the children intimately, have the closest relationship, and of course the moral right to legislate for their children. Schools expect parents to have by far the best ability and opportunity to resolve underlying psychological issues affecting behaviour.

I'm sure this girl's educational issues can be resolved, but it's going to take a parent to address the problems in her life that are really affecting her. She needs to know that she is loved, that she has rules in her life, and those rules are there for her benefit *because* she is loved. This is not the time to allow problems to become bigger; action needs to be taken now, not later. She sounds as if she desperately needs you. Now isn't the time to be getting bogged down with what teacher said what, and when, and whether children should be taught pottery in detentions.

Run, Forrest! SENCO tactics for sprinting kids

Dear Tom

I am the SENCO and I'm working out tactics for dealing with a Year 3 boy who loves to run – out of lessons, away from people, and all around school. I never chase him, and we all give him space to return to classes. I reward him for good behaviour and that works a bit; nothing obvious sets him off – he just does it when he feels like it – but we're all going mad figuring out ways of dealing with him. Any advice would be gratefully received! Thanks.

Has he been evaluated by the Ed. Psych? Running away might be compulsive behaviour, fear of peers, anxiety; a whole raft of underlying issues. If there is something rooted inside him that prompts this behaviour against his will, then it's an issue beyond mere classroom management to address; it will take a psychologist's approach, and I won't commit the sin of presuming to know which strategy would work with him.

On the other hand it might just be misbehaviour, and a symptom of unwillingness to participate or behave in an approved manner. What does he say to you when you speak to him about it? Does he justify his actions somehow? That is your 'in', your clue to dealing with the behaviour, because you might be able to reason with him, and present the situation back to him in a way that he can understand (e.g. emphasize how much time it wastes, how much it damages his education, how much it disappoints his mum – whatever works). Or perhaps he doesn't rationalize it in any way, and just says 'he wants to', in which case normal sanctions need to apply in order to emphasize to him that he's not more important than the rest of his class, that he needs an education, and that grown-ups largely know what's best for him.

I'm worried that by tolerating the behaviour he learns subliminally that it is a) acceptable and b) a good strategy to get out of lessons. Certainly don't chase him, in case that's the response he's looking for. Like I say, the things he tells you about his own behaviour will be the key to understanding the strategy you need to deal with this.

What to say in interviews

Hi Tom!

As a TA I'm often asked in interviews about how I handle bad behaviour in the classroom; I never know what to say. Sorry if this isn't exactly a behaviour advice question!

It sure sounds like a behaviour question to me :-) When you get asked about scenarios where children misbehave, I would recommend the following strategies/things to say at interview:

Refer at all times to the school Behaviour Policy whenever misbehaviour occurs. If you don't know what system your school uses, then find out. If it doesn't have a policy then get out. Run!

Defer behaviour control at all times to the teacher; the TA's role is supportive, and the pupils need to see that the teacher is the main authority in the room, otherwise it confuses them and undermines the teacher. Then the pupils can start playing both adults off against each other in a tedious, heart-breaking round of 'he said/but she said'. This doesn't mean bend over and brace yourself; it just means that you should be in touch with how your teacher wants behaviour handled. I used to have a TA who would shush the children whenever they squeaked, which ended up being more disruptive than the pupils themselves. I ended up having to shush her. Permanently.

Communicate with the teacher prior to the lesson to establish ground rules and patterns of control, which pupils to work with, and what you do if they go off task.

My son is in hell with bullies

Dear Tom

Some Year 9 boys are bullying my Year 7 son, starting from last term. I never knew how bad it was until he came home in floods of tears. They mock him so much about how he looks that he has asked me – seriously – if he can have plastic surgery when he's older.

I know who they are because I've phoned the form tutor, and I was told they would be spoken to. Well, if they were it had no effect because the bullying is still going on. How can I stop this happening to my son? Should I speak to the boys' parents?

This must be horrible for you and your son. I have enormous

amounts of sympathy for your son if he is a victim of this. Some points to consider.

If you want to speed up the process, get active with the school; schedule a meeting with the head of year/person responsible ASAP, to discuss what is being done. If you do this I guarantee that they will go up a gear, because no one likes to go to a meeting with nothing to report (somewhat cynical I know, but true nonetheless).

At the very least the school can insist that the two parties stay well out of each others' way; that way, if there is contact again, clear liability and fault can be assigned. Proving bullying is extremely hard, as it's often one word against another. To be fair, it *should* be hard to prove; unfortunately, kids being kids, false allegations are all too easy to make (of course I'm not suggesting your son is doing so, merely making the point that the school might not look as if it's doing much, but is actually trying to be fair. After all, it would be just as bad if they came down hard on innocents – that would be just another form of bullying). Still, if the teachers are keeping an eye on the situation then it should be relatively easy to spot who the aggressors are, and who the victim.

If he can, your son should try to stand up to them verbally. I certainly wouldn't advise your son to box them on the nose, despite how satisfying it would be in the short term. First of all, it gives the school legitimate cause to exclude *him*, and secondly it will only escalate the violence, raise the stakes and prolong the situation.

Bullies bully because it gives them self-esteem. They pick their victims on the criterion that they will allow them to do so – essentially they pick people who smell like victims. Again I'm not implying that your son is weak, merely that there is something about his character that is kind enough to suggest to nasty kids that he won't cause them too much trouble. If bullies think that the victim will sting them back a bit, they'll lose interest because generally they're not looking for an actual fight, just the possibility of putting another person down to make themselves look better. So smart, sassy answers back at them as publicly as possible could help. Try to encourage your son not to show any emotion; that simply feeds their egos, that they can get a rise out of him. Laughing at them is another way.

Bullies often don't think they are bullies. They probably reckon it's just sport. So sometimes a talking-to can help them realize that their actions are hurting another. Of course, they may realize fine what they are doing, so sharp sanctions can have the desired result too.

Tread carefully – parents will defend their children to the last breath, if they feel like they are under attack. Wouldn't you do the same for your son? If you do speak to the other parent (which could be extremely useful if you have a good relationship with her) then do so in a very non-confrontational way. Explain that your son is really upset and that you know her son probably doesn't mean to be nasty, etc. and could she have a word? If you get her on side it's like having a howitzer in a sword fight, but if you get her back up it could mean trench warfare.

My daughter got a smack: what should I do?

Dear Tom

My daughter recently moved to a new school. She's always had a wonderful academic and behavioural record, and loves lessons. Then a big, older girl gave her a painful slap in the face for no real reason; my daughter is too kind to retaliate, so she has just gone into a kind of shock.

My daughter finds it hard to sleep now, and doesn't want to go back because she's frightened of this girl, who smiled at her the day after the incident. I taught my children to be civilized, and I can't believe that my poor girl is losing interest in academia because of this thug. Please could I have some advice? She cries all the time now, like a baby, and I want to know if the school has done the right thing.

Being hit *inside* a school is just as serious as being hit *outside* a school. You are perfectly within your rights to call the police and make an allegation of assault. The police might be reluctant to proceed as it's a 'school matter' but if you insist then they have to take action. Perhaps you could inform the school about it *before* you do so and see if that has a stimulating effect on their response to the issue. Too often schools view assault as 'normal' behaviour and it's not, as your daughter has found.

As to the shock, I greatly sympathize – violence can be deeply distressing, particularly if you're not used to it. Be there for her, encourage her, tell her that it's not her fault, and that you're working to make sure the other girl is punished. Perhaps take her somewhere for the weekend to take her mind off it? This could be the time to go somewhere nice.

You and your daughter deserve much, much better than what the school is doing for you right now, and as a parent sometimes you have to make it happen.

It's a dog's life as a cover supervisor

Dear Tom

Before I start my PGCE next year, I'm working as a cover supervisor. With all the sickies going on I have a full timetable. Most classes are OK – hard, but OK. But two year nine classes are taking me to the limit. I get them a lot – they won't stop talking, they chuck stuff around the room, and most don't do any work. Few instructions are followed. I do set detentions though. Any tips on winning them over, given that my timetable is so unpredictable? Thanks.

Cover supervisors deserve mention in the New Year Honours lists, IMHO. All the pain of supply, plus the bonus comments of, 'you're not a real teacher'. It sounds like you've made a good start with them, despite their surliness, and of course Year 9 classes are legendary for their rebelliousness, so you're not alone.

The good news is that you'll be there long enough to get most of them on task, most of the time. What is essential is that anyone who doesn't turn up to your detentions then gets followed up, so make sure your paperwork is done, and pass them on to a reliable member of the senior team/HOD for follow-up. Just as importantly, find out what that person proposes to do with them, and demand (politely) that something *does* happen. Then, if they act up again, do the same thing. And do it again. And again, until they learn that it's not worth it, that you will follow up, and that your lessons are lessons, and not an extension of play time.

It's when we slack off, and let things slide, that they learn that they can get away with it. So teach them a different lesson. My often repeated mantra is, 'you're not stuck in the room with them – they're stuck in the room with you.' So don't dread seeing them. Look at it as an opportunity to get stuck into the behaviour. Don't exhaust yourself during lessons with shouting and arguing with them. Be calm (it's a job, after all, not a holy battle of wills) and just peacefully take names in the morning and kick ass in the evening, as Eminem might say were he to teach in England.

What is a 'managed' move?

Dear Tom

I'm a teacher, and I need some advice for my sister in-law, who recently had a call from her daughter's Head. She was asked to attend an interview about recommending a managed move for her daughter to another school. After a lot of upset in her family life (divorces, relatives dying, etc.) she had a bit of a bad history in Year 9, plus she's got a bit of a temper. When she had her phone confiscated, she ran out of the room in a huff; as she did so, an item she threw hit the teacher. Now the Head says this is an assault, and she should go for good.

I don't understand. There was an SEN pupil at my old school who hit people, but she never had a 'managed move'. So what is a managed move, what advice do I give to my sister, and what are her rights? Thanks a lot.

Generally, unless a child is being permanently excluded, any move has to be authorised by the parent or guardian. In this case, the parent might be presented with the threat of a PE and is given the alternative to take the daughter out of school and into a new one voluntarily before that happens. In this way she avoids a bad record. It might also be a good thing for the pupil, as perhaps she needs a fresh start somewhere else.

Of course the parents can always refuse, in which case they might face a long struggle with the school, the governors and the LA. Alternatively the school may have a weak hand, and be looking for an easy way to exclude the pupil, in which case the parents only have to say, 'No – let's look at some more options.'

If the pupil is facing a managed move then in my experience this means that there is a considerable file of extreme and dangerous behaviour weighing against her. Even if she is experiencing difficult times at home, I must say that she can't use this as an excuse for aggression and disruption.

Typhoid Mary of naughtiness: can a teacher cause disruption in another's lesson?

Dear Tom

I walked into someone else's class today where three boys suddenly starting playing up. These boys have a terrible reputation and the behaviour I saw is what I have seen numerous times, so I ignored it in order not to undermine their teacher – or so I thought. But then in front of the class she said, 'Don't starting playing up just because Miss (blank) is here.' Later the teacher said that they were extremely well behaved, but as soon as I walked in they kicked off. I wasn't sure how to react. These boys had to be removed by me only a few lessons ago so she could get on with a lesson! Is it possible she's right?

Hmm, it sounds like the class teacher was simply embarrassed about you seeing bad behaviour in her lesson. And because her inner demons were shouting at her *'you're a rubbish teacher! See? Even Miss X can see it!'*, she responded by vocalizing her worst fears, maybe even transferring the real object of her guilty emotions (her negative perceptions of her own teaching) on to you as a fetish (and I mean that in the psychological sense, not the Channel 5 way).

Ask her if she needs any support. Perhaps ask her what she did with the boys. Try coaching rather than lecturing, of course. If you feel she really needs support then speak to her line manager – tactfully.

Accused of incompetency

Dear Tom

I teach a group of students on a carousel basis, so I only saw them for about ten weeks at the start of term; at this time I clearly indicated their deadlines for coursework, responsibilities, etc. Of course, some missed the deadlines anyway, so I sent letters home and asked them to see me for help. I passed out reminders in their registers and told other teachers to remind them. Now they're accusing me of incompetency! The SLT have said that it was my responsibility to get the coursework in, no matter what! Surely I did all I could – maybe more – and that somehow it has to be up to them to deliver what's expected of them?

A spineless accusation. Morally we can distinguish between actions that are expected of us, actions that we are expected *not* to do, and actions in between that are neither – we may do them or not.

We are expected to deliver the syllabus. We are expected to advise and coach them to produce coursework. But we are also clearly expected *not* to write the work for them. The amount of pressure we put on them to achieve the coursework is what's under discussion here. The problem is, the more pressure we put on them to complete, the less independent learning and initiative they display, which is pretty much one of the main aims of the work itself. It could be argued that putting kids into detention to achieve this (which incidentally I would also do out of necessity, not out of desire) is the opposite of the spirit of the challenge.

In the Teaching and Learning equation, an enormous emphasis is placed on the teacher's responsibility to achieve results; yet simultaneously we are judged largely on the basis of what the student is doing. It's a cunning business this: getting them to do the maximum amount while we do the minimum, and often it seems that we are asked to do one thing (encourage independent learning, for instance), while realizing that we need to do something else to achieve the end results (exam grades, course work, module essays) that the system looks for.

You sound as if you did a lot to make this happen. If you reported the situation well in advance to your line manager, then what did they advise? If they were silent, or happy with what you were doing, then you have a cloak of invincibility in this matter, as blame can trickle up as well as down. Not that I'm suggesting this is a scenario that needs blame to be allocated particularly. If you wanted to find that anywhere, I'd start having a squint in the direction of the students who were told what they had to do, when they had to do it … and then didn't.

Who will teach the teachers? Creating an INSET on behaviour

Dear Tom

I run a school Learning Support Unit, and I've been asked to put together a staff day focusing on behaviour at school, and I wondered if you had any suggestions. I don't want it to become just another day of griping about how rotten kids are. Thanks.

Here's the headline: one day isn't going to develop their skills, but you might be able to make them think about what they do already. I have a few suggestions. Video training sessions. Before the day, enlist some teachers who are prepared to be videoed teaching classes – say 15-minute segments of teaching. Recruiting will be the hard part, but if you look I'm sure you'll find some teachers who would be happy to do so; they will probably be quite able at BM, and hopefully rather thick-skinned too. There's no legal problem using videos in classes – even the major unions are OK with it, as long as the camera isn't trained on the teacher and used as a stick to beat them with. In this case the teachers would have to agree to be filmed.

Then the training group observes these videos and attempts to learn from them: SWOT analysis, what went well, what could have been done differently, etc. It's a brilliant way to get teachers to think about real life situations and how to deal with them. BM is a verb, and needs to be seen and imitated to be improved, so this is a great way to observe a lesson without becoming part of it (of course the camera does, but you'd be amazed how quickly most classes start to ignore it. It's like week three of *Big Brother*, by which point they're all skewering voodoo dolls of each other). These sessions are also great fun – it's gripping, rather than the usual training day disasters featuring coloured felt tips, A2 paper, brainstorming etc.

If you feel that it will descend into a bitching session then you could anticipate this by giving everyone questionnaires before the day, asking them specific questions, gripes etc. about BM. That way you can collate, interpret and represent the content of the staff body's thoughts and feelings in a meaningful way to them on the day itself. This means their views are taken into account, and opinions are given a forum for expression (written ones are usually more thought-through than verbal ones anyway). Incidentally, if you feel that people are bursting to express themselves negatively, that is a clear signal for SLT that something is seriously wrong in the staff consciousness; people feel they don't have a chance to express themselves, be heard, or make a difference. Just a thought.

Broken links in the Chain of Command: do SLT do enough?

Dear Tom

I read recently on the BBC website that heads and SLT, although they have lots of power in school, often fail to support staff as much as they should when it comes to behaviour matters. What's your opinion on this report, and do you think this criticism will make Heads and SLT react more to behaviour problems in the classroom?

Hmm, alas my experience of human behaviour in all positions (not merely managerial ones) is that people will often fail to act unless there is pressure to do so. This isn't a terribly cynical view of human behaviour, just an acknowledgment that people have hundreds of priorities, pressures and needs, and satisfying them all requires prioritization – and sometimes, a few of those priorities get bumped down the order of importance, or fall off the table entirely.

People in any position of responsibility often act in such a way to satisfy the needs of the ones above them in the food chain, before they address the needs of those 'below' them. It's simply an easier way to live – if you can keep your boss happy, then chances are your life will be easier. After all, they have the power to make you unhappy ...

The point of this jibber jabber is that senior managers will often not respond to a mere report – hell, they're surrounded by reports, they eat them for breakfast, same way teachers get adverts for INSETS in their pigeonholes. SLT can shrug a report off like sweat. What prompts action is usually when there is some external demand made on them (Hume would call it the 'external cause') that forces them to change – an imminent OfSTED, a line manager review etc; something externally assessed and quantifiable. Often something connected to a performance-linked pay issue. But this is human nature, not a gripe about SLT. And of course, there are other factors that can instigate behaviour change in management, not the least of which is a sense of duty, professional responsibility, honour, justice, etc. … These occur too. But a report has to become something a whole lot less ethereal before it starts to tickle the armpits of senior management.

Of course, on a related issue, SLT have a profound effect on the whole school behaviour policy, theoretically and in practice. All leadership trickles down from the top, so if the Head and his/her team drop the ball on behaviour, that all filters back to the classroom and the corridor. If the pupils know that behaviour problems will, eventually, lead to the Big Room then they'll think twice about pushing their luck with the teacher. But if the sanctions start to dissipate like mist as soon as they go above the HOD/HOL level, or just as damagingly, if they apply only sometimes, then the kids will know – they'll *know* – that they can get away with breaking the rules.

The worst thing I heard in a previous school's playground? One kid says to another, 'What did the Head say to you when you didn't show up for detention?' Other kid says, 'Nothing. Just talked to me, told me not to do it again.'

This is like trying to run a society with judges, policemen and courts, but no prisons. There needs to be a terminus for bad behaviour, somewhere that it *goes*; otherwise, the students realize that we've only got water pistols and splurge guns.

I would like to see it compulsory for all schools to have a designated member of SLT responsible for behaviour, and then that SLT member given support and protected time in order to perform his or her job. Then that member of staff (backed up by whatever framework of support staff is deemed necessary) could be a visible presence, an ultimate sanction, and a reminder to the general populace that all is well, that order prevails, and that everyone can go about their lives safely and securely.

I'd probably give that designated member of staff a special title. Like 'Head Teacher'. That has a snappy sound to it.

Somebody stole a day from my life! Are INSETs any use for behaviour?

Dear Tom

My school has agreed to pay for classroom management training to support my professional development. I'm not looking for a specific company but what should I look for when signing up? I need a one/two day course.

Many thanks

Behaviour management is a doing word (despite grammatical appearances otherwise) so I recommend courses that involve you role-playing scenarios with actors/colleagues. It's amazing how easy it is to fall into your unconscious behaviour routines, despite being perfectly aware that you're not actually dealing with a pupil.

I would also recommend courses that allow you to observe video-taped scenarios (either the ones you have created or filmed in mock/real class situations) as it's great practice actually to *see* kids misbehave and the teacher's reactions, particularly when you're not directly involved in it. Often it's hard to get the most out of a behaviour observation in school, as (not unlike quantum physics) we, the observer, get caught up in the experiment.

I would be extremely suspicious of any INSET or course that expects you to sit still and be lectured at all day. I would also check to see if the person delivering the course is either still in, or has recently been in, the type of educational environments you're interested in. Beware behaviour experts who have only ever taught in Swiss finishing schools for the daughters of diplomats ... Give them a quick *Google* first, check 'em out. And personally (and here I admit bias) I would advise you give courses a wide berth that approach behaviour management from a terribly academic point of view. Of course, there's loads of theory behind behaviour, but managing it as a teacher is mostly attitude and action, not over-intellectualizing.

Oh yes: any course that advertises 'Better behaviour through empathy/hugs/cuddles/chakra alignment' etc should be reported to the Ministry.

The hidden cost of a cheap laugh: the dangers of undermining colleagues

Dear Tom

I read recently in the TES that a teacher was having problems controlling a class, but when another (unpopular) teacher walked in and out again, she found that by laughing with the class about the teacher, she found they bonded, and afterwards she found behaviour much easier to manage. Do you think laughter is important as a behaviour management tool?

While I applaud any tactic that strengthens relationships between pupils and staff, I would also question the greater implication of doing so at the expense of professional solidarity. By giggling at the exiting teacher, the writer demonstrated a behavioural lead to the class, that it is acceptable to consider teachers as figures of fun. Perhaps in this instance it had a subsidiary effect that was beneficial, but it also would have the effect of legitimizing the mockery of the teaching staff in general, and that teacher specifically.

I wonder how much damage this incident could cause to the teacher individually. Perhaps the pupils in the class would have lost a little respect for him, and things were made a little harder for him. It's impossible to measure, of course. But I would expect my colleagues to bite their tongues -- I mean really bite them, not just suppress a snort of laughter – and ignore the situation.

Of course, this might have the effect of making us seem a bit po-faced. After all, there are times when I feel like rolling my eyes at the behaviour of teachers. But tacitly to approve of their public mockery is humiliating and unprofessional. Of course I sympathize with the writer, and the pressure to use any strategy in order to motivate and engage them affects us all.

Laughter is, of course, famously a medicine. But that doesn't mean it's a cure all, or that everyone needs it all of the time. In fact sometimes medicine is downright dangerous. Laughter is a primate's way of communicating a placatory fear response; in effect it means 'Please don't hurt me, I'm harmless.' Of course in humans it's much more sophisticated, but it is normally used to express solidarity and mutual friendliness. When your relationship with a class is in its infancy, they need to see you looking sober and serious so that they know you mean business. If you start smiling too early (yes, the old advice re: Christmas deadlines and teeth-baring are true) then you imply that you want them to like you. Instead, keep it solemn until you can afford to let them relax a bit, and you can too. It doesn't work in reverse, and if you're too nice at first it takes a hell of a lot of effort to reel the behaviour back in.

Great relationships with the kids sometimes take time. Laughing with them is the next level, and is usually a sign that you can do greater things with them in the classroom. But don't be tempted to use short cuts. It's like bribery – a short term gain, but at what cost ...?

The sins of the father: parental violence against teachers

Dear Tom

I was 'nearly' assaulted this week by a parent. He swore loudly at me, and stood up angrily; pushing the table he was behind violently towards me. My HOD had to stand between us because he thought he was going to hit me. But the school hasn't supported me at all, and in fact has asked my HOD to phone the 'gentleman' to apologise for how things turned out!!

Now I feel very insecure in school, if this kind of abuse is allowed. I've been told I could bring this to the police, but I'm not sure how to go about it.

That's horrible, and it's depressing how much grief some front-line teachers are expected to take from parents and pupils in a school context that would have us dialling 999 outside of work. It's something I saw a lot when I worked in the entertainment industry, where customers were mollycoddled and kowtowed to, while the staff who were assaulted or intimidated were expected to apologize and wipe the table. In effect this is what you're being asked to do.

Too *right* you should do something about it. I'm glad your colleagues have supported you and vaguely appalled at the reaction you say the school has taken. What you need to do will take some guts.

Tell your line manager that you want the parent banned from entering the school premises. This is a no-brainer. If someone flung a chair or table at me I'd be on to the Old Bill before they left the room; at the very least you deserve the right of working in a safe environment. And if a parent proves that they cannot express themselves politely then they need sanctions, just like the kids do. If the school won't agree to this then you need to make them agree. Tell them you will pursue this further with the police if they won't. Talk to your union rep and see if you can mobilize some support from your fellow members into something organized and orchestrated.

If SLT can't be bothered to take action (which is by far the easiest line for them to take) then you need to make them uncomfortable. It's tragic that you have to do this to make it happen, but you do. Manage upwards.

I'm no legal expert, but I believe that the legal definition of assault is the threat to commit bodily harm (and battery is the carrying out of the threat) so this man could legitimately be liable for this charge. A threat can be non-verbal, and if someone had to intervene (good witness) then there is clear evidence of intent to harm or intimidate. Either way you shouldn't have to put up with it. It's what unions were designed to help with.

Kick up a fuss. If enough of you take action, you might actually be able to change policy and improve the lives of others around you.

The Sheep and the Goats; helping a school to nail the bullies

Dear Tom

I do some work with a local youth club. There's a slightly isolated boy who comes there and he trusts me. Now he's told me that the kids at his school make his life a misery. His school is apparently a good one, but he worries that if he tells his teachers then he'll look weak, and that he should just be a man and tough it out.

This week they pushed him too far and he fought back ... and then got in trouble for fighting. When he told me this he burst into tears. Part of the problem is that the teachers now think he's partly responsible so they won't help. He feels his only options left are to fight back. His parents don't care, I'm told.

I told him to tell the Head. He asked if I could come into school and speak to SLT with him, but I'm not sure I can. Should I phone the school instead and let them know what he tells me?

I sympathize with your position and the boy's; teenagers can be vicious as any adult.

I actually sympathize with the boy's retaliation in some ways – not because I applaud it but because it's a perfectly logical response to his situation. He's being bullied, and nobody has given him a way out of it, so his options are to live a life of shame, or retaliate in the only way he knows how. Advice to 'put up with it,' 'ignore it' or similar is as detestable as it is useless. He knows what children in playgrounds and men in prisons know intuitively: if you hit them, they might think twice about hitting you again.

Unfortunately he may only encourage their bullying, knowing that they can get a rise out of him, or better still, get him to over-react and then get in trouble. I imagine to a harasser that would be a particularly sweet outcome.

Now *you* need to give him a strategy; this problem has fallen into your lap, and doing nothing isn't an option any more. First of all, make sure he isn't exaggerating, or being melodramatic. I know that this is potentially a sop to the bullies, but be sure that he really *is* being victimized. You've seen nasty comments on social forums. Good, that gives you evidence. Could he bring along another friend to speak to you who would support his story? I know it sounds harsh on him, but remember that his alleged bullies need to enjoy the same benefit of the doubt you give him. Gather something concrete that could convince a neutral party.

If you're convinced that his claims are real then I recommend that you contact the boy's school directly yourself. Arrange a meeting time; remember that some teachers/staff are happy to come into school early or later in order to accommodate third party lifestyles. Show them what you know, and stress that you are worried that his claims aren't being taken seriously. Remind them that the school has a duty of care to its students. If anything happened to him the school could be held responsible.

Contact the parents and let them know what you're doing. Do so politely and hopefully in a spirit of cooperation. By and large most parents would be too glad to hear that someone is helping their son. But also, they might be able to shed light on the background to the situation (see above) that might strengthen or weaken the validity of his claims.

If what he says is true, then he needs your support and strength more than anything else right now. You might just be his only lifeline. It's a big responsibility, but it belongs to you now. If he isn't helped now, he could fall into patterns of behaviour that could damage or ruin his academic career, and fracture his self-respect. But with assistance, this might be turned around.

The teacher's too cool for school: TA thinks the teacher is soft

Dear Tom

I'm a TA in a tough school (Year 6), where at least nine of the kids have statements for a variety of issues. I'm assigned to one boy in particular, but I help out overall. The pupils (and others) are terribly hard to keep a handle on: they're so squirmy, and fuss, and tut, and fret about everything, sticking their noses into everyone's business. I know that most of them are incredibly insecure, and one boy even storms out of class when he gets in a huff. The teacher is unbelievably patient and never blows her stack, but sometimes I wish she would. If the class isn't reasonably quiet, how can anyone learn?

One thing that is very important to know here is the attitude of the teacher to the situation; I would speak to her and find out what her impressions of the situation are. Are the statemented/less able/SEN pupils in the class making satisfactory progress? Is the behaviour acceptable enough not to impede learning? Is the behaviour sufficient to allow satisfactory teaching? How are the other members of the classroom coping with the current levels of noise and behaviour?

Once you have answered these questions you will know if there is a significant problem. A quiet class isn't always an engaged, learning class, and a busy noisy classroom isn't always a bad one (although if you're like me and you prefer the sound of silence, it's teeth-grindingly annoying). If the teacher is quiet and calm, perhaps she is satisfied with the learning environment, in which case your task is to bite your tongue and just support that learning, despite how you feel about the noise. Every teacher has their own style, even if we sometimes wish they didn't. Of course if you can see significant difficulties with their learning that the teacher hasn't noticed, then it is only right to bring it to your colleague's attention.

If you feel that the teacher is failing to deal with serious issues then liaise with her over seating plans that separate the instigators, ensure that their work is differentiated down to the paper colour, and praise them whenever they do anything right, reassuring them that they are capable. Critical behaviour almost always masks issues of insecurity and fear of failure, so address that with them. Put their work on the walls. Everything short of a hug.

8 | Being a teacher- how to cope with the pressure

Have you hit The Wall yet?

In my career I have faced angry drunks, mob brawls, kitchens on fire and a nightclub plunged into darkness while the emergency exits were padlocked. None of these experiences has been as stressful as teaching. I say this to reassure anyone in education who is freaking out because classes are twisting them into crazy shapes like a pipe cleaner.

Every teacher I have ever met runs the rapids at first. Some of them have rough rides for years to come, and some of those eventually leave the job and do something less stressful, like playing chicken inside a hessian sack on a railway line in the dark. If you've freaked out for any reason during your career then you can breathe a sigh; this means you are perfectly normal. I'm no Überteacher, but I rate my behaviour control (I better had, or this book is a fairy tale); and I had many, many long dark staff meetings of the soul about bad behaviour in my classes, especially in my first year. I left lessons paralysed with self-doubt and crushing introspection. At home I would be working every evening until ten o'clock, planning lessons that I knew would be dashed against a cliff face of indifference. I had tears in my eyes on more than one occasion. And I had the benefit of coming to teaching in my thirties, after a long career dealing with roughs and toughs in bars.

So why is it so stressful? For most people reading this, the answer is obvious; but let's analyze it a bit to see if we can do anything about it.

First of all the hours are long: early starts and many, many interminable meetings after school. Parents' evenings and presentations. Lunch duties. Secondly, influencing other people is very, very difficult. You have *no* direct control over what someone else does, unless you have wired them to electrodes (in which case email me with schematics). You also have a lot of responsibility; the knowledge that you have to get scores of pupils through exams, syllabuses etc.

– or even *teach* them – is the burden of Atlas. Plus it's not something you can simply achieve directly through your actions (see above).

Furthermore, some pupils are extremely unpleasant. We aren't allowed to be equally unpleasant to them. These two points taken together combine to create a horrible sense of worthlessness; they can treat us like dirt, and we have a limited range of responses. In effect, we look powerless.

Finally, teachers are often so hard on themselves they make Catholic flagellants look *laissez faire*. We judge ourselves remorselessly on our shortcomings or our perceived ones.

One way of looking at stress is to see what stress is actually *for*. After all, it must serve some function, biologically, or be the result of a biological process. The answer lies in the fight or flight mechanism of most animals. Millions of years ago, our ancestors evolved this survival response to dangerous situations; faced with a sabre-toothed tiger or cranky mammoth, they had numerous options that boiled down to two: did they step up and take the bugger down, or did they realise that in a fair fight, enormous clawed paws beats tiny pink opposable digits every time, like scissors beats paper?

Whichever one they chose, they found that their bodies flipped into action in order to support their brave but foolish choices: as soon as they realised danger was all around (*Wet Wet Wet's* less successful Darwinian follow up), every system in the human body stood to attention. The heart rate soared, gushing blood that would be needed to power the muscles; breathing rates increased, but breathing became simultaneously shallower in order to maximise the oxygen that dissolved into the blood stream; blood was diverted from the gut to the muscles so that they would benefit from this fuel boost. Adrenalin poured out of glands in order to make all this happen. The posture would change; legs would bend slightly so that our ancestors could run, kick, whatever; height was lowered to make sudden movements quicker; the shoulders came up and the head retracted; in the male animal testicles would be automatically drawn in to protect this most precious treasure. Dozens of other tricks and triggers tripped off around the body like mousetraps.

Just as importantly a raft of mental changes took place; combat focused the mind fabulously – rather than being able to drift lazily across a variety of tasks, they became focused, able to think about nothing other than the threat they faced. This prevented them from being clobbered while they worried about whose job it was to dust the cave that weekend. With all of these natural enhancements, they stood a much better chance of dealing with whatever was promising to clean their clocks.

Natural, yes, but tremendously unbalanced. This wasn't a state you wanted to be in for long. The body couldn't maintain this terrific readiness indefinitely, and there was a price to pay; if combat or flight didn't occur, then eventually all the superpowers wore off, leaving our mono browed grandfathers exhausted and numb. If the combat readiness was too prolonged, other secondary mechanisms would be triggered: defecation, urination, salivation and shock to name a few.

Fast forward a few thousand years. The cavemen now wear matching tie/shirt sets from St Michael. The mammoths have been replaced with school children. But the mechanism is exactly the same. Teachers find themselves in a threatening environment (a new school, for instance), in a class with unpleasant and challenging students who constantly bait him or her. So the body, feeling threatened, does exactly what it was built to do: get ready for a barney, or a quick exit.

You already know the symptoms: the blood has fled from the gut to the muscles, so you don't feel hungry; this might even extend to nausea. Heart rate shoots up, and you breathe more quickly. Suddenly you find it hard to focus on anything other than challenging pupils. But your body starts to get confused: you have neither run from the classroom, nor battered them with a frying pan (I'm guessing here). What's going on? For some reason you are still in the presence of the threat, but you haven't done anything about it. So the body keeps you on red alert. Eventually, if this keeps happening day in and day out, the teacher starts to fear going into school; feels depressed; feels inadequate and lonely; feels like nobody could be less suited for the job than they are.

And that's what stress is: a sense of frustration between what you'd like to do and what you can do. An awareness of the gap between your existing state and your desired one. I'm not actually suggesting that you want to tear them apart with your teeth, or run up a tree. Actually, maybe I am. But that's irrelevant; you can't (I repeat, you can't) do either. So what do you do?

Some things you need to know

I'm perfectly aware that when you feel depressed or blue, words are not enough. But they can be part of the process, so here are a few things to bear in mind:

1. Every teacher finds teaching hard for a *long* time. Every single

one. And as this book shows (if nothing else), the harder the school, the harder the job.

2. Any feelings of stress are a perfectly natural reaction (see above).
3. You aren't rubbish. You're learning how to become a teacher, that's all.
4. You aren't rubbish (part 2). You simply hate not being competent and confident.
5. You probably weren't taught very well how to control classes. That's not your fault.
6. Pupils respond in the first instance to strength; they need to be reassured with the security of your discipline. If they think you're too nice, they will challenge you repeatedly.
7. As an unfamiliar presence, they won't automatically defer to your authority, so you'll have to build up authority with them.
8. That takes time, as all relationships take time (unless you're a sailor on shore leave).
9. It's going to hurt for a while. Seriously, get used to it.
10. But like most pain, it won't last forever. Like having a filling drilled, there is a positive end to it all.

Some of those propositions may feel hard to believe, but they are facts beyond further reduction. Trust me, I teach philosophy so I know what I'm taking about (that never works, incidentally. Why is it that people always take the advice of other specialists – say, plumbers or lawyers – seriously, but as soon as you say 'I'm a moral philosopher,' everyone thinks they can have a punt? Honestly. We get no respect ...)

Be a teacher

Now you need to do something a bit harder: get yourself thinking like a teacher. This is achievable by anyone, no matter what your background, be you tyrant or tree-hugger. Teaching is a skill, not a collection of facts. It certainly doesn't have a rule book on how to behave, or a list of prescribed 'teacher' behaviours for every situation. It's a place you get your head into, an attitude (or as Aristotle would say, a collection of character and mental virtues that define a role. Trust me). What's the attitude? I'll mention a few:

1. You're the boss of the room. You can interpret that in many, many ways. Some people run the class like a train network, some like a nursery, but there is a thread that binds them all together:

you are in charge. Everyone in the room has rights, yes. Every child matters. But your wishes are predominant. They have to be: children will not organize and teach themselves without guidance. Anyone who thinks otherwise is a utopian armchair jockey. Children must be trained by adults, until they become interesting enough to say something intelligent, rather than merely charming.

2. Their behaviour is their responsibility. It's not your fault if they're foul, feral, or flinging Doritos at each other. It's up to you to do something about it, but ultimately, they are then ones deciding to do it. Do *not* beat yourself up when a child misbehaves. Deal with the misbehaviour.

3. Be consistent. I've mentioned this dozens of times in my responses, but it is essential. If you say you're going to do something, then do it.

4. Don't take them home with you. (Seriously, don't: I went to a DFE cluster meeting about it.) By this I mean that *they* don't sit at home worrying all night if they've hurt your feelings, or feeling impotent with rage that they're not as good a student as they should be. No: they're downloading YouTube clips about public executions on to their iPhones. So don't sit at home and stew about them.

5. They are kids. Pustulent and disagreeable at times, wonderful and shiny at others. You're a grown-up. You've probably had sex, smoked, voted and travelled the world a bit. They might pretend to be big and hard, but that's standard behaviour for teenagers, to play at being a grown-up. What do you care what a child thinks of you? Seriously. So Jasmine thinks you're *bare rude*. So the hell what? Fonzie says Jasmine can sit on it. There are 6 billion people in the world. 6 billion opinions on everything. Are you going to listen to all of them?

6. They don't know you. To them you're just another adult, a restriction on their Geneva-convened rights to talk in lessons and Twitter about the best bits in *Saw IX*. Don't take anything personally. Some of the more aggressive ones will know how to go for the jugular (despite being unable to spell it) and say things that echo your own fears: 'you're rubbish,' 'you can't control the class very well, Miss,' etc. Ignore it. They are winding you up. Take names and move on.

7. You're not there to be liked, you're there to teach them. It's what you're paid to do, so up to a point, just grit your teeth and bear it. It's what being a professional is all about.

8. Eventually you will win. And when you win, they win.

For whom the bell tolls

It tolls for thee, brother. The end of the day bell, that is. I mentioned above that you shouldn't take school home with you, but what should you do?

◆ **Remember the points, above**. Many of us tend to treat our jobs as an extension of our self-esteem; if we're valued at work then we must be valuable people. Unfortunately this externalization of our self-regard makes it vulnerable to attack, and if things don't go well at work, or we perceive them not to be, then it puts dents in your ego you could serve soup in. Be aware of this when it's happening.

◆ **Get some perspective.** It's a hell of an important job, true, but that doesn't mean that every detail, every stumble or frustration is a disaster, any more than any tiny win is a triumph. Learn to see that just because Robyn or Robert scorned your ability to teach doesn't mean that the sky will fall, or that you are a miserable failure at life, love and work. Perspective is a hard thing to gain through introspection; it is far easier to achieve through action. How do you keep a perspective on the importance of your job? Do other things. Do things that are *not* your job. If you have a hobby, continue to pursue it. Do you have friends? Make arrangements to see them, and treat them as seriously as appointments with mobbish parents.

Oh, the pressure to re-prioritize your life will be crushing – of course it is, you've got so much work to do – but you're not a machine that teaches. You're a human being, and we need a balanced lifestyle, just as much as you need a balanced diet, in order to stay sane. Meet friends who don't teach (please tell me you have some) and talk to them about teaching. They will revel in your gory stories, and you'll be talking about your job in an analytic way rather than just living in it. Plus they will comment about it like tourists, and you'll see what normal people think. Teaching will seem more like something that you do as part of your life, rather than your life itself, more important than breathing.

◆ **Do things that are nothing to do with teaching**: climb a mountain, walk to the pub, whatever. Go and see a play; watch a spider spin a web; cook dinner with gypsies; I don't know, do what you do. Whenever teachers return from holidays, you know how they always say they feel recharged? That's what perspective is. You can have that all year round, if you blend the different interests in your life together.

But, you say, *I'm so terribly busy! I just can't find the time to go abseiling off the Louvre when I have three sets of books to mark for last Wednesday!*

◆ **Rubbish. Get your priorities sorted**. You aren't any good to classes if you burn down to the wick. Work as hard as you need to, and then stop; grant yourself the time and space to be human. This *is* important, and more important than a set of Year 8 books. The stars will stay stuck to the night sky if you return books a day late, believe me (I have extensively tested this theory). The ravens will remain in the Tower of London if you neglect to laminate a hundred Golden Time vouchers. It really will be OK. What *will* be a disaster is if you allow yourself to be run into the ground. That's why unions were created, and despite even their best intentions there are still tremendous pressures in teaching to overextend yourself. Don't. Save that for emergencies. Your day-to-day job isn't a constant emergency.

◆ **Get healthy.** When the mind is stretched to breaking point, do something with the body (make sure it's yours). Go for a jog, if you're that sort of masochist; a walk will do. Hard exercise is terrific if you have the mentality for it; an hour in a gym will give you an hour where you're not thinking so much about your crumbling classes, and more about the unusual aromas that other people's bodies possess. It also serves an enormously important task of using up all that adrenalin that your body has been pumping out for fight-or-flight. Remember, your body is expecting some action, right? So give it some action. Any kind of exercise will help with this, so get your body into motion. I'm not sure if Wii Sports counts as exercise, but I'll presume it does (in the same way that Kia-Ora counts as one of your five-a-day).

Also, when you feel healthier and fitter then you're able to deal with stress more easily. So even if the thought of running a treadmill fills you with dread (dread mill?) then find something active that can fit into your lifestyle. For me it was cycling to work, although London traffic had a tendency to press every stress button I possessed before work had even started.

◆ **Get some sleep** (God, I sound like your mother. I'll be telling you to cut down on wine and eat healthily next. Actually I will: mind crossing those roads now). So you're working till one every morning planning lessons. What are you, an idiot? Get some sleep. I presume you get up at stupid o'clock anyway to make morning briefing, so don't punish yourself by stealing sleep from yourself at the end of the day. We need about 8 hours of sleep a night, give or take. Give yourself it. And keep your sleeping pattern regular, i.e. go to bed at roughly the same time every day. It's been proven that your sleep is much deeper and rewarding if you do this.

Avoid caffeinated drinks or alcohol too late at night. Caffeine stays in your system for hours, and keeps you awake but not necessarily in a good way. Even if you fall asleep, your sleep will be more shallow and unsatisfying. Same with alcohol; it might knock you out, but it's not exactly the sleep of babes. Same goes for other 'medications' (you know who you are) … None of these are suitable substitutes for what our bodies are meant to do naturally: clock off when we're tired to heal, mentally and physically. We're still not sure what sleep actually does, but that's because we're not as smart as we think we are. So let's just remember that it's important and not try anything fancy like staying up for a week, OK?

◆ **Ask for help at school**. Don't labour away by yourself like a martyr; you may be rewarded in Heaven, but you'll get clobbered in this life. School staff are a team, and even if you're new, there are people you can and should lean on when times get tough. You'll do the same for them some day. So talk to your mentor, your line manager, your buddy, your SLT – whoever can help. Get them to observe you if you want tips on specific aspects of your teaching. Ask them if you can observe them for you to do the same.

If specific students are giving you grief then speak to their Head of Learning/Year Head and ask for advice. They should be happy to help, and shame on them if they're not.

◆ **Follow the school procedures**, especially on discipline. The students should know that if they challenge you then they're also taking on the whole school, and most of them don't have the guts to do that. The knowledge that any student who crosses you will eventually receive justice has an amazing power to dissolve teacher tension, because one of the reasons we get stressed is the belief that the kids can abuse us with impunity. Well, they can't. Just be patient, and do the paperwork. Remember that 75 per cent of behaviour management happens outside the classroom. It can be slow and time-consuming, but it is devastating if used consistently and effectively. Give them some of that for a while, and most of your malcontents will settle down.

Feeling powerless and useless can shatter your self-esteem; in serious cases it can lead to symptoms of depression, and for those prone to depression anyway, it can be a trigger for a long spell of darkness. So it makes sense to do what you can do to offset these symptoms. And that's one of the most encouraging things about it: there *are* things you can do to minimise the stressful aspects of the job, rather than sit back and be a helpless victim of circumstances. Knowing that there are things you can *do* is tremendously empowering, so make sure you try most of the things in the list above. You are *not* a victim, you are practically a miracle of nature: a rational, highly trained, independent, valuable and competent man or woman with a huge amount to offer other people, students and colleagues.

You are, of course, a teacher. Good luck, in all things, and spread the love.

Further Reading

One of my main premises is that controlling classes shouldn't rely on a PhD in conflict resolution, so I would never expect anyone to wade tearfully through every issue of *Asperger's Quarterly Review* in order to learn how to control a class. But if anyone is interested in learning more about this fascinating subject, either through curiosity or a desire to develop their understanding of good control, then you could do worse than take a look at some of these books and resources. Inclusion in this section doesn't confer my uncritical patronage on everything they claim, but it does indicate that it contains matter relevant to the issues I have been discussing.

Anthropology

Carrithers, M., *Why Humans Have Cultures*, Oxford University Press, 1992

Morris, D., *The Naked Ape*, Corgi Books, 1969

School Practice

Blum, P., Surviving and Succeeding in Difficult Classrooms, Routledge Falmer, 1998

Leaman, L., Managing Very Challenging Behaviour, Continuum Books, 2005

Websites

Bennett, T., *The Behaviour Forum*, tes.co.uk. Even despite my modest thoughts, still one of the best resources for any teacher looking for support from other professionals.

Politics, Philosophy and Economics

Aristotle, *The Politics*, Penguin 1962

Burke, E., *On Government Politics and Society*, Fontana, 1975
Galbraith, J.K., *The World Economy Since The Wars*, Sinclair-Stevenson, 1994
Hobbes, T., *The Leviathan*, Penguin Classics, 1982
Hume, D., *Enquiries Concerning Human Understanding*, Oxford University Press, 1989
Levitt, S.D., Dubner, S.J., *Freakonomics*, Penguin Books, 2006
MacIntyre, A., *After Virtue*, University of Notre Dame Press, 1981
Mill, J. S., *On Liberty*, Penguin Books, 1985
Plato, *The Republic*, Penguin, 1955
Rousseau, J.J., *The Social Contract And Discourses*, Everyman, 1988

Literature

Golding, W., *The Lord Of The Flies*, Faber and Faber, 2002
Orwell, G, *1984*, Penguin Classics, 2004

Psychology, pop or otherwise

Brown, D, *Tricks Of The Mind*, Channel 4 Books, 2007
Gilbert, P., *Overcoming Depression*, Robinson Publishing Ltd, 2000
Gladwell, M., *Blink*, Penguin Books, 2005
Goldstein, N J., *Yes – 50 secrets From The Science Of Persuasion*, Profile Books, 2007

Other

Dixon, P., *Rhetoric*, Methuen and Co Ltd., 1971
Various, *The Scout Handbook*, Page Bros., 1980

Index